D0209525

MOB TOWN

MOB TOWN

A History of Crime and Disorder in the East End

JOHN BENNETT

YALE UNIVERSITY PRESS
NEW HAVEN AND LONDON

Copyright © 2017 John Bennett

All rights reserved. This book may not be reproduced in whole or in part, in any form (beyond that copying permitted by Sections 107 and 108 of the U.S. Copyright Law and except by reviewers for the public press) without written permission from the publishers.

For information about this and other Yale University Press publications, please contact:

U.S. Office: sales.press@yale.edu   yalebooks.com
Europe Office: sales@yaleup.co.uk   yalebooks.co.uk

Set in Minion Pro by IDSUK (DataConnection) Ltd
Printed in Great Britain by TJ International Ltd, Padstow, Cornwall

Library of Congress Control Number: 2017942335

ISBN 978-0-300-22195-4

A catalogue record for this book is available from the British Library.

10 9 8 7 6 5 4 3 2 1

This book is dedicated to my wife Laura and our families,
both at home and abroad

Contents

CONTENTS

Introduction

And away went the coach up Whitechapel, to the admiration of the whole population of that pretty densely populated quarter.

'Not a wery nice neighbourhood, this, Sir,' said Sam, with a touch of the hat, which always preceded his entering into conversation with his master.

'It is not indeed, Sam,' replied Mr. Pickwick, surveying the crowded and filthy street through which they were passing.

Charles Dickens, *The Pickwick Papers* (1836–37)[1]

The East End, like the whole of London itself, can be said to be all things to all people; throughout its history it has been respected and reviled, lauded and feared, neglected and indulged, used and abused. The amount of change the East End has been subjected to through the centuries has made it an almost continuously shifting landscape of diverse industry, architecture, religion, politics and social class. This should make this particular part of the capital difficult to define (as one would define, say, the West End, which most would associate almost solely with entertainment and indulgence). The ever-changing East End should by rights avoid simplistic categorisation, yet the very name still conjures up stereotypes, some of which have prevailed for decades or even centuries.

Recently, with the regeneration of key locales within the area, particularly following the reinvention of Docklands as a world-class financial hub, the metamorphosis of key neighbourhoods like Spitalfields and Shoreditch into some of London's coolest quarters, and the gradual creep of the City into its territory (the neighbourhood around Aldgate East is known today by property developers as 'City Fringe'), this contradictory area is now favourably regarded for the richness of its modern culture. But many who actively seek out the distractions of the East End today would probably have given it a wide berth as little as thirty years ago. This author distinctly remembers the Spitalfields of the 1980s as a plethora of battered sweatshops, decaying houses and market detritus, with the homeless and the destitute a significant presence, the like of which was unimaginable around his home in the suburbs. Likewise, Wapping, neglected and mainly deserted following the closure of the docks more than a decade earlier, presented an unearthly warren of streets overshadowed by grim warehouses, with the air of an unsettling dystopia. Then as now, for many it was the numerous street markets – Petticoat Lane, Brick Lane and Club Row, to name the most famous – that continued to give the East End life, and thirty years ago these hubs of activity echoed with the cockney street-patter that was even then becoming a noticeably diminishing cliché.

And if it is clichés one is after, the East End of that time was abundant with them: sooty terraces of damp, mice-ridden homes with outdoor lavatories, the front doorsteps nevertheless kept spotless out of pride; the cheeky market trader whose business was not always as legitimate as he would have you believe; Pearly Kings and Queens in all their finery; small dark pubs, fiercely guarded by the locals as they revelled in the atmosphere of light ale fumes, cigarette smoke and the slightly discordant jangle of a piano; grubby-faced children playing in the streets, taking boisterous joy from whatever bits of disregarded rubbish they could turn into playthings; gnarled and destitute meths drinkers crowded round a constantly lit fire on a bombsite. All of this is dreadfully simplistic, of course, but these oft-evoked – and now predominantly extinct – perceptions were once the norm (and were probably accompanied by the irrepressible pub piano and a dozen rough-and-ready East Enders singing 'Knees Up Mother Brown').

But the other element of East End life that appears to linger in the collective memory, deservedly or not, is its criminality. Like the much-evoked hardship and poverty associated with London east of the City, so the subject of lawlessness refuses to go away. It is somewhat unfortunate that the East End has had a number of high-profile cases which have served to make criminal behaviour a frequent focal point to those who study its history; the legends of Jack the Ripper and the Kray twins continue to fire the public's imagination, and other dramas such as the Siege of Sidney Street and the Battle of Cable Street remain recurrent reference points. Popular fiction has reinforced the East End's villainous reputation through the works of Charles Dickens, Arthur Morrison and Sax Rohmer. Non-fiction, particularly reportage from the second half of the nineteenth century, kept the reading public abreast of all that was considered morally wanting in this apparently insalubrious quarter.

It was the latter material, particularly prevalent during the Whitechapel murders of 1888, when all eyes were peering into London's underbelly, that cemented the East End's reputation for crime and vice in the decades that followed. But whilst the motives for crimes like those perpetrated by the Ripper were less discernible, many examples of unlawful behaviour east of Aldgate Pump had immediately recognisable causes, often as a result of the district's setting within the geography of the metropolis. Its proximity to the City boundaries and the docks provided many situations which could be exploited by the criminal-minded, whether it was through greed, need, or as a result of frictions and tensions such as those surrounding race, religion or politics. Some episodes, naturally, escape categorisation. Thus the criminal history of the East End of London is a rather large subject, for in between the major *causes célèbres* – and there have been many – sit a plethora of incidents which, despite having less impact in their day and having quickly been obscured by the mists of time, remain no less important in regard to what they tell us about lawlessness in the East End of London, and its causes.

But in the same way that the East End defies simplistic categorisation in terms of its character, so it possesses unclear borders. One could well ask, 'What and *where* is the East End?' The boundaries tend to expand or contract depending on which authority one consults. The *Encyclopaedia Britannica*, for example, has the East End beginning at Aldgate Pump, at the confluence of Leadenhall and Fenchurch Streets: this is a fair assumption, for beyond lies Whitechapel, certainly the heart of the East End in many people's minds. Gardiner's Corner – once the site of a prominent department store[2] – at the busy junction where Whitechapel High Street, Commercial Street and Leman Street (and, once, also Commercial Road) intersect, has been another suggested starting point. From here, the immediately adjacent East End is Whitechapel, Spitalfields and Mile End, its southernmost point bordered by the natural boundary of the River Thames, taking in Wapping, Limehouse, Shadwell and Poplar. But where does it end? It is here that the East End becomes more than just a physical entity. Robert Sinclair emphatically stated that 'I see no reason to use the phrase "East End" unless very exceptionally to indicate the sense of somebody's mind.'[3] This concept of 'state of mind' is a perceptive one: often the citizens of districts such as Hoxton and Dalston, or more distant locales like Plaistow or even Romford (the latter being most definitely in Essex), consider themselves East Enders. Indeed, such a label, despite the often-sullied reputation of the place, is often worn as a badge of honour, for being an East Ender sets one apart as tough, resourceful and unique to London, carrying with it a sort of independence. William Booth, founder of the Salvation Army, alluded to such uniqueness when he commented that 'one seems to be conscious of it in the streets. It may be in the faces of the people . . . or it may lie in the sounds one hears or in the character of the people.'[4] That said, the concept of the East End denizen as a breed unto him or herself is yet another cliché – the place is too diverse to maintain such an ideal, especially today.

For our purposes, the East End shall be – as it has been defined by a number of commentators – bordered by the City to the west, the Thames to the south, the neighbourhoods of Bethnal Green and Shoreditch to the north, and where the River Lea drives through Bow to the east: a district which since 1965 has been the London Borough of Tower Hamlets.[5] There is much history and turbulence here: civil disorder, dissent, industrial sabotage, theft (both petty and large-scale), housebreaking, gang warfare, racist violence, prostitution, violent assault and murder. Less commonly considered themes come in the form of child neglect and infanticide, illegal gambling, drunkenness and corruption.

From such rich seams of criminality come myths and legends: two in particular, the Jack the Ripper murders and the Kray twins, have stretched far beyond their original context, even becoming part of a wider entertainment industry. This is perhaps one of the reasons – overexposure being another – why these two subjects are often given short shrift by writers who delve into the wider history of the East End. They are often looked down upon, not because they are unimportant, but almost as though any lengthy consideration of these two infamous cases might imbue any study of the wider context with an unwanted and crass populism. Here I must make my position clear: to look at East End crime with anything less than a token nod to these two contentious subjects would be missing the point, and I refuse to pass them off as tiresome and clichéd. They are as much a part of the criminality of the area as anything else, and merit wider consideration.

The Ripper murders, born of the district's social conditions in the late nineteenth century, affected the area in significant ways, inspiring other incidents which combined to make the East End a major international focal point. The Ripper crimes highlighted social injustice and crushing squalor, becoming a means by which historians today can gain a much more detailed sense of life in London at the time. This is one of the Ripper's legacies, along with the belief that such focus inspired rapid improvement in the infrastructure and conditions of the East End. (The mystery of the murderer's identity and the long-running quest to name him once and for all, however, constitute a legacy that, for our purposes, shall be avoided.) The Krays, saddled with the same sensationalism today, are again an important part of the criminal milieu of their particular era, the ultimate conglomeration of generations of villains who went before them. Their unique thirst for power and recognition made them truly stand out, and when they were imprisoned for murder in 1969, they warranted front-page coverage in the national press. The ultimate manifestation of east London villainy, they are impossible to ignore, and like the Whitechapel murderer, find their place here, amidst the chaos, without prejudice or hype.

Trawling through the centuries of crime in east London, it was soon apparent to this author that choices would have to be made: naturally it would be impossible to report every burglary, street fight or petty felony that has taken place over a period of almost half a millennium. Fortunately, themes arise at various stages, be it periods of political unrest, rising trends in certain crimes, or notorious cases, all of which warrant considerable attention. In between those, like the mortar that holds together the bricks of a larger construction, come more minor cases, worthy of mention either for their audacity and uniqueness, or, in some cases, because they are so unusual or surreal. This book thus weaves its way through the criminal life of the East End chronologically, ensuring that it devotes appropriate time to the bigger cases and themes of the time, while acknowledging lesser deeds along the way. The criminal East End awaits our scrutiny.

I must acknowledge the following people for their assistance, advice and support during the writing of this book, some of whom have been instrumental, past and present, in forging my further understanding of the East End and its criminality: firstly I must thank my commissioning editor at Yale, Heather McCallum, who was the driving force behind this project, who had confidence in me and who fought hard to help me cobble the initial proposal into shape, as well as showing great reserves of patience during its production: without her this book would not exist; also Stephen Halliday, for his initial enthusiasm for the project and words of encouragement and advice; and my wife Laura, for her support and incredible patience during the production of this book as I went through what the late Bill Fishman once called 'the burden of writing'. Special mention must also go to Richard Jones, who has been helpful beyond words – his support and generosity regarding newspaper archives and his ability to ferret out some unique stories have contributed to this book significantly; Stefan Dickers and his team at the Bishopsgate Institute, who have been a tremendous resource, their skill in finding just what I have been looking for at the right time making a challenging job that bit easier; Malcolm Hamilton-Barr, Christopher Lloyd (now retired) and the staff of Tower Hamlets Library and Archives, who provided many years of invaluable research material which has informed not only this book but many of my former projects; similarly, the staff at the National Archives, London Metropolitan Archives and Hackney Archives. I would also like to thank, in no particular order, the following for their contributions, support and inspiration, no matter how great or small: Michael Adkins, Laurie Allen, the Altab Ali Foundation, David V. Barnett, Dave Barrington, Paul Begg, Jacob Blandy, Ross Bradshaw, June Brown, Neil Bell, Alfred and Brenda Bennett, John Chambers, the staff of the City of London Police Museum (particularly

Catherine Coultard), Robert Clack, the *East London Advertiser*, Dennis Ellam, Jonathan Evans, the late Professor Bill Fishman, Philip Hutchinson, the late Ken Leech, Rachel Lichtenstein, Rachael Lonsdale, Marika Lysandrou, the Metropolitan Police History Society, David Moffatt, the late Adrian Phypers, Mark Ripper, Stephen Ryder, the late Chris Scott, Iain Sinclair, Toynbee Hall Archives, Jerry White and Scott Wood.

CHAPTER 1

Beyond the City Wall

Also without the bars both the sides of the street be pestered with cottages and alleys, even up to Whitechapel church, and almost half a mile beyond it, into the common field; all which ought to be open and free for all men . . . in some places it scarce remaineth a sufficient highway for the meeting of carriages and droves of cattle; much less is there any fair, pleasant, or wholesome way for people to walk on foot; which is no small blemish to so famous a city to have so unsavoury and unseemly an entrance or passage thereunto.

John Stow, *The Survey of London* (1908)[1]

As early as the late sixteenth century, London east of the (then extant) City wall, past the Tower of London and Aldgate, was not to everyone's taste. The above description of the main road out of Aldgate through Whitechapel, written by the English historian and antiquarian John Stow in his important *Survey of London* (first published in 1598), reveals a lamentation for what is lost through development, an affliction of observers of east London even today. Stow was well placed to see some of these earlier developments, but was quick to remark on what little good they did for the general wholesomeness of the area. A good example comes in his descriptions of the riverside from St Katharine's to Wapping, which had undergone similar new building within Stow's lifetime, creating 'a continual street, or filthy strait passage, with alleys of small tenements, or cottages'. Stow mentions a place of execution on a raised area of land at East Smithfield and suggests that its relocation had made the area less notorious and thus acceptable for development.

Execution Dock

This original gallows, close to the neighbourhood of St Katharine's, was the primary place of execution for maritime crimes. Since the reign of Edward III, all crimes committed at sea, in home waters or abroad, had fallen under the jurisdiction of the British Admiralty, and capital punishment was applied to acts of mutiny, piracy, murders on the high seas, and violations of the later Articles of War governing the behaviour of naval sailors, which included the act of sodomy.[2] Offenders were held at Marshalsea prison in Southwark or at Newgate, and after their trial would be led with no small amount of ceremony to the scaffold to meet their fate. Once there, the condemned prisoner was expected to give a final speech in which he would confess, and ultimately atone for, his crimes before warning the assembled crowds against a life of wrongdoing. Often, however, this became an opportunity for the doomed miscreant to rail against and expose the perceived corruption of the authorities. The death penalty for acts of piracy in particular was intended to be cruel, and a shortened rope was used, which meant a shorter drop and a less reliable guarantee of instantaneous death; thus the dying criminal would be gradually asphyxiated while his legs squirmed in what was popularly referred to as the 'Marshal's Dance' (after the High Court marshal who presided over the grisly proceedings).

Alongside those crimes committed out at sea, increased trade on the river, and the establishment of a number of wharves at Shadwell, Ratcliffe and particularly Wapping, resulted in a rise in crimes associated with the River Thames. Two examples reveal that both British and foreign individuals met their end at the riverside gallows: the first was in 1440, when a ship returning from Flanders was intercepted in British waters by pirates who cut the throats of the crew and sank the vessel, resulting in the deaths of women and children, for which two men were convicted, hanged and suspended in chains at St Katharine's; the second was in 1495, when two Dutchmen made the journey from Newgate to Wapping and there were 'hanged in the watir', suggesting that by this time, the site of maritime executions had been moved to what became known as Execution Dock.[3]

Although its exact location has been disputed over the years, Execution Dock, situated by the banks of the Thames at the low tidemark at Wapping, and thus at the boundary of the Admiralty's jurisdiction, has become a name synonymous with river piracy, smuggling, mutiny and the brutal punishment of a bygone age, and could well be considered to be the East End's first infamous association with criminality.[4] Wapping was the place where the state's justice was made visible and purposefully put on display for wider public consumption, thus becoming a symbol of the omnipotence of the monarch's authority. Executions generally took place on a Saturday, timed to coincide with low tide, and as a result became highly popular spectacles.[5] The dead body would be chained to a stake at the low watermark and left there until three tides had washed over it, before being tarred and displayed on a gibbet farther east at Blackwall, Woolwich or Tilbury, as a warning to others who might have been tempted to take on Britain's seafaring power. Execution Dock was deemed fit for purpose for a good 400 years, despite changes in procedure; sometime between 1786 and 1815 the practice of securing a body in the river after hanging ceased, and in 1834, cases normally heard by the High Court of the Admiralty were transferred to the Central Criminal Court: only then did the public

3

executions at Wapping stop. The last were held in December 1830, when William Watts and George Davis were hanged for piracy.

Maps depicting London in the latter part of the sixteenth century demonstrate the sort of urban growth described by Stow, and the early construction of houses and other properties by the all-important river made the Thameside locations of St Katharine's, East Smithfield and Wapping significant locations of early East End development. As is evident from a map showing London around 1560,[6] numerous buildings lined the main thoroughfares, stretching east as far as Limehouse, and those closest to the river appear tightly clustered, suggesting Stow's 'alleys of small tenements'. As for the growth of east London farther north, roads beside the wall of the City were becoming apparent, with significant lanes like Houndsditch and Hogge Lane[7] etched into the still predominantly rural landscape, with only the main road through Whitechapel showing any eastward expansion comparable to that of the area by the Thames; even then it stretched only as far as the church of St Mary Matfelon.[8] The hamlet of Stebunheth (modern Stepney), with the ancient church of St Dunstan's as its focal point, sat amongst fields and marshland, and the largely open and pleasant aspect of the area made it popular for entertainments of all kinds such as hunting, pageants and festivals. But its location set apart from the City of London also made it an early breeding ground for dissent, and as early as the sixteenth century the embryonic East End had become the exile's choice.

The outsiders

In the early 1500s, Protestant reform, challenging the accepted doctrine of the Catholic Church, was spreading throughout Europe; Martin Luther, rejecting the teaching and practices of the papacy, had set out his ideas in his *Ninety-five Theses* in 1517, and his refusal to retract his writings led to excommunication by the pope and to his being branded an outlaw by the

Holy Roman Emperor, Charles V, in 1520. But these writings were quickly disseminated throughout Europe, and in England found early favour in the southeast, particularly around the ports. Stepney became a fertile oasis of dissent as Luther's ideas, and later those of John Calvin, trickled in with the European mainlanders alighting from their ships moored on the Thames east of London Bridge. Stepney was ideally placed; part of the oath taken by freemen of the City of London stated that 'ye shall know no gatherings, conventicles nor conspiracies made against the King's peace,'[9] and thus meetings could be held in relative safety away from the nervous civil and religious authorities who did all they could to clamp down on the growing Nonconformism.

Such heresy, when exposed, could be punishable by death: William Jerome, vicar of St Dunstan's, had opened himself up to the ire of the Church by preaching a thunderous sermon attacking the Act of Six Articles,[10] and calling the burgesses of Parliament 'butterflies, fools and knaves';[11] he was burned at the stake as a Lutheran in 1540. Cuthbert Sympson, deacon of the Congregational Church at Islington, was charged as a dissenter in 1558, and tortured and burned at the stake in Smithfield when informants revealed his secret meetings to the authorities. Such congregations invariably took place in Wapping, St Katharine's and Ratcliffe and were attended by foreigners, including visitors from Holland and France, whose presence served to arouse the great suspicion of the owners of the properties where the meetings were held.[12]

One feels that the stranglehold of the powerful City, and the efforts by many to sidestep its rules and conventions, had much to do with the slowly developing, contradictory – and ungovernable – nature of the land beyond its eastern boundaries. It may have been a delightful place to hold festivals and healthy outdoor pursuits, but the staging of plays was a different matter entirely; indeed, the positioning of a number of playhouses about the eastern suburbs has often been cited as another indicator of the East End's willingness to accept the unconventional.

London's first permanent theatre, built as a receiving house for travelling players, was the Red Lion in Whitechapel. The theatre, situated along the Whitechapel Road towards Mile End,[13] was built in 1567 by a grocer, John Brayne, in the garden of Red Lion farm. It was a single-gallery multi-sided theatre with a fixed stage measuring 40 by 30 feet, equipped with trapdoors. A 30-foot-high turret, for aerial stunts, also served to mark it prominently within the landscape. It is believed that only one play was ever performed there, *The Story of Samson*, and the location, out in the rural suburbs and thus not particularly accessible during less favourable weather, meant that the theatre was short-lived.[14] In 1572, the mayor and Corporation of London banned the staging of plays within the City boundaries, specifically to halt the congregation of crowds of strangers as a preventive measure against the spread of plague. Three years later, all players were formally expelled from the City; but the act of banishing players and blocking the performing of plays was not just on health grounds, for there were many who voiced other concerns.

Following the construction of the more durable Theatre in 1576 and the Curtain in 1577, both in Shoreditch,[15] a number of anti-theatrical tracts appeared, denouncing the concept of theatre and those who participated in it or who enjoyed its pleasures. It was felt that the plays were often lewd and profane, that play actors were mostly vagrant, irresponsible and immoral people; that taverns and disreputable houses were always found in the vicinity of theatres, and that the theatre itself was a public danger in the way of spreading disease.[16]

Sermons at Paul's Cross saw outspoken detractors of the theatre such as Thomas White, vicar of St Dunstan's in the West, declare that 'the cause of plague is sinne if you looke to it well: and the cause of sinne are playes: therefore the cause of plagues are playes'.[17] Other moral concerns were pronounced to the effect that the playhouses operated on the Sabbath and their popularity meant that the public was more concerned with watching 'vain playes and enterludes' than attending church.[18] And in an age when boys were required to play female roles, the opinion widely held amongst Puritan critics of the stage was that the actor 'was bound by the very necessities of his craft to infringe the divine law which forbade one sex to wear the costume of the other'.[19]

In early 1581, the Theatre in Shoreditch became the focus of accusations of unruliness, and John Brayne and John Burbage, proprietors of the playhouse, were charged with bringing together unlawful gatherings, where 'great affrays assaults tumults and quasi-insurrections and divers other misdeeds and enormities have been then and there done and perpetrated by very ill-disposed persons to the great disturbance of the peace of the Lady the Queen'.[20] Despite the feelings of the distraction-seeking public, the authorities of the City and other agencies labelled actors squarely as undesirables, with plays seen as a conduit for licentious and criminal behaviour and the playhouses providing venues for such collective depravity. Because such theatres were located outside the City's jurisdiction, the putting on of plays in such dedicated settings avoided any *official* categorisation of unlawfulness. Nonetheless, it would taint such districts with a reputation for disreputable habits, and those who lived in the districts of Southwark, Shoreditch, Finsbury and the area between Aldgate and Stepney were looked down upon as unruly. Certainly, the reputation of the suburban resident of early London as being boisterous and unmanageable was given a boost in the seventeenth century during a series of notable civil disturbances in which the East End played an integral part.

Revellers, riots and bawds

By the onset of the 1600s, the riverside neighbourhoods were still the most populated, industrious, and thus flourishing, part of the fledgling East End. Over 50 per cent of baptisms in the first decade of the seventeenth century took place in Ratcliffe (the most populated of the riverside hamlets), Shadwell, Limehouse and Poplar, dwarfing the figures recorded in the immediate outlying areas to the north, namely Bethnal Green, Spitalfields and Mile End, which still remained largely undeveloped. With innumerable ships playing the waiting game, moored along the riverside stairs awaiting access to the busy Pool of London close by London Bridge, many of the area's inhabitants were linked to maritime pursuits; not only was there a transient population of mariners, but local trades reflected the necessary and obvious links to the Thames, including small shipbuilders, makers of ropes and sails, smiths, and other providers of essentials such as tailors, shoemakers and builders.[21] Naturally there were many lodging houses and inns to provide shelter and sustenance for the mariners, and with that came facilities to cater for baser pleasures.

Medieval London's major district for such distractions was situated in Southwark, across the river from the Pool of London, and thus easily accessible to the scores of sailors and workers on the river; it became known for its theatres, bull- and bear-baiting pits, brothels and taverns. Presided over by the bishop of Winchester, away from the City authorities, this garden of earthly delights was allowed to flourish, particularly as prostitution had been licensed there since 1162. The brothels, or 'stews' as they were known, were deemed a necessary safety-valve, allowing men to let off steam, and were governed 'according to the old customs that had been there used time out of mind'.[22] This sex trade, thus sanctioned, was felt to be the lesser of innumerable evils, keeping the sex-hungry male away from what were deemed more depraved acts such as sodomy and masturbation, whilst at the same time filling the coffers of the bishop.

The riverside east of the City had its own outlet of inns and unsanctioned bawdy houses; famously, the Pelican in Wapping would come to be known as 'the Devil's Tavern', owing to its disreputable clientele, a place where many a plot of robbery and smuggling was hatched.[23]

Several inns, such as the Artichoke, the Malt Shovel and the Gunboat in the increasingly cluttered district of Ratcliffe Highway, were the haunts of prostitutes,[24] many of whom had come from mainland Europe and thus could be relied upon to provide individual expertise and to satisfy all tastes – Flemish women in particular were noted for their sexual proficiency and imagination. Venetian courtesans, meanwhile, were too expensive for the rank-and-file sailor, and catered instead for aristocrats, wealthy merchants and even members of the royal court. A number of bawdy houses run by Dutch women were recorded in East Smithfield.[25]

The brothels of the eastern suburbs close to the riverside became, along with those in other neighbourhoods, the target for unruliness and mob violence in the early to mid-seventeenth century. Shrove Tuesday, like any great holiday, had traditionally been a time of merriment, a boisterous festival which invariably ended in civil disturbance, and in London the green light for such rowdy behaviour was embraced by the younger menfolk, namely apprentices. Perhaps triggered by the arrival of Lent when all vices and indulgences would face a compulsory pause, and in what has been suggested as an attempt to remove temptation, theatres and brothels became a target for the young men's riotous revelries, as recorded in a play of the time:

Farewell all ye good boies in merry London,
Nere shall we more upon Shore-Tuesday meete
And plucke down houses of iniquitie.[26]

One bordello in Shoreditch was attacked so often in the years 1612–14 that it was ultimately demolished.[27] In all, twenty-four such disturbances took place in the London suburbs on Shrove Tuesday between 1606 and 1641, with one, on 4 March 1617, targeting brothels in Wapping and St Katharine's: John Chamberlain wrote 'how at Wapping they pulled down seven or eight houses and defaced five times as many, besides other outrages, as beating the sheriff from his horse with stones, and doing much other hurt too long to write . . . we shall see some of them hanged next week as it is more than time they were.'[28]

Damaris Page, perhaps one of the best known of the East End brothel-keepers of this period, was affected by the disturbances of 1668, which became known as the Bawdy House Riots. Page was born in Stepney around 1620 into extreme poverty, a situation which would certainly have pushed her into prostitution at an early age. In 1655, she faced the hangman's noose when an attempted abortion on one Eleanor Pooley resulted in the young woman's death, Page having thrust a two-pronged fork into Pooley's abdomen to a depth of about 4.5 inches. Page herself made it known she was pregnant at the time of her conviction and thus pleaded for clemency; the child was stillborn at Newgate prison. Ultimately Damaris Page was pardoned and allowed to go free after three years, continuing her old ways.[29] From then on, she forged a successful career as a brothel-keeper on the Ratcliffe Highway, special-ising in personal services for sailors and merchants, which earnt her the nickname 'the great bawd of the seamen'.[30] Before long she was buying up more property to house her businesses, which were extremely lucra-tive. One of her brothels, on Rosemary Lane near East Smithfield, catered for prominent naval officers, and this resulted in a mutually beneficial relationship; Page is believed to have been instrumental in assisting press gangs to acquire new naval recruits, thus leaving many wives without support – a situation that would have led many of these now vulnerable women to resort to prostitution, usually in one of Page's many houses. It is said that one sea captain was moved to state that 'as long as Damaris Page lived he was sure he should not lack men'.[31] This made Page unpopular amongst those indisposed to her particular line of work, and so, at the onset of the Bawdy House Riots during Easter week 1668, her houses became a target for the mob.

These disturbances were nothing unusual in that they occurred during a holiday period, and as the innumerable Shrove Tuesday incidents of previous years show, such occasions were typically punctuated with attacks on brothels and other places of supposed 'ill virtue' by rowdy young men. However, the events of 23–25 March 1668 lasted three days and ultimately involved thousands of perpetrators. It is difficult to believe that these riots were merely the work of mischief on the part of young apprentices, as the rioters were well organised, with captains placed at the head of each group. Political slogans such as 'Down with the Red Coats!' and 'Reformation and Reducement!' were frequently heard during the disturbances, as well as threats to tear down Whitehall itself, suggesting a political origin rather than traditional high-jinks.[32] Another cause was believed to be dissent triggered by a recent proclamation by Charles II which cracked down on private lay worship for Nonconformists while ignoring the existence of illegal brothels[33] (after all, the king and members of his court patronised many such houses, including those run by Damaris Page). And thus, when the bawdy houses of Shoreditch, Poplar and East Smithfield found themselves the target of these tumults, the ransacking of Page's properties became a prime objective. The result was a significant loss of revenue for this most prominent of bawds, and Page went before a magistrate as a victim of the riots. Despite her being an unmarried woman and a brothel-keeper at that, she was looked upon favourably and even stood as a key witness against one of the instigators of the riots, Robert Sharpless.[34]

The predicament of Damaris Page and her sisters-in-trade also resulted in the publication of a number of satirical pamphlets, the most famous being *The Poor-Whore's Petition*. In this, Page and contemporary madam Elizabeth Cresswell[35] appeared to have put their name to a plea to the king's mistress, Lady Castlemaine, to remunerate the affected brothel-keepers to help rebuild their houses and their businesses. Lady Castlemaine was a known prostitute and it is very possible that the petition was a satirical piece composed by a third party, making comment on the perceived licentiousness of Charles II's court. Indeed, Samuel Pepys noted that Lady Castlemaine was 'horribly vexed' by the publication; perhaps due to his strong links to the royal court, he made the disappointed judgement that 'the times are loose, and come to a great disregard of the King, or Court, or Government'.[36]

It is from this troubled period that an interesting tale emerges from the bawdy houses of Ratcliffe, namely the case of Thomas Savage and Hannah Blay. Savage was born into an honest family in St Giles-in-the-Fields, but had been apprenticed to a vintner at the Ship Tavern, Ratcliffe Cross, with whom he led a profligate life for several years. Introduced to a brothel in Ratcliffe by a sailor friend, he met Hannah Blay, described as 'a vile common strumpet', with whom he fell into an unholy partnership of drinking, thieving and whoring, by his own admission spending many a Sabbath in her company rather than at church. Blay soon became tired of the young man's offerings of drink and reckless amusement in return for her services and made it clear that if he was to spend more time with her, he would have to produce hard cash for the privilege. The only place where Savage knew he could easily obtain money was from his master, from whom he had never previously stolen, mainly because the maid was always present. When Blay heard this, she batted aside his caution: 'Knock her brains out, and I'll receive the money, and go anywhere with you beyond sea, to avoid the stroke of justice.'[37]

When the fateful day came, Blay got Savage drunk on burnt brandy. Going to his master's house, the reluctant robber sneaked in by a back door, only to be confronted by the maid and other servants at dinner. The maid chastised him about his reckless life, which only served to rile Savage who, at that moment, decided that the maid would after all meet the fate demanded by Hannah Blay. Waiting until the master and servants were at church and he was alone with her, he seized the opportunity. Savage began smashing objects with a hammer which he had acquired from a back room in the house, to deliberately annoy the maid. When she admonished him for this, he provoked her further by standing on a newly cleaned dresser in his dirty shoes, and she scolded him even more. Savage threw the hammer at her head. Troubled by a brief moment of doubt, he was then taken over by the necessity of his task and he beat the maid with the hammer until she was dead. Having done so, Savage broke open his master's cupboard and took a bag containing the considerable amount of £600 which he conveyed to Blay, though he was unwilling to part with the spoils.

Back in Greenwich, Savage became wracked with guilt, but his problems only increased when the bag of money was noticed by the mistress of the house he was staying in. It was not long before news of the robbery and murder reached her and, piecing together the incident, her troubled lodger and his recently acquired fortune, she dispatched a number of men to find Savage, which they soon did, in a tavern, sitting alone with his head upon the table in a drunken stupor. Ultimately, Savage was convicted of the crimes and sentenced to death. But his execution at Ratcliffe Cross did not go according to plan:

he was turned off the cart, and struggled for a while, heaving up his body. Which a young man, his friend, perceiving, he struck him several blows upon his breast with all his strength, to put him out of his pain, till no motion could be perceived in him. Wherefore after he had hung a considerable time, and was to all appearance dead, the people moving away, the sheriff ordered him to be cut down, when, being received into the arms of some of his friends, he was conveyed into a house not far from the place of execution. There being laid upon a table, he began, to the astonishment of the beholders, to breathe, and rattle in the throat, so that it was evident life was whole in him. Hereupon he was carried from thence to a bed in the same house, where he breathed more strongly, and opened his eyes and mouth, though his teeth were set before, and he offered to speak, but could not recover the use of his tongue.[38]

Once news of Savage's recovery had spread, sheriff's officers arrived and quickly took him back to the place of execution where, on this attempt, the hanging was successful. The body was taken to Islington where it was buried on 28 October 1668. At the time of his execution, Thomas Savage was only seventeen years old.

CHAPTER 2

Economic Conflict

The Prosecutor depos'd, That as he was coming from Bow to London, and near Bow Church, the Prisoner ask'd him if he was going to London, he said yes, and he said he would bear him Company, and that as they were going along, he Knock'd him down, and afterwards took him by the Handkerchief about his Neck, and drag'd him out of the Path, pull'd out a Pistol, and threaten'd, that if he made any Noise, he would shoot him through the Head . . .

William Summerfield's Old Bailey deposition (1723)[1]

The first half of the seventeenth century had seen gradual urban growth east of the City walls, and whilst the cluttered neighbourhoods of the riverside and Shoreditch continued to be the focus of much boisterousness, the quiet fields between them, most notably the Spittle Field,[2] Goodman's Fields and the large Lolesworth Field, were divided up by landowners and sold to builders, creating a series of streets flanked by houses, gardens and smaller 'tenter' fields used for stretching cloth. The market on the Spittle Field had been in operation since Charles I granted its charter in 1638, and though this once open land was now much diminished, the encroachment of property on all sides created a defining area in which the market could continue to flourish. Significant building had taken place north of Whitechapel High Street as far as Brick Lane to the east, and many of the streets developed during the middle period of the seventeenth century are still with us in name and form, such as Wentworth Street, Bell Lane and Fashion Street. Others, like Flower and Dean Street, Thrawl Street and Dorset Street, whose original presence or name is lost to us now, would later become epicentres of local poverty and vice.[3]

Your money or your life

The predominantly rural aspect of the area east of these new developments certainly influenced the kind of lawlessness found there in the late seventeenth and early eighteenth centuries. Unsurprisingly, animal theft, predominantly of horses, was common – the equivalent of dealing in stolen vehicles today. The long, desolate and lonely roads past Mile End were also prime stalking grounds for highwaymen and 'footpads'. The crime of highway robbery had been removed from benefit of clergy in 1531. This legal loophole had, since the twelfth century, allowed clergymen to be tried solely by an ecclesiastical court rather than a secular one, and sentencing for such crimes did not always result in the death penalty, as it did in ordinary courts. By the sixteenth century, the criterion for pleading benefit of clergy had changed, and it was therefore available to any citizen who had the ability to read. A number of offences were still deemed 'unclergyable', however, including murder, rape, treason, poisoning, burglary, witchcraft and pickpocketing; highway robbery, considered to be violent theft, fell into that category, and was thus invariably punishable by death. And so, as travellers risked using the main road to Essex passing through Mile End, Bow and Stratford, so those who robbed them risked their own lives in perpetrating the crime.

16

The road between Mile End and Bow was a particularly hazardous stretch to travel on, and even from the late seventeenth century highway robbery was common there. In February 1680, Justice Northe, his wife and son, and another woman, were violently robbed by three men and a woman who 'did use them in a most barbarous manner', stealing a pearl necklace worth over £100, 4 shillings in cash, a cravat, a handkerchief, a scarf, and rings of considerable value. The robbery was interrupted by men who had come to meet the coach and a standoff ensued. The robbers fled on foot and the darkness made identification of the felons almost impossible; however, when two of the robbers, Frances Phillips and William Harris, went to pawn some of the articles at a later date, their participation was discovered and they were sentenced to death at the subsequent Old Bailey trial.[4]

Often, the risk taken by the highway robbers was great in relation to the spoils gained by the crime. William Johnson and his wife were robbed of little more than a steel box, a handkerchief and £5 in cash while travelling to Romford on that same stretch of highway between Mile End and Bow. Five men were involved, John Hutchings, Joseph Redwell, Henry Paffet, Richard Kent and Thomas Williams, all of whom were found guilty of highway robbery and sentenced to death.[5] Six months later, Peter Anderson netted a reasonably profitable haul from two men, Samuel Blackburn and Samuel Newton, as they travelled at night through the fields near Bow. The two travellers were relieved of two coats, two swords, a pair of fringed gloves, a belt, rings, buckles, and 12 shillings by Anderson and three unknown accomplices. When his case came to trial, Anderson, charged with two counts of highway robbery, claimed to have been at home in bed at the time of the robbery, but, unable to prove it, he too received the death penalty.[6]

By the beginning of the eighteenth century, highway robbery was becoming alarmingly commonplace, as innumerable Old Bailey cases,

17

particularly from the 1720s, attest. Indeed, in 1728, a report to James Stuart stated that

> Highway robberies prevail in England more than in any other nation of Europe. Are not the persons who commit them frequently such as are unwilling to make their distress public, and, finding themselves sunk in spite of industry, grow desperate and run the risk of an ignominious death to satisfy these voracious harpies the Whigs that occasion all their misery.[7]

Much of this increase, as the report suggested, was said to be a reaction to what was seen as the 'gross inequality and misery deliberately produced by a narrowly based elite that had allied itself to usurping dynasties', namely the House of Orange, the reign of Queen Anne and the House of Hanover.[8] Social injustice – and the hardships that resulted from it – sometimes produced sympathy for highway robbers and in some ways made them popular figures and even folk heroes in the minds of the people. Some had their quirks, such as considered politeness, or making promises never to hurt women, giving them the allure of the 'gentleman' criminal – a moral blurriness that would reach its peak in east London in the mid-twentieth century. Despite this, the often violent methods that many highwaymen used were looked upon with distaste, no matter how the general populace might have felt about the somewhat dubious sense of social righteousness being enacted. One victim, Richard Tisdale, was robbed of £3, a watch and a ring after being knocked down by the thief, Jonathan Batt, who yelled, 'Damn you, you dog, I have you down, lie still you son of a bitch, deliver your Money.'[9] John Howse was targeted by James Stagles, who was armed with a pistol which he had fired at the coach in order to make it stop. Howse was robbed of some money and two pocket-pieces before Stagles declared that he would shoot him if he did not get out of his way.[10] This, like the previously encountered incidents, took place on the road between Mile End and Bow, which had become the eastern suburbs' venue of choice for highway robbery since the creation of Mile End Gate around 1714, one of many turnpikes which had sprung up on the main roads into London in the wake of the Turnpike Act of 1663.[11] By necessity, robbers were compelled to operate beyond the turnpike, as any transit requiring passage through the manned gate would leave the criminals open to challenge and identification.

Highway robbery certainly had its share of noted characters, some of whom have become legendary: individuals such as James MacLaine, Claude Duvall and John 'Sixteen String Jack' Rann have become quasi-fictional characters in literature and the media at large, but it is Richard 'Dick' Turpin who has overshadowed them all in terms of fame and mythology. So much has been written about this infamous character that it is often impossible to separate fact from fiction.[12] Believed to have been born in Hempstead in Essex in 1705, it is said that he followed his father's trade as a butcher and was apprenticed in Whitechapel before being dismissed owing to 'the impropriety of his behaviour, and the brutality of his manners'.[13] Turpin's life of criminality, first as part of a gang which terrorised Essex and Epping Forest and later as a roving highwayman, meant that descriptions of him were often circulated; in 1734, the London Gazette described him thus: 'Richard Turpin, a butcher by trade, is a tall fresh-coloured man, very much marked with the small pox, about 26 years of age, about five feet nine inches high, lived some time ago in Whitechapel and did lately lodge somewhere about Millbank, Westminster, wears a blue grey coat and a natural wig.'[14]

Despite the often-mentioned associations with Whitechapel, Dick Turpin's connections with the East End are nonetheless flimsy. However, the incident that instigated a downturn in his fortunes did take place there in 1737. By this time Turpin had teamed up with Matthew King, who had originally been targeted as one of the notorious highwayman's many victims: the robbery did not go according to plan, for –

unbeknownst to Turpin – King was a jobbing highwayman in his own right, and proved more than a match. An account of their alleged first meeting is recounted in an early nineteenth-century chapbook:

> King, the highwayman, as he was returning . . . to London, being well dressed and mounted, Turpin seeing him have the appearance of a substantial gentleman . . . bid him stand and deliver, and therewith producing his pistols, King fell a laughing at him, and said, 'What dog rob dog! Come, come brother Turpin, if you don't know me, I know you, and should be glad of your company.'[15]

Thus began a lucrative but relatively short-lived alliance. In May 1737 they robbed a Mr Joseph Major in Epping Forest and took his horse, named Whitestockings,[16] which King subsequently had stabled at the Red Lion on Whitechapel High Street.[17] The mare was traced to the inn and, it being made known that the owners of the horses there would soon be returning for them, a vigil was mounted; King was soon apprehended as he attempted to collect the animal. He claimed to have legitimately bought Whitestockings, but in the process also managed to divulge that his brother, John,[18] and Turpin were waiting for him in Goodman's Field, where they were duly found. John King was taken, but shots were fired and Matthew King was hit in the left breast. In the confusion, Turpin got away and went into hiding. The following morning, three men went to a lodging house in nearby Wellclose Square, where Turpin was staying, but he was forewarned by the lady proprietor and made good his escape across the rooftops. The King brothers were sent before Justice Ricketts and John was committed to Newgate; Matthew, after it was discovered that he was likely to make a recovery from his gunshot wound, was committed to Bridewell.[19]

It has commonly been stated that it was Turpin who shot King, although it is not certain whether this was done in error, or to facilitate his escape, or whether it was intended as punishment for King's subsequent disclosure of his accomplices' whereabouts. (It has also often been said that King eventually died from his injury, despite several newspaper accounts of his expected recovery.) Whatever the case, Turpin was a wanted man, and secreted himself in a hideout in Epping Forest where he was spotted by gamekeeper Thomas Morris, who challenged the notorious robber and was shot dead. Now certainly wanted as a killer as well as a thief (which suggests the murder of Morris was Turpin's first), a bounty of £200 (approximately £17,000 in today's money) was offered for his capture.[20] He settled in York using the alias John Palmer, where, after his true identity was discovered following several other misdemeanours, he was executed on 7 April 1739: 'Turpin behaved in an undaunted manner; as he mounted the ladder, feeling his right leg tremble, he spoke a few words to the topsman, then threw himself off, and expir'd in five minutes.'[21]

The lawless nature of individuals like Dick Turpin and, also notably, Captain William Kidd – who was famously hanged at Execution Dock in 1701 for piracy[22] – cannot be said to be a result of any direct association with the East End per se. Their characters or deeds were not fashioned by any specific cause exclusive to east London's troublesome suburbs, yet the fact that they are well-known historical criminal figures who fleetingly touched the East End during key points in their lives (or deaths) helps to reinforce the sense that this part of London had a dark heart. Populist history guides, when speaking of early Whitechapel, revel in the Red Lion story, suggesting that from that fateful moment in May 1737, Dick Turpin leapt upon his trusty steed, Black Bess, and made the lengthy flight to York in record time. Of course, it never happened that way, but as the histories of various pubs and inns on the route north from London suggest (usually unreliably), there is much to be gained from the claim that Turpin stalked your neighbourhood or drank ale from your cellar. Arguably, Dick Turpin, who almost from the moment of his death has been transformed by what has been written about him from a mere thug and murderer into 'a bold and daring highwayman, a gentleman of the road, a protector of the weak and oppressed',[23] is probably the first of many major, one might say legendary, criminal figures associated with the East End, albeit tentatively – figures whose activities would imprint themselves indelibly onto this part of London's rather troubled psyche.

The angry mob

By the beginning of the eighteenth century, on the eastern side of Brick Lane, the development of Mile End New Town, effectively an extension of Spitalfields and Bethnal Green, was proceeding slowly, with much of its sporadic housing being inhabited by 'handicraft tradesmen … labourers and artificers'.[24] Such trades included silk-weaving, which initially centred on Spitalfields before later spreading farther north and east. It was the prevalence of silk-weavers in this newly developing district which would have a profound effect on its character.

Although the weaving industry had been present in the Spitalfields area for some considerable time, a major boost came with the revocation of the Edict of Nantes in France in 1685. This edict, signed in 1598, had granted Protestant Huguenots significant rights in what was essentially a strongly Catholic country, freeing them from persecution as heretics and instigating a new era of secularism and tolerance. The revocation of the edict, activated by King Louis XIV's Edict of Fontainebleau in 1685, immediately scrubbed all of the basic civil rights enjoyed by the Protestants for decades, resulting in renewed, often ferocious, persecution. All Protestant ministers were given two weeks to leave the country unless they converted to Catholicism, and whereas all other Protestants were prohibited from leaving France, the persecution, which often involved acts of torture, caused many, believed to be upwards of 40,000, to flee to other nations close by, often at great personal risk.[25] By 1687,

London had become home to over 30,000 French refugees, with a high proportion settling outside the City walls in the rapidly growing neighbourhoods east of Bishopsgate.[26] Here they took some comfort in an area known for its Nonconformism and strong links to Protestantism: in a later reprinting of Stow's *Survey of London*, the editor, John Strype, spoke highly of these new citizens: 'Here they have found quiet and security, and settled themselves in their several trades and occupations; weavers especially . . . And this benefit also to the neighbourhood, that these strangers may serve for patterns of thrift, honesty, industry, and sobriety as well.'[27]

But it was not all plain sailing to begin with. In 1683, just a few years prior to the refugee surge, enough immigrant weavers had settled in Spitalfields to fuel discontent among the indigenous craftsmen who, already hit by recession, became angry over the threat to trade posed by these newcomers. It reached such an extent that, at one point, it was advised that a troop of cavalrymen be stationed nearby in Whitechapel to quell any potential disorder.[28] Whilst the existing weavers there initially resented the foreigners, concerned about their credentials and the quality of their work, the French soon established themselves, showing that their silks were of high quality, and in this expanding London suburb the industry thrived. With growing trust and respect, initial difficulties and poverty were overcome, while legislation banning imported silks from France and other European countries allowed the Spitalfields weavers to dominate, and with that came wealth. The sudden development of handsome properties to the north and east of Spitalfields market created a number of communities dominated by French weavers in what are now Elder, Fleur-de-lis, Folgate, Princelet, Fournier and Wilkes Streets.[29]

John Strype, himself from a refugee silk-weaving family, wrote of the new Spitalfields at this time in much the same way as Stow had described the riverside hamlets over a century before: 'Within this parish, formerly, in the Memory of some, pleasant fields for the Citizens to walk in and for good House-wives to whiten their Cloths. Now all but built into Streets, with a very convenient Market-place, and a Tabernacle for Divine Worship.'[30] The mention of a seemingly single 'Tabernacle' does not, however, do justice to the significant presence of Nonconformist places of worship in Spitalfields, now on the increase as Protestant Huguenots built a number of chapels to cater for their swelling numbers. By 1700, there were nine such places of worship in the area, including Brown's Lane (modern Hanbury Street) behind Spital Square, Wheeler Street, Crispin Street and Parliament Court. On Brick Lane, at the corner of what would soon become Church Street (today's Fournier Street), a temporary wooden hut served as a French church for almost sixty years before being rebuilt in 1743 as L'Eglise de l'Hôpital or La Neuve Eglise,[31] an annex to L'Eglise Protestante in Threadneedle Street in the City.

Newly formed parishes, a result of the growing population of the eastern hamlets, had made the construction of new churches in the East End a necessity, but the notable presence of Nonconformism in the area now made it a priority in the eyes of the authorities. By the more tolerant eighteenth century, such alternative religious observance was hardly a crime, but the new parishes were deemed ideal locales in which to install places of worship allied to the Church of England, and to thus assert Anglican authority over the Nonconformists. The resulting Commission for the Building of Fifty New Churches of 1711 resulted in the construction of three splendid churches in the East End, designed by Nicholas Hawksmoor, between 1714 and 1730: St George-in-the-East, St Anne's Limehouse and Christ Church Spitalfields, the latter remaining one of the East End's most notable and impressive landmarks.[32]

During this time, the fierce competition in the skilled trades resulted in a series of disturbances which were a direct result of the weavers' ardent desire to cling to their livelihoods in the face of perceived threats. One such menace was the increased popularity of printed calico, imported from India by the East India Company, which as early as 1708 was becoming the material of choice for the dresses of London society ladies and for home furnishings. By 1719, the journalist, pamphleteer and author Daniel Defoe, an outspoken mouthpiece for the weavers, was commenting that the streets were 'crowded with calico madams' and their homes 'stuff'd with calico furniture'.[33] The survival of the silk-weaving industry was considered of great importance and the relative cheapness of this imported material threatened to undermine the livelihoods of those who worked in it, from weavers and throwers to merchants and importers. The anger against this commercial intrusion manifested itself in strongly worded broadsheets, such as the 'Ballad of Spittlefields, or the Weavers Complaint Against the Calico Madams (To the tune of Apples for Gold)':

In the Ages of Old,
We Traded for Gold,
Our merchants were thriving and Wealthy:
We had silks for our Store,
Warm Wool for our Poor,
And Drugs for the Sick and Unhealthy:
And Drugs for the Sick and Unhealthy.

But now we bring Home
The Froth and the Scum
To Dress up the Trapes like a gay-Dame:
And Ev'ry She Clown Gets a Pye-spotted gown,
And sets up for a Callicoe Madam.
O! tawdery Callico Madam . . .

To neglect their own Works,
Employ pagans and turks,
And let foreign Trump'ry o'er spread 'em:

Shut up their own Door,

And starve their own Poor,

For a tawdery Callico Madam.

O! this Tatterdemalion Madam.[34]

Serious unrest began in June 1719, when as many as 4,000 weavers assembled in Spitalfields and around the Mint (then based at the Tower of London) in protest at calico imports. Tempers frayed and violence ensued. Further demonstrations saw to it that calico works were attacked and, more disturbingly, women wearing the offensive material were set upon, sometimes having their clothing torn from their backs, or worse. In one incident, a weaver threatened Rebecca Tate of the White Lion in Rosemary Lane, Whitechapel, with a knife for wearing a calico gown, 'and swore he would either cut the callicoe or stab her to the heart'.[35] John Larmony and Mary Martoon of Shoreditch were acquitted of assaulting Elizabeth Price in a ferocious attack that also resulted in the stealing of money. When Price was seen wearing a calico gown, Larmony cried out, ' "Callicoe, Callicoe; Weavers, Weavers!" Whereupon a great Number came down and tore her Gown off all but the Sleeve, her Pocket, the Head of her Riding Hood, and abus'd her very much.' During the fracas, Martoon was heard to call Price a 'Calico Bitch'.[36] Husbands sometimes offered the attackers money to leave their wives alone, but this was often to no avail, and one gentleman 'had his brains beat out' for having the audacity to make such an offer. One weaver was killed with a cleaver when a butcher attempted to defend his wife from the mob.[37]

The press of the day made much of the behaviour of the demonstrators, stating that it was 'notorious how they tore [a victim's] clothes and would not spare so much as her under petticoat'.[38] The unrest also gave the regular criminal the opportunity to benefit from the chaos, with robberies and random assaults also being recorded amidst the hubbub; on one occasion, 'three fellows under pretence of being weavers, when they were downright thieves' robbed a woman as they tore her gown.[39] The riots were perceived as something of a class war, too, for the poorer weavers were seen to be targeting the middle and upper classes. Protesters also felt that the wearing of calico was unpatriotic, and thus xenophobia, with calico representing a form of 'foreign invasion', fuelled the discord. The genuine weavers, perhaps because they were fired up by a legitimate grievance, were often treated leniently by the authorities, and many were acquitted in court; but as the disturbances and assaults on women continued into 1720, harsher punishments were meted out, perhaps as a deterrent. One weaver in July of that year was convicted of tearing a woman's calico gown off her back and 'using her very barbarously in the fields near Hoxton', language which suggests sexual assault: the man was sentenced to transportation for seven years.[40]

The passing of the Calico Act of 1720 was a reaction as much to the rioting as it was to the threat of a downturn in domestic industry caused by imports. Loopholes in previous acts had done little to stop the growth of such alien commodities, but the tougher 1720 act, which banned all imported calico, attempted to finally give English trades priority and assurance, and ultimately put a halt to the violence. Thus it was felt that anybody who continued to instigate such hostility after the passing of the act had no real cause to do so other than for reasons of sheer wanton lawlessness; weavers who persisted in tearing calico gowns and assaulting those who wore them were looked down upon even by their early champions, and punishment became severe.

As the eighteenth century entered its first decades, then, we see that the causes of great public unrest in east London were economic in origin, as opposed to being on religious or moral grounds. Suddenly, the East End had a viable workforce, rapidly increasing in number with the arrival of immigrant artisans and those who were called upon to build their homes and workshops. The weavers of this newly built-up London suburb would pass their skills on to the indigenous population who

27

would gradually spread the industry towards Bethnal Green and Mile End New Town. It would not be long before the master weavers began seeing the benefits of using a less expensive workforce, predominantly made up of recently arrived immigrants who were prepared to work for significantly lower wages than their English or French counterparts. Before long there would be, in the words of one contemporary, 'great discontents and murmurings through all this Mobbish part of the Town'.[41]

Such problems came to the fore in 1736 when the church of St Leonard's in Shoreditch was being rebuilt. The church, believed to be Saxon in origin, had been enlarged over the centuries, but by the eighteenth century significant structural problems had begun to challenge the integrity and safety of the building. The headwaters of the River Walbrook passed close by, making the foundations unstable, particularly as the floor of the church sat 8 feet below ground level. Around 1713, high winds carried away part of the steeple, and three years later part of the tower collapsed: one observer noted that 'the walls of the old church rent asunder, with a frightful sound, during Divine service, and a considerable quantity of mortar falling, the congregation fled on all sides to the doors, where they severely injured each other by their efforts to escape'.[42] A new church was thus deemed necessary, and construction began in 1736, to the designs of the recently appointed City of London architect George Dance the Elder, whose other notable projects included St Botolph's in Aldgate (1741–44) and the Mansion House in the City (1739–52).

It was not long before a story began to spread that English workmen involved in the construction of the church were being dismissed and replaced by Irish labourers who, it was said, were 'letting themselves out to all sort of labour considerably cheaper than the English labourers have; and numbers of them being employed by the weavers upon the like terms'.[43] It was suggested that the generally impoverished Irish were willing to accept less than two-thirds the wages of their English colleagues. This was deemed utterly unacceptable, and in July 1736 violence broke out in Shoreditch, neighbouring Spitalfields, and around the area of Rosemary Lane and Cable Street (part of which bore the name 'Knockfergus', allegedly due to its significant Irish community):

This Strife being fomented by Rumours, fighting Matches, and National Animosity, at last raised to such a Pitch, that it appeared like a civil War . . . In short, it is known that the Mischief would have ended, if the Care and Vigilance of her Majesty had not put a stop to it, by ordering some Horse and Foot Guards to patrole through Shore-ditch and Spittle-fields.[44]

On 30 July, Robert Page, William Rod and Thomas Putrode, described by the authorities as 'Persons of evil Minds', along with several others, smashed windows and broke down doors of houses around Leman Street and Cable Street to cries of 'Down with the Irish!' Their target was the home of Graves Atkin who, after becoming aware of his peril, fled with his family and went into hiding. Other properties were attacked nearby; Richard Burton, having assured the mob that he was not Irish, appeared to have avoided any violence until a woman shouted out that he was lying. It was only the arrival of Justice Phillips and a group of soldiers that saved him from serious harm after the assailants recommenced their assault. James Farrel's house in Rose and Crown Alley was violently attacked, leaving not a single window unbroken. His door was smashed, a board was thrown into the house (which struck his terrified wife on the thigh) and Farrel took flight out of a back window in fear for his life.[45] Page, Rod and Putrode ventured a flimsy defence at the Old Bailey a few months later, claiming they were bystanders who were erroneously apprehended by the soldiers; they were found guilty nonetheless and imprisoned on two counts of rioting and assault.[46]

Over 100 rioters, again shouting 'Down with the Irish!', attacked John Waldon's public house, the Bull and Butcher on Cable Street, that same night. Accompanied by his lodgers and assisted by his neighbours, Waldon escaped over an 8-foot wall, leaving the pub to the mercy of the attackers who had more than simply anti-Irish sentiments on their minds – using his absence as an opportunity to steal meat on display in the windows.

The re-employment of English workers helped to quell this brief, but violent, period of unrest. Notices with the title 'A Kind Caution to Rioters and to All the Inhabitants of the Neighbourhood' were also posted in public places around the key locales of the troubles, warning of the repercussions of instigating such attacks on people and property, and announcing that 'the offenders therein shall be judged Felons, and shall suffer Death as in Case of Felony without Benefit of Clergy'.[47] It is important to note, however, that the reasons behind such disturbances – the perceived undercutting of indigenous labour by immigrant workers – did not exist in isolation, for religion also played its part. The 1730s was witnessing a period of alarm at the 'growth of Popery', a fear that would be magnified in significantly Protestant areas such as the burgeoning East End; now that the Huguenots were increasingly assimilated into the community, Catholicism, in the form of these Irish immigrants, was coming to be considered a significant threat.[48]

The complicated labour arrangements, demands for higher pay, and concerns over competition which were embedded within the weaving industry meant that trouble was never very far away, despite the authorities' regular attempts to pour oil on troubled waters. High duties on imported silks, enforced to protect the indigenous weavers from foreign competition, increased incidents of smuggling, which proved very hard to eliminate. Nevertheless, the weavers worked hard and played hard and were often criticised for idleness and drunkenness during their valuable time off. Many pubs served the weaving community, including the Crown and Shuttle, the Mulberry Tree, the Thrower's Arms, and a number of establishments known as the Weaver's Arms.[49] Indeed, it was written that 'Everybody knows that there is a vast number of journeymen weavers, tailors, clothworkers, and twenty other handicrafts, who, if by four days' labour in a week they can maintain themselves, will hardly be persuaded to work, the fifth.'[50]

Before long, the masters sidestepped the usual apprenticeships and collective agreements, and once again economic forces began to dictate the order of things. Again, work was farmed out to cheaper employees, some of whom were expected to work for exploitative levels of pay, and masters were increasingly turning to machine looms as a means of production. In 1762, journeymen weavers put together a book of pricings, listing the piecework rates they were prepared to work for; this was rejected by the masters, fuelling further discontent. Consequently, weavers began to come together to make their opinions felt: targeted employers, essentially those who were deemed guilty of pricing out the journeymen with cheap and inferior labour, received threatening letters, their property was stoned and, ultimately, major violence broke out. Spitalfields, naturally, was a hotbed of such disturbances, with gangs of 'cutters' breaking into weavers' workshops, cutting silks off looms, damaging the looms themselves, and causing no small amount of havoc. On one occasion, after the home of a master weaver was broken into, the mob 'placed his effigy in a cart, with a halter about his neck, an executioner on one side, and a coffin on the other; and after drawing it through the streets they hanged it on a gibbet, then burnt it to ashes and afterwards dispersed.'[51]

Despite the passing of an Act of Parliament in 1765 which made it a felony (punishable by death) to break into any property to damage or destroy silk goods in the process of manufacture, further disturbances over pay erupted in 1765, 1767 and 1768. However, this was merely the curtain-raiser for the events of 1769, which later became known as the

31

Spitalfield Riots. Disastrously, that year, employers attempted to enforce a wage cut, and in response weavers galvanised themselves into organised groups and clubs as a form of resistance. One club known as the Bold Defiance, or the Defiance Sloop, based itself at the Dolphin in Cock Lane, Shoreditch (roughly the site of today's Redchurch Street), and imposed levies on anybody who owned a loom in order to finance their 'fighting fund'. It was nothing short of extortion; and those weavers who refused to contribute were also targeted by the mob. One prominent local employer, Lewis Chauvet of Crispin Street, Spitalfields, barred his employees from contributing to such societies and thus felt the wrath of the militant weavers. In August 1769, large numbers of cutters sought out Chauvet's workers, demanding that they pay up, and fighting broke out, resulting in serious injuries on both sides. On the nights of 24 and 25 August, gangs of cutters raided Chauvet's workshops, removing silk from up to sixty looms, and causing damage to the value of £400.[52] Further attacks ensued across Spitalfields, and on some nights, with sometimes thousands of weavers causing chaos, the army were called in to deal with the deteriorating situation, and pistol-fire could be heard ringing through the streets.

Thomas and Mary Poor were impoverished master weavers who, during the troubles, had sought nightly refuge away from the Spitalfields area. In their enforced absence, their home was broken into on two occasions by a gang who committed their customary damage; in the second incident, their son William, who was home alone, narrowly avoided serious injury by managing to placate the angry invaders.[53] The rather dubious evidence ventured by the Poors implicated weavers John Doyle (or D'Oyle) and John Valline (or Valloine), who were tried at the Old Bailey in October 1769 for breaking into the property with 'intent to cut and destroy a certain quantity of silk manufactory in a loom, and also . . . to cut and destroy a loom'.[54] Just over a fortnight before the trial, a party of soldiers assembled at the Dolphin and raided it, finding there a number of 'riotous ill disposed persons, chiefly weavers under the denomination of cutters'. The weavers came together quickly, producing a formidable display of arms, including pistols and cutlasses, which gave the soldiers little choice but to begin firing their own weapons. The standoff lasted three hours, resulting in the deaths of weavers and soldiers, and the arrest of four men.[55]

With the apparent cost of damage sustained in the 1769 riots believed to be in the region of £150,000[56] (approximately £10 million in today's money), the authorities were now coming down hard on the rioters: John Doyle and John Valline were sentenced to death by hanging. As the first individuals successfully convicted of crimes in relation to the disturbances in Spitalfields, an example was made of them: instead of being executed at Newgate, they were to meet their end in Bethnal Green, within the extended weaving community, as a powerful message to other militant weavers. At the scene of the public execution (outside the Salmon and Ball public house at the junction of Bethnal Green Road and today's Cambridge Heath Road), sympathetic crowds attempted to disrupt the proceedings prior to the prisoners' arrival by throwing bricks, tiles and stones while the gallows were being put up.

Once the convicted men reached the scene, the throwing of objects petered out. Before their deaths, both Doyle and Valline declared their innocence, and Doyle in particular spoke eloquently, though bitterly, of his predicament, making the suggestion that his conviction was in no small way facilitated by offers of money in order to loosen up witnesses' tongues: 'I John Doyle, do hereby declare as my last dying words in the presence of my Almighty God, that I am as innocent of the fact I am now to die for as the child unborn. Let my blood lay to that wicked man who has purchased it with gold and them notorious wretches who swore it falsely away.'[57]

The consequences of the events of 1765–69 resulted in the passing of the Spitalfields Act of 1773, designed to regulate rates of pay in the industry, agreed upon by deputations of master and journeyman weavers, and subsequently ratified by magistrates. The act was further modified in 1792 and again in 1811, when female weavers were finally represented, and this much-needed legislation ensured peace until it was repealed in 1824, by which time the silk-weaving industry was entering a steady and ultimately terminal decline.

Such routine troubles continued to mark the East End, despite its pockets of pleasantness and fortune, as a place to be avoided at times. The district was becoming rapidly more populated and busy, and, away from the more draconian City authorities, and in the absence of truly organised policing, it had gradually become a favoured stomping ground for the outsider, the thief, the prostitute and the beggar: for where there is an established population, there are many targets for villainy.

CHAPTER 3

Mounting Problems

Wherever evils and crimes exist in Society, which have not only been felt by the innocent and useful part of the community to be noxious and oppressive, but also declared, by the Laws of the Land, to be objects deserving punishment – Where such evils are even found to increase, notwithstanding Legislative Regulations established with an immediate view to prevention, the conclusion to be drawn is obvious. Something is wanting in addition to the mere Letter of the Law, which shall operate more effectively to the relief and security of Society.

Patrick Colquhoun, *A Treatise on the Commerce and Police of the River Thames* (1800)[1]

The edges of the Whitechapel Road beyond St Mary's church were becoming noticeably built up by the end of the eighteenth century, although many of the already extant side streets beyond Baker's Row (now the southern part of Vallance Road) and the New Road were essentially embryonic thoroughfares which barely stretched for a few hundred

35

yards before dwindling into footpaths across wide-open spaces. To the south of Whitechapel Road, isolated trackways beyond the Whitechapel Field Gate, behind the recently built London Hospital[2] and the ancient Mile End Green, took travellers along lonely roads to Stepney Green and Shadwell. To the north, pathways crossed open land delineated by evocatively named spaces such as White Cap Green, Coverley's Fields, Spicer's Field and Hare Field. Parts of this land had been used for the digging of clay for bricks, and towards Bethnal Green could become waterlogged, hence the area known as Hare Marsh.

Two streets, Ducking Pond Lane and Ducking Pond Row, got their names from a sizeable pond situated alongside White Cap Green, the largest of several waterlogged holes in the area.[3] It was formed by the Black Ditch, a now lost river, which rose in Shoreditch and passed through Hare Marsh, then south to Whitechapel, before running down to Poplar and Limehouse, where it ultimately emptied into the Thames at Limekiln Dock. The pond itself was first recorded in the 1740s,[4] and served for a while as the local community's ducking pond, where individuals were given humiliating and uncomfortable punishments for a range of misdemeanours, most notoriously for practising black magic. Some cases of witchcraft recorded in Stepney and Whitechapel during the 1650s stand out: Elizabeth Lanam went on trial before the Middlesex Sessions after John Cooke 'languished and wasted in his body' supposedly at her behest; Adam and Mary Isgare, Richard Cooke and Mary Pettyman were believed to have died after Grace Boxe, alias Cherry, practised witchcraft upon them over a period of three months in 1654; and Elizabeth Crowley, a 'common witch and inchantress', was said to have dealt the same fate to Ellen Turner, whose body 'was wasted consumed pined and lamed'.[5]

The most high-profile case in the East End was that of Joan Peterson of Spruce's Island, Shadwell,[6] the so-called 'Witch of Wapping', who was deemed to be both a 'bad' and a 'good' witch, in that she was said to have performed charitable cures as much as grave mischief, although she was also 'known to heal the sick in a manner more suggestive than satisfactory'.[7] In this way she was believed to have cured a man of the headaches, which had troubled him for some time, by having him drink a potion; and for one woman who came to Peterson asking if she could revive her sick cow, which she believed had been struck down by another witch, another vague remedy was forthcoming. But to offend Peterson was rash indeed; on one occasion, after a man called Christopher Wilson refused to pay her the agreed fee after having been apparently cured of his ailments, she yelled at him, 'You had better have given me my money, for you shall be ten times worse than ever you were!' Wilson's fate was ghastly: he is said to have fallen into strange fits after which he rotted and died.[8]

Another incident that blurred the divisions between the real and unreal worlds saw a sick child visited by a large black cat, which once struck promptly vanished. A woman who set upon the cat soon discovered that the leg with which she had attempted to kick the mysterious animal had swollen up and become very sore. Witnesses believed that Peterson, who was a neighbour, had deliberately caused the child's illness and that the cat itself was a manifestation of her dark influence. Such tales, of which there were many more, were brought up in Peterson's subsequent trial for witchcraft at the Old Bailey in April 1652, and they were enough to see her condemned to death at Tyburn.[9]

By the eighteenth century, fears of sorcery and resulting witch hunts had significantly decreased from this earlier pitch, but the ducking pond could be used for other offences, such as dishonest trading, prostitution or bearing an illegitimate child. Another use was the humiliation of the public nuisance known as a common scold, or *communis rixatrix*, a woman (the law only applied to women in this case) who habitually broke the peace by arguing and quarrelling noisily with others. If convicted, the sentence for such women was to be placed in a certain engine of correction called the trebucket, castigatory, or cucking stool, which in the Saxon language signifies the scolding stool; though now it is frequently corrupted into ducking stool, because the residue of the judgment is, that, when she is so placed therein, she shall be plunged in the water for her punishment.[10]

Out in the fields

The open space beyond the ducking pond was a quiet locale, off the beaten track, where footpads could lure potential victims, as well as providing a useful means of escape from crimes perpetrated on more built-up thoroughfares. This sometimes marshy expanse was witness to one particularly horrific case in April 1771, when a Spitalfields pattern drawer, Daniel Clarke, was seized by a morally incensed mob hell-bent on justice, and brutally murdered.

In September 1769, during the height of the weavers' riots, Clarke's home in Artillery Lane had been targeted by cutters who had broken into the property and caused considerable damage to numerous silks and equipment. Subsequently, William Eastman was charged with causing malicious damage to a silk manufactory and tried at the Old Bailey, where he was found guilty and sentenced to death.[11] Clarke was a key witness and was now considered by the strongly unified cutters to be 'a monster in human shape, the fear of whom kept several families in a starving condition by keeping them from their principal support thro the apprehensions of being informed against'.[12] This suggests that Clarke did not just testify against Eastman, but may have been blackmailing others involved in the cutting who had managed to escape justice.

It was not until April 1771 that the angry cutters caught up with Clarke. He was recognised on Half Nichol Street in Shoreditch by two men who proceeded to beat him, wounding his face. Clarke managed to get away and found temporary refuge in the house of Mary Snee in Cock Lane where he had his injuries cleaned, sending Mrs Snee's daughter to fetch his pistols from his house. When Clarke momentarily went outside to collect the guns, he was seen by his assailants who had now been joined by others; one man threatened him with a stick and Clarke threatened to shoot him, but he was unable to discharge the pistols and ran back inside the house. Mrs Snee's home was set upon, with cries of 'Damn him!' and 'Turn him out . . . hang him, or burn him, or drown him, or do something or other to him; damn him turn him out!'[13] Clarke took flight over the garden wall and headed into Spitalfields where the mob caught up with him in White Lion Street. Witnesses stood helpless as, at one point, Clarke was stripped to the waist and whipped. He was dragged through Quaker Street and then to Hare Street (part of what is now Cheshire Street) where a gate led into Hare Field, a brickfield which at that time was pockmarked with small ponds due to wet weather. The growing crowd, which now consisted of several children, wanted to dunk him in the ponds, but none they could find were deemed sufficiently deep to supply the required punishment. Then the mob came to one that was about waist-deep, threw Clarke into it, and proceeded to pelt him with stones and brickbats. He was pulled out and pushed in again as the crowd continued their assault. The water reddened with Clarke's blood.

After a sustained battering lasting a good two hours,[14] during which Clarke was repeatedly hit on the head with bricks, he was dragged out of the pond with the aim of finally getting him to a hospital. Justice was deemed to have been done for the time being, but, terribly wounded, Clarke collapsed and died in front of the crowd. In the aftermath, Justice Wilmot, whose home was nearby, received an anonymous threatening letter telling him in no uncertain terms that he would pay with his blood if he persisted in his attempts to track down and persecute the offenders, thus depriving more weaver families of their livelihoods.[15] In the end, three men, Henry Stroud, Robert Campbell and Anstis Horsford, were tried, convicted and sentenced to death for the murder of Daniel Clarke; they were hanged in a field in Bethnal Green on 14 July 1771, close to where they had so brutally ended Clarke's life.[16]

On the other side of Whitechapel Road, the isolated tracts of open land, wedged between developments around St Dunstan's, along Stepney Green and Shadwell, and divided by the New Road, White Horse Lane and other embryonic thoroughfares, offered continual opportunities for the roving criminal. One such was Peter Conway, who at the age of nineteen had been sentenced to whipping after being convicted of stealing two live ducks in Hackney in 1768.[17] Two years later, he found himself facing the death penalty for the more serious crime of highway robbery when he was indicted, along with three others, of robbing a surgeon and apothecary, Thomas Brewer, on the New Road. Conway was the only one of the four who was acquitted; the others were all executed.[18] But before the year was out, he would face trial for murder.

Again, the original motive was robbery. Conway and accomplices William Jackson, Michael Richardson and a man named Fox bought a case of pistols and loaded them with small pieces of pewter, clipped from the handles of spoons,[19] before venturing out the following night into the lanes behind Mile End Green. In Redman's Grove they confronted William Venables and his companion, a Mr Rogers, but Jackson, feeling that the two men might be too strong to overpower, backed off. Conway pushed on, however, demanding that Venables, described as 'the lustiest of the two', 'stand and deliver his money'.[20] Indeed, Venables was certainly a match for his assailants and managed to knock down Richardson and Fox twice, but it was a short-lived defence, for as Richardson recovered himself he fired his pistol at Venables, the makeshift shot entering the lower part of his head through the jawbone. Conway followed suit, shooting Rogers in the forehead, just above the eye; both men died instantly. The little gang fled towards Wapping, via

Ratcliffe Highway, and perhaps fuelled with a bravura born of adrenaline, robbed a man of 18 shillings on the way.[21]

Conway and Richardson were tried for the murders of Venables and Rogers in July 1770. Press reports of the time declare that the defendants often carelessly incriminated themselves as they answered questions, giving the court every reason to convict them: the jury took only five minutes to reach its verdict.[22] Significantly, the authorities responded to these events, suggesting a growing realisation of how dangerous such neighbourhoods had become:

> In consequence of the above most heinous Murders, the Hamlet of Mile End have laudably ordered an increase of Nine Watchmen in the most dangerous Parts about the Avenues of the fatal spot where the unhappy Victims, Mr. Venables and Mr. Rogers, fell. The watchmen are to be stout, resolute Men, accommodated with boxes, and provided with Fire Arms and Great Coats; their pay 7s. a week. One of the stands is to be in the Grove.[23]

Authority responds

It is fair to say that the policing of the metropolis at this time bore little resemblance to the way it is today. In many ways, the early forms of policing in London relied strongly on the will of the people, who were expected to, and often did, apprehend criminals of their own volition, usually as a crime was being committed. They were also expected to notify a justice of the peace, a local trusted citizen who had accepted the role of upholding the law, of any felonies committed. It was the Justice of the Peace Act of 1361 which served to replace knights as defenders of the common law and the king's peace, a role that still exists today in the form of the magistrate. Justices of the peace were also permitted to appoint constables who would join with watchmen (who were paid by the local community) to apprehend criminals, although they were under no obligation to investigate or prosecute crimes, effectively requiring them to act as and when a crime was committed.

Fears of rising crime in the late seventeenth century, and the offer of handsome rewards for the apprehension of criminals, led to the arrival of thief-takers, private individuals who used their knowledge of the underworld to profit from the rewards on offer. Not only would they expose criminals; sometimes they would negotiate between felon and victim for the return of any stolen goods. But they also took corrupt advantage of their target's precarious situation by blackmailing, and it is no surprise that individuals were sometimes convicted of non-existent crimes, all to the benefit of the thief-taker's purse. Despite this, and the ignominious reputations of notorious thief-takers such as Jonathan Wild,[24] the authorities continued to encourage legitimate thief-taking, considering it to be the lesser of two evils, as apprehending villains without the help of the thief-takers would have been far more difficult.

In order to make it easier for people to report crimes (and thus to encourage them to do so), in the 1730s magistrates set up 'rotation offices' where citizens could find a justice of the peace at set hours. These were installed in both the City and Middlesex (within which Greater London now sits), the most prominent being in Bow Street, Covent Garden. It was here that Henry and John Fielding hired thief-takers on a retainer, sending them out to investigate and apprehend criminals wherever a crime had been reported. Although these men preferred the title of principal officers of Bow Street, they became widely known in London as the Bow Street Runners. The Fieldings also collected and disseminated information about crimes and suspected criminals, and Bow Street developed into a central network for criminal intelligence, a most important development. Horse patrols were also introduced, staffed by part-time constables, providing a more visible presence on the main thoroughfares as a deterrent to crime, particularly highway robbery. By 1792 there were seven police offices in the City, Middlesex and Westminster, each with three stipendiary magistrates and six constables.

It would be the East End, by this time no longer separated from the City by wall and gates,[25] which would see the first manifestation of a properly established police force, which from 1798 served the riverside wharves and the busy Pool of London from its base in Wapping.

Its founder, Patrick Colquhoun, a Scottish-born magistrate, had carved out a formidable reputation as beneficiary to the poor and champion of the wronged. His considerable skill as an investigator and collector of statistical data had made him a respected cog in the machinery of legislative reform, and his influence was widely felt in the East End. Amongst other acts, he did 'incalculable good, by acting with a committee of benevolent Quakers in drawing the attention of the public to the preparation of cheap and wholesome soups for the poor in Spitalfields', as well as 'preventing and detecting the depredations committed on the property of silk weavers'. But Colquhoun also devoted much of his time to investigating crime and its causes, particularly in his role as magistrate of the Tower Hamlets. He was no lover of public houses, which he could plainly see were 'receptacles of idleness and dissipation', and was responsible for framing and creating various regulations which were adopted by the licensing magistrates of the district. Aware that laws in themselves were insufficient to 'unquestionably give a seasonable check to immorality and delinquency; so as by their prevention not only to protect the rights of innocence, but also increase the number of the useful members of the community, and render punishments less frequent and necessary', Colquhoun created his plan for a more organised and regulated police force.[26]

It was the commercial powerhouse of London's river which would first benefit from this new concept. By the 1790s, theft and looting of ships moored in the Pool of London and the many riverside wharves farther east had reached an intolerable level. Colquhoun's talent for generating statistics revealed a shocking tally of plunder. Goods from the West India Company's ships, such as raw sugar, rum, coffee, pimento, ginger and dye-woods, were regularly being pilfered, to the value of £150,000; the cost of stolen East India goods from the Mediterranean, America and the Baltics was even more severe at £250,000. Combined with materials from the ships themselves, such as tacking, cord, sails, pitch and provisions, the total loss to the river-based merchant companies amounted annually to £500,000.[27] Such figures made the integrity and security of London's gargantuan river industry a priority, and in 1797 Colquhoun joined forces with master mariner and magistrate John Harriott, who had already been pushing for a centralised river police force, meeting with little interest from the City authorities. Colquhoun's statistics must have been a wake-up call for those with the power to activate the plan, and with the added input of philosopher and social reformer Jeremy Bentham, the West India Merchants and Planters Marine Police Institution was approved for government funding in July 1798. With an initial investment of £4,200, this initially private agency, with Colquhoun serving as superintending magistrate and Harriott as resident magistrate, employed around fifty men charged with the onerous task of policing the 33,000 workers on the river, a third of whom were deemed to be corrupt.

Although the agency's initial acceptance had been on a trial basis, with funding for one year, that first year was a major success: the new police force had 'established their worth by saving £122,000 worth of cargo and by the rescuing of several lives'. Naturally it was not popular with those who sought to profit from stealing from the Thames cargoes. On the evening of 16 October 1798, in reaction to the arrest of two coal-heavers, the institution's headquarters in Wapping was attacked by a stone-throwing mob. Before long it was apparent that the crowd were going nowhere, and that their increasing fervour would put the magistrates

44

inside at great risk. A pistol was fired out of a window, causing a temporary dispersal, but the crowd soon reconvened. Colquhoun came outside and read the Riot Act, at which point a riot did indeed ensue; as tempers flared, the crowd were 'swearing they would have the office down; that they would blow up the bloody office'.[28] Paving slabs, some weighing as much as 20 pounds, were torn out of the ground and hurled at the building and at officers who had come outside to try to quell the unrest.

In the tumult, pistol shots were fired from within the crowd, killing one rioter and an officer, Gabriel Franks. Although it was never determined who had fired the fatal shots, the two fatalities were deemed to have been caused by the same weapon.[29] Ultimately, one man, James Eyres (or Ayres), was brought to trial for the officer's murder, although he could not be identified as Franks's killer. However, the very act of being involved in the riot against the offices of a magistrate was deemed a severe offence in itself. The trial judge decreed that 'All persons who take an active part in a riot are answerable, by the sound policy of our law, for all the dreadful consequences which are most likely, and most unfortunately for you, in the late tumult and outrage, have ensued.'[30] Eyres was found guilty and sentenced to death and dissection on 9 January 1799, but was given a respite at His Majesty's pleasure on the day of his execution. Gabriel Franks would find a sad place in history as the first British police officer – recognisable in the form we know today – to die in the line of duty.

That same year the West India Dock Act was passed, authorising the construction of the first great non-tidal dock in the East End, to be situated on the northern part of the Isle of Dogs. This massive undertaking, which would effectively slice through the bow-shaped peninsula and isolate the communities to its south, was a response to the overcrowding on the river itself: the new facility would permit ships to dock in dedicated basins, surrounded by colossal warehouses for the instant loading and unloading of produce and goods. Security was at almost paranoid

45

levels, with the entire dock surrounded by a nigh-on impenetrable wall, topped with iron railings and complemented by a water-filled ditch, 'making illicit entry virtually impossible'.[31] Such strict security measures posed a threat to the river police's validity, but the value of Harriott and Colquhoun's brainchild was not forgotten; the Police Act of 1800 transformed it into a public body, renamed the Marine Police Establishment, to cover all shipping on the tidal Thames and its tributaries. The West India Docks opened in 1802, and the survival of the river police was assured, despite their being joined by other high-security complexes in the East End in the early 1800s.[32]

Villains, imagined and real

There cannot be many who have not heard the story of Sweeney Todd, the infamous 'Demon Barber', who during the late eighteenth century slashed his way through innumerable unsuspecting customers in his establishment in Fleet Street, before having their flesh baked into pies by his lover, Mrs Lovett. It is a perennial tale of horror, much reinterpreted in popular entertainment, in books, films and even musicals. It has been generally accepted that Todd never actually existed and that, like Bram Stoker's Count Dracula, he is an amalgam of different sources, a composite of obscure horror tales, known murderers, folklore and the very human fear of cannibalism. Very few claim that Todd is anything other than the fictional murderer first depicted in a mid-eighteenth-century 'penny dreadful', *The String of Pearls*,[33] although a few writers believe otherwise. The late Peter Haining, author of two books on Todd,[34] claimed that he had discovered undeniable evidence that he actually existed (claims that have not been corroborated by others):

I pored over archives in London and Washington, looked at 18th-century maps and scrutinised contemporary publications. They

46

revealed that Todd's life and crimes were more intriguing, more curious and more gruesome than previously suspected. Moreover, his background conforms to the psychological profiles of serial killers built up by modern police criminologists.

The Demon Barber's crimes, it turns out, are no urban myth.[35]

It is perhaps interesting that the supposed real-life Sweeney Todd was a product of the East End – a child Haining described as having 'breathed the fetid air of the East End slums' (a largely incorrect description of the Spitalfields area at that time, it should be said).[36] According to Haining, Todd was born on 26 October 1756, at either 85, 87 or 89 Brick Lane,[37] to impoverished silk-weavers – his mother barely twenty years of age, and his father an incorrigible alcoholic who regularly beat his wife and son. The boy shed no tear when his parents disappeared in 1768, after which he embarked upon his nascent life of crime, ending up in Newgate prison at the age of fourteen. There he was apparently apprenticed to the barber who shaved the heads of condemned men, the man from whom he learned his notorious skills. Upon his release, Todd set himself up as a barber, first on Hyde Park Corner, then, famously, at his address in Fleet Street. The rest of the story, culminating in Sweeney Todd's execution for his murders in 1802, is well known. Unfortunately, there is no record of any such trial or execution, or of the childhood imprisonment in Newgate. It would seem unwise, then, to dwell on this notorious character as a genuine individual whose criminality found its trigger in the darkness of east London.

Sweeney Todd was not the only legendary criminal character served up by the late eighteenth century. Isaac 'Ikey' Solomon fits comfortably into the East End's 'Who's Who' of crime, and, like Dick Turpin decades before, has earned a place in subsequent literary offerings for his alleged feats of criminality and audacity.

Solomon, one of nine children, was born around 1785 into a criminally disposed family in Gravel Lane, close to Petticoat Lane on the western fringe of the East End, and his life of lawlessness was in no small part influenced by his father, Henry, who was a 'fence', or receiver of stolen goods.[38] As a young boy he was soon supplementing his job as a fruit-seller by passing off forged coins, and before long he was picking pockets and committing robbery with the intention of selling on the spoils, following in the footsteps of his father.[39] In April 1810, the young Isaac, along with accomplice Joel Joseph, was caught after stealing the purse of ironmonger's agent Thomas Dodd in Greenwich. Such was their criminal profile by this time that the arresting officer, John Vickery, knew the two thieves by sight, and when they were searched a suspiciously large amount of money was found about their persons; Joseph, who initially seemed to have nothing on him, was told to remove his neckerchief, and when he refused, Officer Vickery did it for him, discovering £37 worth of banknotes secreted within.[40]

This felony earned Solomon a sentence of transportation to Australia where he should have spent the rest of his days; however, for reasons that are no longer known, he was put on the prison hulk *Zetland* at Chatham,[41] where he remained for four years until either he managed to escape or, as the Newgate Calendar suggests, was released in error when a fellow prisoner bearing the same name was given a pardon.[42] Returning to east London, Solomon set himself up as a jeweller and pawnbroker on Bell Lane in Spitalfields, resuming his career as a thief and dealer in stolen goods, in which profession he was 'probably one of the most successful in London'.[43] It has often been claimed that during this period Solomon may also have been a 'kidsman', somebody who trained impoverished children in the art of thieving in return for shelter and an 'education' of sorts. Years later, Henry Mayhew would describe how these fledgling criminals learnt the tricks of the trade:

A coat is suspended from a wall with a bell attached to it and the boy attempts to take a handkerchief from the pocket without the bell ringing. Until he can do this with proficiency he is not considered well trained. Another method is for the trainer to walk up and down the room with a handkerchief in the tail of his coat and the ragged boys amuse themselves by abstracting it until they learn to do it in an adroit manner.[44]

Solomon had a number of close calls with the law, until finally being arrested in April 1827 for housebreaking, robbery and receiving stolen property. Committed for trial, he was incarcerated at Newgate. On a writ of *habeas corpus*, Solomon was taken to the Court of King's Bench, where, on rejection of the application, he was driven back to Newgate; but, unbeknownst to the authorities, Solomon's father-in-law was driving the coach, and managed to make a diversion through Petticoat Lane where family and friends conducted an ambush and set Solomon free. He fled first to Denmark, then to New York and the United States, where he heard via the press that his wife Hannah (whom he had married in 1807) had been targeted by the authorities; convicted of receiving, she had been transported to Tasmania, along with their four youngest children.

Solomon arrived in Hobart in October 1828, effectively a fugitive from British justice. However, as he had not committed any crimes in Tasmania, he was able to set himself up in business as a tobacconist and general store-keeper. A warrant for his arrest and extradition to Britain was applied for but took a year to arrive, whereupon he was arrested in November 1829. Again, a writ of *habeas corpus* was applied for and, owing to technical problems with the arrest warrant, Solomon was granted bail at £2,000 with four sureties of £500. Friends and associates in Hobart were unable to raise the considerable sum and he was put on the ship *Prince Regent* and returned to Britain to face trial.[45]

By this time, Solomon's exploits had earned him the distinction of having his eventful life set down in print: in 1829 a 'Former Police

49

Officer' published an account of the story so far, with the lengthy title *Adventures, Memoirs, Former Trial, Transportation, & Escapes of that Notorious Fence, and Receiver of Stolen Goods, Isaac Solomons* [*sic*], one of several pamphlets published during this period which seem to have been popular with the public.[46] On 8 July 1830, Solomon appeared at the Old Bailey facing eight indictments of housebreaking, burglary, simple larceny and receiving. He was found guilty on two of the charges and sentenced to fourteen years' transportation, back to Australia, where he would remain, even after being granted his freedom in 1844, until his death in Hobart on 3 September 1850.[47]

As a Jewish fence, well known for his exploits and written about in the mass media, Ikey Solomon is believed, rightly or wrongly, to have been the inspiration for Charles Dickens's infamous character Fagin from *Oliver Twist*. The two share similarities as criminally minded Jews, and their depictions in popular fiction have also correspondingly led to accusations of anti-Semitism. Dickens himself was so strongly criticised for emphasising Fagin's race and religion at every turn that in subsequent editions of the novel he removed over 180 instances of the word 'Jew' from the text.[48] Later, in *Our Mutual Friend*, Dickens created the benign Jew, Mr Riah, claimed by some critics to be an apology for Fagin and an attempt to redress the balance and appease his critics. Over 150 years after the publication of *Oliver Twist*, Bryce Courtenay's historical novel *The Potato Factory*, based on Ikey Solomon's story, attracted similar disapproval, with one critic writing that 'It is hard to imagine any book in English, this side of the Holocaust, in which Jews are depicted in such a derogatory manner.'[49] The alleged links between Solomon and one of Charles Dickens's most resilient characters has always been the subject of debate; another possible model is the character of Monipodio, the leader of a seventeenth-century gang of Sevillan thieves who was a main character in Miguel de Cervantes's 1613 short story *Rinconete y Cortadillo*.[50]

Whether Isaac Solomon inspired the character of Fagin or not, his audacious escapes, turns of luck and ultimate freedom confirmed him as a literary anti-hero and an embodiment of the East End criminal's tendency to stick two metaphorical fingers up to the establishment, much to the delight of many.

CHAPTER 4

The Growth of Infamy

Ratcliffe Highway is a public thoroughfare in a most chaotic quarter of eastern or nautical London; and at this time (viz., in 1812) ... apart from the manifold ruffianism, shrouded impenetrably under the mixed hats and turbans of men whose past was untraceable to any European eye, it is well known that the navy (especially, in time of war, the commercial navy) of Christendom is the sure receptacle of all the murderers and ruffians whose crimes have given them a motive for withdrawing themselves for a season from the public eye.

Thomas De Quincey, 'On Murder Considered as One of the Fine Arts' (1857)[1]

Despite its xenophobic overtones, Thomas De Quincey's description of the Ratcliffe Highway ably describes the busy thoroughfare's seedy reputation in the early years of the nineteenth century. The rolling population of mariners supplied the area with an unenviable number of transient rogues, as well as providing those same rogues with unwitting victims ripe for the exploiting. The prostitutes of the highway were well known, providing the

52

composers of sea shanties with ample material for bawdy songs, invariably named after the infamous street. The following example also gives a nod to the drinking, violence and robbery endemic to the time and place:

> As I was a-walking down Wapping
> I stepped into Ratcliffe Highway,
> And there I went into an alehouse
> To spend all that night and next day.
>
> Two charming young girls sat beside me,
> They asked if I'd money to sport.
> 'Bring a bottle of wine, change a guinea.
> I see you are one of the sort.'
>
> The bottle was placed on the table
> With glasses for every one;
> When I asked for the change of my guinea
> She gave me the verse of a song.
>
> The bottle that stood on the table
> I quick at her head did let fly,
> And down on the ground she did tumble
> And loudly for mercy did cry.
>
> The gold watch that hung on the mantel
> I into my pocket did slip;
> And, darn my old shoes, didn't I trick her,
> And soon got aboard of my ship.

'I should not like a son of mine to be born or bred in Ratcliffe Highway,' wrote J. Ewing Ritchie years later, adding that a casual stroll along its length would be 'sure to shock more senses than one. In beastliness I think it surpasses Cologne with its seven and thirty stenches, or even Bristol or a Welsh town.'[2]

The Ratcliffe Highway murders

The linen-draper's shop of former mariner Timothy Marr stood at 29 Ratcliffe Highway, between Artichoke Hill and John's Hill, in a block 'composed of a compact square of dwelling houses encircling a piece of ground for the general use of the inhabitants, to which there is no passage out through the premises of the neighbours.'[3] Marr had moved into the premises with his young wife Celia, their baby son Timothy junior, apprentice James Gowan (or Biggs, according to some reports), and servant Elizabeth Jewell in April 1811. Just before midnight on 7 December, as preparations were being made for the next day's trading, Marr sent Elizabeth out to pay a baker's bill and procure some oysters for a late supper. She returned fifteen to twenty minutes later unsuccessful on both counts, only to find the door of the shop locked from within and the shutters firmly fixed over the windows. Ringing the shop bell and knocking on the door received no response, but it did attract the attention of the watchman, George Olney, who promptly called upon Mr Murray, owner of the pawnbroker's next door. Murray was able to climb over his back wall and gain access to Marr's shop from the rear, and upon entering found a lamp which he used to make his way around the silent house. The dim light soon revealed the first of the horrors that had befallen the Marr household that night, acts of 'refined cruelty . . . hardly surpassed in the annals of depravity':[4] on the floor was the apprentice Gowan, 'lying on his face, at the further part of the shop, with his brains knocked out, part of them actually covering the ceiling, and blood on the wall and counter.'[5]

Murray's cries drew others to the house. As he went to the front door to let them in, he found Mrs Marr lifeless, still bleeding from shocking head wounds. Behind the counter lay Timothy Marr, battered to death. Appallingly, the baby was found dead in the kitchen, still in its cradle, 'with one of its cheeks entirely knocked in with the violence of a blow and its throat cut from ear to ear'.[6] With this the Thames Police were called, the first officer to arrive being Charles Horton, who inspected the horrific scene. Curiously, £152 in banknotes – a considerable sum – was found in the shop, as well as money on Timothy Marr's person, suggesting that either the murderers had been interrupted in the act of robbery, or that there was some other motive behind the killings, such as revenge. A ripping chisel was found on the floor, as well as a carpenter's maul, caked with fresh blood and hair. Footprints, undoubtedly belonging to the assailants, were discovered leading out through the back door.

Some witnesses claimed to have seen some men running in the direction of Wapping from an empty house in Pennington Street, and enquiries soon led to three Portuguese sailors who were taken into custody as suspects. They were quickly released when they were able to prove that they were travelling from Gravesend at the time of the incident.[7] A number of other individuals were detained, to no avail, including a former servant-girl named Wilkie, who was alleged to have made threats against the pregnant Mrs Marr following her dismissal some months before.[8] Timothy Marr's brother was also detained for questioning over an earlier disagreement, as was the carpenter who had been working in the shop earlier that day, but all had solid alibis. The post-mortem examinations, carried out by surgeon Walter Salter, were published in the press following the inquest at the Jolly Sailor public house, revealing to all the true barbarity of the crimes.

Following the inquest, the bodies of the Marr family, their wounds on display, were laid out in the Ratcliffe Highway shop for inspection by the public, before being interred in the grounds of St George-in-the-East church, in a single grave, on 15 December. The modest ceremony attracted 'an immense crowd . . . but the utmost decorum prevailed'.[9] In the hope of speeding up the apprehension of the murderers, a reward of £50 had already been offered by the parish and bills to that effect were pasted up around the district.[10] Within days of the announcement, a further £20 was added by the magistrates of the Thames police office.[11] The bloodstained maul, perhaps the only sound piece of evidence in this grotesque mystery, was cleaned on 19 December, revealing the initials 'J.P.' or 'I.P.' engraved upon it. At last, here was something that could provide the investigation with some direction. But it did not come soon enough for another family living nearby – who were massacred in an almost identical way.

Earlier that evening, John Williamson, publican of the King's Arms in New Gravel Lane, Wapping, had noticed a man lurking around his premises and listening at the front door, and had alerted a local constable to the presence of this suspicious character. Not long after, between 11 p.m. and midnight, the neighbourhood heard cries issuing from the public house. The first to arrive at the King's Arms witnessed a young man, naked save for a shirt, climbing down a series of knotted bedsheets from a second-storey window. The man, John Turner, a lodger at the inn, was in a terrified state and told those assembled that 'murderers were in the house, committing dreadful acts of blood on the whole family'.[12] The front door was forced and, with the help of Mr Anderson, a neighbour who had only recently purchased a pot of ale from the premises, the doors of the cellar were broken open. The dead body of John Williamson was found on the cellar stairs; he had received a wound to the head, his leg had been broken by a strong blow, one hand had been almost entirely severed, and his throat was dreadfully cut.[13] At the same time Williamson's dead wife was discovered in the sitting-room, lying by the fireplace with a severely fractured skull and a cut throat from which blood was still gushing. Nearby was the maid, lying on her side with appalling skull fractures and a cut to the throat so severe that it had penetrated to the spine.

Amazingly, the Williamsons' 14-year-old niece, Kitty Stilwell, was found upstairs in her bed, unharmed and totally unaware of the carnage that had taken place beneath her. She was swiftly removed from the scene.[14]

In a scenario similar to the Marr murders, the killers had escaped on foot from the back of the house. A crowbar was found by the body of John Williamson, but it was still the maul, recovered at the scene of murders in Ratcliffe Highway, that offered the best hope of a solution. In addition, further rewards, by now totalling £710, were being offered by the local parishes and the government for the capture of the murderers of both families.[15] On 24 December it was discovered that the maul had belonged to a sailor named John Peterson, who was away at the time of the murders but who had recently been lodging at the Pear Tree public house in Cinnamon Street, Wapping. The landlord of the inn, Mr Vermiloe, who was at that time in debtors' prison, had tipped off the authorities, and constables went to the Pear Tree to inspect Peterson's belongings which were being stored there, confirming that the maul was indeed missing. Suspicion had fallen upon three men, one of whom, John Williams – 'a man of middle stature, slenderly built, rather thin but wiry, tolerably muscular, and clear of all superfluous flesh', and whose hair was 'something between an orange and a yellow colour'[16] – presented a plethora of circumstances that made him a person of significant interest. All three were detained at Coldbath Fields prison.

Williams, himself a lodger at the Pear Tree, would have had access to Peterson's maul; he had apparently been seen drinking in the King's Arms on the evening of the Williamson murders, and an earlier comment to the effect that he had no money was deemed suspicious when it was discovered that he later appeared to have plenty. It was also suggested he had some history with Timothy Marr, differences having occurred when they were both at sea together. He had also been seen with blood on his torn shirt, according to him the result of brawl over a card game. Williams had alibis as to his whereabouts following his alleged visit to the King's

57

Arms (where he was well known), and put the money down to having pawned some clothes; but the alibis were not checked by the authorities, and other reports which could have cast doubt on the case against Williams were ignored. On Friday, 27 December, with further evidence against him mounting, he was to be taken from prison to Shadwell police office for further questioning, but was found hanging in his cell.

With the death of John Williams, the authorities felt satisfied that at least one of the perpetrators of these atrocities had taken his own life, although any possible accomplices were still at large. Others were questioned, but to little effect, and with the potential remaining for further murders, vigilantes began to patrol the terrified neighbourhoods where the crimes had occurred:

> The whole of Ratcliffe, Shadwell, &c. is now like a garrisoned town: the inhabitants have associated, and patrol all the streets, courts, and alleys, every night from nine o'clock until five in the morning. They all carry fire-arms; and not an improper character now dares to appear out at night. The poorer inhabitants who cannot afford to procure fire-arms, bring their dogs along with them; and the utmost security now prevails in this lately terrified neighbourhood.[17]

The Ratcliffe Highway murders, as they would become collectively known, caused fear on an unprecedented scale throughout London. Thomas Macaulay wrote many years later of 'the state of London just after the murder of Marr and Williamson; the terror which was on every face; the careful barring of doors; the providing of blunderbusses and watchmen's rattles. We know of a shopkeeper who on that occasion sold 300 rattles in about ten hours.'[18] Such palpable apprehension also brought the law enforcement practices of the East End under close scrutiny, and well-attended parish meetings were held across the district. In Ratcliffe, it was decided that every housekeeper be involved in a rota of patrols which would add up to four divisions of thirteen men. Poplar, which was principally populated by Irish labourers and seamen, added an extra watchman to its tally of five. The most energetic revisions came, unsurprisingly, in Wapping and Shadwell; in the former, all the incumbent watchmen were dismissed and a new force of thirty-six 'able and diligent men', armed with cutlasses, pistols and rattles, were installed. Voluntary assistance from any other parishioners was openly encouraged to increase security in the area.[19]

With such alarm prevalent in the district, the death of Williams offered the authorities some convenient closure to a rushed inquiry, albeit one that was left incomplete.[20] A scapegoat had been provided, and even though there was no evidence that Williams had committed the murders, the perceived wisdom of his complicity was willingly accepted by the population, and the maligned suicide's interment was given a lurid fanfare. On New Year's Eve, the body was taken on a cart, followed by a considerable crowd, to the crossroads of Cannon Street Road and Cable Street for burial, the ripping chisel and maul found at the Marr home prominently displayed on either side of Williams's head. Along the way, the cavalcade passed the scenes of both murders, pausing for a while at each. (It was perhaps not unexpected that thieves should attempt to prey on the crowd, and two notorious local characters, Bob Barney and George Driscoll, were arrested for picking pockets.[21]) The body of Williams was dropped into a hole, the proportions of which meant that the corpse lay almost upright, and a stake was driven through the heart, 'amidst the acclamations of thousands of spectators'. The hole was then filled to the top with quicklime and the paving stones were replaced.[22]

There is a peculiar epilogue to Williams's interment beneath the crossroads. In August 1886, the Commercial Gas Co. was excavating the site to lay gas pipes when Williams's skeleton was discovered by workmen, the stake still lodged between the ribs. The bones were distributed amongst morbid collectors and the skull was taken by the owner of the Crown and Dolphin pub nearby, where it was said to have been on display for many years.

Ethnic flashpoint

The overcrowded melting pot that constituted the district made notorious by the 1811 murders, 'terrorized and divided by religion, by ethnicity, by property, by country of origin',[23] could still produce its own specific brand of disorder and violence. This occasionally manifested itself within specific immigrant communities, who were often subdivided into separate gangs or sects. By the second decade of the nineteenth century, up to 500 Chinese lascars employed by the East India Company were residing in King David Fort in Shadwell, an overcrowded barracks, where they were underfed and frequently mistreated.[24] By this time, lascars made up nearly two-thirds of the merchant service, many of them being unceremoniously dumped at Wapping after their gruelling six-month voyages from the Orient. They were looked down upon by their English hosts who regarded them uncharitably as 'senseless worshippers of dumb idols' and 'practically and abominably wicked'.[25]

On one extraordinary occasion, the harsh conditions in the fort conspired to make the dense Chinese community implode upon itself with notable violence. In September 1813, two factions, the 'Chenies' and the 'Chin Choo', set upon each other with tremendous savagery with blades, some of which were as large as cutlasses, and anything else that could be used as a weapon. The superintendent ordered that the gates be closed to prevent the offenders from escaping, and although the disturbance began to die down when constables arrived, some of those who had come to quell the riot and confiscate knives were pelted with tiles torn from the roof of the barracks.[26] Once the fracas had ceased, it was discovered that one participant was dead, his bowels ripped open, and seven others were taken to the London Hospital with serious injuries, two of whom subsequently died. It was discovered that the fracas all stemmed from a card game between a Chenies and a Chin Choo the day before. A mere 1s 6d had been lost in the game, which the loser refused to pay, so they had 'renewed the contest the following day with knives', calling on their respective comrades for assistance.[27]

The 1813 riot revealed deficiencies in provision for the Asian sailors' needs, and following an inquiry (published in 1815) it was reported that the accommodation at Shadwell was ' "totally wanting" from the point of view of health and hygiene, with "no regular hospital, nor any sufficient means of separating the diseased from those in health"'.[28] Apparently, in a one-year period up to April 1814, over 120 lascars had died in the barracks and it was revealed that inmates were starved and beaten.[29] Conditions were ultimately improved as a result of such findings. The Chinese of east London, despite the occasional eruptions of internal aggression, were considered to have a tendency towards self-reliance, something that would serve them in good stead in the decades ahead: they would begin to make parts of Shadwell, Poplar and Limehouse their own, creating London's first 'Chinatown'.

The Boss of Bethnal Green

The actions of the authorities in the above cases suggested that bad habits and criminality were not just the preserve of the rowdy east Londoner. Protocol could be bent to assuage the fears of the public, to enable those in positions of power to save face, or to hide maltreatment and neglect. Corruption within the proto-police force in London at that time revealed the all too tempting misuse of power which such responsibilities could allow.

A most dramatic exponent of the misuse of authority during the period was Joseph Merceron, the 'Boss of Bethnal Green', whose actions during the early nineteenth century are only recently being regarded with the historian's scrutiny. Merceron was born in 1764 to a family of Spitalfields pawnbrokers, but passed up the opportunity to follow in his parents' footsteps with a voracious appetite for upward social mobility which would see him come to wield extraordinary power and influence throughout his professional life, two attributes he would abuse for considerable personal gain.

Starting off as a lowly lottery clerk, Merceron gained steady promotion owing to his charisma and apparent integrity, and increasingly found himself in positions of authority where local financial matters were concerned. With local government based predominantly within the church parishes, Merceron regularly attended vestry meetings where his slick and persuasive demeanour won many friends and supporters. Before long he was voted in as church warden of St Matthew, Bethnal Green, giving him considerable power over church funds for the poor; it was here that his criminal career began in earnest. As well as arbitrarily controlling funds for the needy, he commanded influence over licences for public houses, a sure-fire way of garnering popularity and control from what was seen as a vital public service. Licences could be granted for reasonable fees, and Merceron would cut rates or increase them depending on how he felt about the individual ratepayer. Ultimately, his stranglehold on the parish's finances allowed him to cream off large sums of money through dubious expense claims. He later sat on the Commission for the Peace for Middlesex and the Tower Hamlets, and, despite being a supposed representative for the peace, was an enthusiast of bull-running and dog-fighting. Such barbaric sports caused a great nuisance and were often met with revulsion, but despite local antipathy to such pursuits, Merceron was more than willing to turn a blind eye.

In 1813, his luck almost ran out when he was indicted by Reverend Joshua King, vicar of St Matthew, for 'illegal and corrupt variations of the poor's rates of St Matthew, Bethnal Green',[30] but the ensuing trial was abandoned and Merceron was acquitted. As King later admitted:

I was dissuaded by the person whom I was so unfortunate to employ as my solicitor on the occasion, from being in court at the time of the trials. He contrived to instruct the leading counsel to declare that I had consented to a verdict of acquittal being obtained for the defendant without trial; although I had given positive instructions to proceed with the trials.[31]

Merceron had many people in his pocket by this time, and one can only glean that King's solicitor was one of them, but the acquittal seemingly reinforced perceptions of Merceron as a moral pillar of the community in the eyes of those less conversant with the truth. Legally, he had done nothing wrong, and thus maintained his status as a man of unimpeachable integrity.

Continuing where he left off, and surrounded by a formidable team of supporters and others who were securely under his thumb, Merceron gave the appearance of 'an almost irresistible dictator'.[32] By 1816, he was the owner of eleven public houses and collected rents from at least sixteen more, many of which were considered disreputable.[33] Twice that year his conduct was brought into question, only for his supporters to cast majority votes of complete confidence so that he was re-elected as treasurer of the parish. In time, Merceron's disregard for the lawful appropriation of poor law funds and his apparent total control of the fortunes of many of his parishioners turned his downtrodden neighbourhood of Bethnal Green into a troublesome slum. Many of the public houses either owned by or under the control of Merceron were deemed to be 'nurseries of depravity and vice' and epicentres of 'annoying and disgraceful tumults',[34] and with the Sunday dog-fighting and duck-hunting complemented by bullock-hunting in the streets during weekdays, Bethnal Green was becoming a 'saturnalia of turbulent disorder'.[35]

In 1818 it was discovered that Merceron had silently paid for his legal expenses from the 1813 trial with poor law funds, to the tune of over

£925 (approximately £38,000 in today's money) – 'an illegal appropriation of money to defray the expenses of an act equally illegal committed by the defendant, in his character as treasurer of a sacred fund, into which he, unceremoniously, thrusts his unhallowed hands, to appropriate a part to the most unjustifiable of purposes.'[36] Merceron was found guilty and sentenced to eighteen months' imprisonment with a £200 fine. Considering that at that time people could be executed for less, the sentence appears rather lenient; one imagines some dubious influence working its magic somewhere behind the scenes once again. While Merceron was incarcerated, his nemesis, Reverend King, left St Matthew; and so, upon his release, finding his old enemy gone, the 'Boss of Bethnal Green' reinstated himself in his former position and continued to work for the parish. From here on in there would be no interference from the authorities and, untroubled by accusations of impropriety for the rest of his professional life, Joseph Merceron died in 1861.

There have been many Joseph Mercerons in history, little dictators who thrived amongst those whom they oppressed with poverty and fear. With more interest in this embryonic gang-lord today revealing his true nature and deeds, it is rather incongruous that Merceron has been respectfully commemorated within the locale he once ruled. Merceron Houses in Globe Road, Bethnal Green, and Merceron Street in Whitechapel may give historic commemoration to an obviously notable public figure, but they reveal nothing of how much he got away with, or the fact that Bethnal Green's once sullied reputation was in part due to the flawed dignitary their appellations honour.

Bobbies and burkers

Great Britain during the early decades of the 1800s was undergoing a revolution in industrial practices. The creation of new technologies was quickly changing the face of agriculture and manufacturing, and the construction of canals and railways, facilitating distribution of more goods than ever before, was changing the urban landscapes of many major towns and cities. East London, with its rapidly appearing docks and factories, became a destination for displaced workers from the home counties who, finding their opportunities for work reduced by the increasing use of machinery in the agricultural trades that had sustained them for generations, travelled there seeking gainful employment. These were the people, often desperately poor, who would fill the factories, carve out the canals, build the railways and besiege the dock gates looking for a day's work.

But with the significant population increase came an increase in crime; in the decade between 1801 and 1811, not only had London's population swelled by 16 per cent, but crime had risen by 55 per cent.[37] The system of watchmen and constables had been under severe strain for years and the success of the Thames Police, a dedicated, organised and salaried police force, had shown the way ahead. Following Patrick Colquhoun's pioneering work on policing the metropolis, further select committees were set up in 1812, 1818 and 1822 to tackle what was seen as a growing crime epidemic. The end result of this energetic thrust to reform policing in London as a whole resulted in the passing of the Metropolitan Police Act in June 1829 and the creation of London's Metropolitan Police Force, dedicated to the maintenance of public order, the prevention of crime and the apprehension of criminals for presentation to the judiciary. The first constables, sporting their characteristic blue uniforms, appeared on the streets in September 1829: they were not well received by all, garnering derisory nicknames such as 'Blue Devils' and 'Raw Lobsters',[38] and, embarrassingly, the first assigned officer, William Atkinson, was dismissed on his first day for drunkenness.[39] Nonetheless, this new police force would later absorb the Bow Street office and the Thames Police and become a template for other organisations around the world, including the City of London's own force, which was created by an Act of Parliament in 1839.

The Metropolitan Police, covering the entire London area (save the City), was split into subdivisions, with east London acquiring two: H-Division (Stepney) had its western border at the City, and stretched east just short of Bow, south to the Thames and north to Bethnal Green; K-Division (West Ham) was responsible for Poplar and the Isle of Dogs, as well as Bow.[40] It would be H-Division, covering Whitechapel, St George-in-the-East, Mile End, Spitalfields, Bethnal Green and parts of Shoreditch, which would famously bear the brunt of much of the East End's criminality in the decades to come.

The arrival of the 'bobby' to London coincided with the last days of that most chilling of crimes known as 'burking'. Named after one of the two most notorious body snatchers of the era, Scotland's Burke and Hare,[41] this grisly act involved the theft of corpses from burial sites to be sold to anatomists for the purposes of dissection. More desperate protagonists were prepared to murder in order to acquire corpses by which to make their profits. The situation had become so serious that newly occupied graves were often guarded by concerned family members for several days at a time, to prevent the newly buried cadaver from being illicitly disinterred and sold on while it remained in a usable condition. Traditionally, only the bodies of executed criminals could be passed on to medical schools for dissection, and this was essentially the only way by which such institutions could come into the possession of a fresh specimen. By the early nineteenth century, however, the number of crimes for which the death penalty was deemed appropriate had diminished dramatically, creating a famine of sorts;[42] an average of only fifty-five people were being executed annually by this time, and with the growth of medical colleges and private anatomical schools, it was believed that up to 500 bodies were needed per year to satisfy demand.[43] In an address to the Webb Street School of Anatomy in December 1831, the physician and sanitary reformer Dr Thomas Southwood Smith announced his despair at the law in regard to the acquisition of corpses for legitimate medical purposes:

Human anatomy cannot be known without the dissection of the human body, yet the possession of a body that has been exhumed for the purpose of dissection (no body except that of a murderer being obtainable in any other mode) is penal; so that you are to be punished for not conforming to a law which you cannot qualify yourself for obeying without breaking.[44]

Burking became a common theme in the press by the beginning of the 1830s. Following on from the discovery of Burke and Hare's crimes and William Burke's highly publicised execution, the practice was forced into the limelight, particularly after some high-profile cases which stemmed from the East End. The case of Elizabeth Ross and her common-law husband Edward Cook was notable in that it was predominantly the evidence of their own son, 12-year-old Edward junior, which saw them face the consequences of the crime. In August 1831, an 84-year-old woman, Caroline Walsh, had taken lodgings at their home in Goodman's Yard, Whitechapel. On the first evening after her arrival, Walsh sat with the family and they all drank coffee, served by Ross; the young Edward also partook of a little and later claimed that it 'made him sleepy, but not sick'.[45] It had the same effect on Walsh, who decided to lie down on the bed in the room, and before long she appeared to be asleep. After a time, Elizabeth Ross walked over to the bed and, in full view of her son, proceeded to cover Walsh's mouth; this she did for at least half an hour. The old woman made small movements as her eyes began to roll. Edward Cook, in the meantime, spent the duration of this incident staring out of a window and not once looked behind him to see what was happening. When Caroline Walsh was still, Ross lifted her body and took it from the room, after which Cook and his son went to bed.

Young Edward found Walsh's body in a sack in the cellar at 8 a.m. the following day. He told nobody. Later that evening, he was looking out of a window when he saw his mother leave the house and walk down

Goodman's Yard, carrying the sack across her shoulder. When he later asked his mother what had happened to the old woman, she merely replied that she had taken her to the London Hospital. It was not long before the disappearance of Caroline Walsh was reported by her concerned granddaughters, Ann Buton and Lydia Basey, who knew the Cooks and were persistent in their concern; in fact, when Buton had first learnt of her grandmother's intention to stay at the Cooks', she had said that 'they would cook her, that they were body snatchers, and would put a pitch-plaster on her, and sell her body at some of the hospitals'.[46] Edward Cook and Elizabeth Ross, when questioned, were unable to account satisfactorily for the disappearance of Caroline Walsh, and were swiftly taken into custody.

It was discovered during numerous enquiries over the following weeks that Ross had been selling off clothing once belonging to Walsh to a number of cloth-dealers at Rag Fair, on Rosemary Lane.[47] Evidence given by young Edward Cook during the hearings at Lambeth Street police office blatantly pointed to the murder of Catherine Walsh by Elizabeth Ross, with the boy maintaining that his father had had no involvement. 'Good God, how could I have borne a son to hang me!' yelled Elizabeth Ross as the boy reeled off more and more incriminating evidence.[48] Put on trial at the Old Bailey on 5 January 1832, Edward Cook would be acquitted of murder the following day, but Ross was found guilty[49] – she was hanged four days later in front of a large and boisterous Newgate crowd. Some press reports found an opportunity to remark on Ross's character: 'The prisoner had been for a long time known at the East end of the town and was of a very violent and revengeful disposition. On one occasion a neighbour having offended her, she in revenge took a fine cat belonging to her, and skinned it alive, and then threw it in agony at the person who offended her.'[50]

Caroline Walsh's body was never found. Cases such as this led to knee-jerk reactions from citizens, suspicious of any mysterious

68

behaviour. Such was the situation in the case of Sarah Skinner, Louisa Covington and George and Sarah Bradley, who were accused of burking in December 1831 after neighbours overheard sounds of violence coming from their home in Severne Place, off Three Colts Lane in Bethnal Green. The cry of 'Hold the Bitch down!' was heard from inside the house, following which some children playing outside shouted 'Burkers!' at the window, scattering when the front door suddenly opened. Later, large boxes were seen being carried from the property, further increasing suspicion about the noisy occupants. Any such misgivings turned out to be groundless, however, when it was revealed during proceedings at Worship Street Magistrates' Court that they were simply rowdy tenants; the suspicious moving of boxes was due to little more than 'shifting about from place to place, and defrauding landlords'.[51]

Two actual body snatchers, William Parrott and John North, were apprehended in January 1829 by watchmen at St George-in-the-East churchyard while attempting to exhume several corpses. In the lead-up to their arrest they had attempted to bribe three watchmen in the Ten Bells public house in Spitalfields; one of the officials, Benjamin King, was asked if his job was 'a very unprofitable business and attended with much trouble', and when he said yes, he and his two colleagues were offered a cut of profits from a grave robbery that could net them between £70 and £80 if they were willing to turn a blind eye. North was keen to acquire fourteen bodies, and, despite his companions suggesting he was being too greedy, the time and date were arranged. In the meantime, the watchmen informed some of their other colleagues and a trap was set. On the night, the team of four grave robbers, having scaled a high wall into the churchyard, began opening graves with 'most extraordinary expedition', but the bodies within were too far gone to be of any use. The grave of a 9-year-old girl was opened, followed by two others, at which point King gave the signal to his men; North and Parrott were arrested but two others escaped. At the resulting trial the chairman 'expressed in strong terms his abhorrence of the vile trade which is every day increasing', and with the jury taking twenty minutes to reach its verdict, North and Parrott were sentenced to nine months' imprisonment with hard labour.[52]

'The Italian Boy'

The most prominent genuine case of this period, however, which took place in Bethnal Green, centred upon the tragic death of an Italian 14-year-old by the name of Carlo Ferrier. Today, Columbia Road is known for its independent shops, trendy coffee bars and, most famously, its flourishing flower market. But in the early nineteenth century, under the name of Crabtree Row, it skirted a vile, filthy slum known as Nova Scotia Gardens, a former brickfield, which consisted of a few cottages built beside a large mound of refuse, and which was noted for its total lack of drainage, omnipresent stench and the prevalence of disease in the surrounding area.[53] It was within this squalid environment that the activities of three men, John Bishop (a resident of Nova Scotia Gardens), Thomas Williams and James May, later known as the 'London burkers', would come to light.

On 5 November 1831, Bishop and May delivered the corpse of a 14-year-old, boy to the King's College School of Anatomy, aiming to secure a payment of 12 guineas. It was received by a porter, William Hill, who noted that the corpse seemed suspiciously fresh, but when he asked the two 'resurrection men' how the boy had died, May merely replied that it was none of their, or his, business. Hill's concern led him to consult the demonstrator of anatomy, Mr Richard Partridge, whose own doubts were raised by specific marks and injuries on the body, and by the obvious fact that the corpse had not been buried. The police were quickly called and Bishop, May and Williams were arrested and remanded into custody. Further examination of the dead boy produced compelling evidence of foul play – a welter of medical information that would not look out of place in a modern forensic examination. It appeared that the teeth had been extracted within a few hours of death and blood clotting under the skull and in the spinal marrow suggested blows with a blunt instrument. The fact that the heart was empty also demonstrated that death came quickly, if not instantaneously, and after a second opinion, it was confirmed that the 'appearance described in the present case could only have been produced by violence'.[54]

The superintendent of police, Joseph Sadler Thomas, made further enquiries. In Newington Causeway, he was given twelve teeth by Thomas Mills, who stated that May had sold them to him for 12 shillings, claiming they belonged to 'a boy between fourteen and fifteen years old'.[55] Inspection of Bishop's lodgings at Nova Scotia Gardens revealed a recently disturbed patch of earth outside which, when dug up, was found to contain the boy's clothes. Tools showing traces of blood were also found in the house itself. With such compelling evidence, Bishop, May and Williams were tried at the Old Bailey for the murder of Carlo Ferrier. All pleaded not guilty: Bishop and May both admitted to the profession of 'resurrection men', although May claimed to have nothing to do with the acquisition of the young boy. Bishop denied the murder of Ferrier and said that his two companions had no idea how he came upon the body, and further maintained that he had never procured a corpse by illegal means. Williams denied everything. Nevertheless, the jury found all three guilty and they were sentenced to death.

With the threat of execution looming over them, Bishop and May went on to make confessions, with Bishop's throwing more light on the death of Carlo Ferrier. On that fateful day, the boy had been abducted by Bishop and Williams, doped with rum laced with laudanum and, once unconscious, drowned headfirst in the small well in Nova Scotia Gardens.[56] The condemned men also admitted two further murders they carried out the same year. Destitute Frances Pigburn had been found sleeping rough in Shoreditch on 9 October, was lured to an empty cottage in Nova Scotia Gardens, and drugged and drowned in the same way as Ferrier, before being sold to a Mr Grainger for 8 guineas. Another young boy was abducted from the pig market in Smithfield where he had been sleeping, and was drugged and drowned in the same manner. His body was sold to a Mr Smith at St Bartholomew's Hospital, again for 8 guineas.[57]

The case of 'the Italian Boy' was a subject of tremendous interest amongst the public, and the execution of the 'London burkers' testified to the effects of such fascination. On the day itself, 600 special constables were assigned to Newgate to keep order amongst the substantial crowds; curiosity and enthralment had reached such a peak that one spectator offered the owner of a property that had a small window facing the prison the handsome sum of 5 guineas for the privilege of being allowed to view the proceedings from it.[58]

The result of such high-profile cases, as mentioned above, was the passing of the Anatomy Act of 1832, a revised version of an earlier act that had been rejected three years previously. The 1832 act finally satisfied the professional needs of physicians, medical students and surgeons (who now had to be licensed), allowing them to use for dissection any corpse that was unclaimed after death. This often meant the deceased being taken from prisons and workhouses, although families were permitted to donate bodies in return for a decent burial, paid for by the appropriate school of anatomy, once they had outlived their use. Such reform conspired to do away with the 'resurrection men', and, despite inevitable attempts by some individuals to continue the grim trade in the immediate aftermath of the Anatomy Act, the days of the burker were numbered.

CHAPTER 5

A Downward Slide

Frequent representations have of late been made to the Lord Mayor, of the alarm excited by a miscreant, who haunted the lanes and lonely places in the neighbourhood of the metropolis for the purpose of terrifying women and children.

Spring-heeled Jack: The Terror of London (1863)[1]

The Terror of London

The 1830s presented a most peculiar criminal offering from the East End's sinister past, when the notorious perpetrator of a series of audacious, but ultimately minor, assaults in the latter part of the decade descended upon the eastern fringes of London and cemented his name in London mythology. For some time during the early years of the nineteenth century, the hamlets to the west and south of London's expanding sprawl had been terrorised by a mysterious, quasi-superhuman creature that had made a habit of accosting young women

73

who dared walk the lonely roads by night. Normally, his victims would be violated by cold, clammy hands with claws, sometimes having their clothing torn, before the horrifying assailant made good his escape, often by leaping over impossibly high obstacles such as walls and hedges. Various descriptions said the man was tall and thin with bulging, sometimes glowing eyes, a horrid face and a high-pitched ringing laugh which emanated from the fiend as he fled. Bizarrely, a number of separate reports claimed that the strange individual spat blue flames, which sometimes temporarily blinded his victims.[2] Needless to say, many of them were left traumatised by their experiences. This bizarre menace would later become known as 'Spring-heeled Jack', tales of whom would persist into the early twentieth century. Martin Coverley, delving beyond the mere sensationalist stories, notes that 'With its sensational storyline and attendant press-generated hysteria, the story of Spring-Heeled Jack ... has become firmly established within the popular imagination as a symbol of Victorian London, his nocturnal activities both intriguing and terrifying the readers of the penny dreadful that shaped his legend.'[3]

By 1837, the character of Spring-heeled Jack had been predominantly terrorising the southern suburbs, but in the following year, reports – which received more significant exposure and reaction from the press and public than before – emanated from the East End. The first incident in the area of this 'pseudo apparition ... in fiend-like guise'[4] saw him manifest himself at Bearbind Cottage, Bearbind Lane (now part of modern Malmesbury Road), described as 'a very lonely spot between the villages of Bow and Old Ford', which was home to a Mr Alsop, a 'gentleman of considerable property', and his three daughters.[5] At about 8.45 p.m. on 20 February, Alsop's 18-year-old daughter Jane answered the frenzied ringing at the gate of the house, to be confronted by a figure enveloped in a cloak who claimed to be a policeman; he then exclaimed, 'For God's sake bring me a light, for we have caught Spring-heeled Jack here in the lane.'[6] Jane did so, yet just as she handed over a lighted candle to the mysterious character he threw off

74

his cape, revealing clothing that resembled white oilskin and a helmet upon his head. The newspaper described his face as 'present[ing] a most hideous and frightful appearance', and as reported on previous occasions, he 'vomited forth a quantity of blue and white flame from his mouth, and his eyes resembled red balls of fire'.[7] He then commenced a most frightening assault on the young lady, clawing at her shoulders with metallic talons and ripping away parts of her dress. It was Jane's elder sister, Mrs Harrison, who heard Jane's cries and successfully pulled the poor girl from the assailant's terrible ravages, dragging her indoors and slamming the front door safely behind them.

Less than a week later, 'Jack' is believed to have struck again, this time at the home of Mr Ashworth of Turner Street, Whitechapel, near the junction with Commercial Road. In this account (which, unlike the Alsop case, was almost entirely ignored by the press), the fiend knocked at the house and asked for Ashworth, but before the boy who answered the call could respond, the mysterious visitor threw off his cloak to reveal his hideous appearance. The boy's screams alerted the family and 'Jack' made off before he was able to commit any more mischief.[8] Three days later, on 28 February, at about 8.30 p.m., Lucy Scales and her sister were leaving their brother's house in Narrow Street, Limehouse, and, as they passed Green Dragon Alley, they noticed someone 'of tall, thin, and gentlemanly appearance' standing nearby.[9] Without warning, the person 'threw open his cloak, exhibited his lamp and puffed a quantity of flame from his mouth' and walked off.[10] The 'flame' was directed at Lucy's face, temporarily relieving her of her eyesight and senses, and she dropped to the ground, suddenly overtaken by violent fits.

Three incidents in little over a week did much to generate a panic which spread beyond the East End. The Morning Post described 'The Spring-heeled Jack Mania' and reported on two tall men, clad in long cloaks and with faces reddened by red ochre and brick-dust, having frightened a 13-year-old boy half to death in west London, claiming to be members of the 'Spring-heeled Jack family'.[11] One Charles Glenville was arrested for 'having frightened a number of women and children into fits, by imitating the silly and dangerous pranks of Spring-heeled Jack' in Kentish Town, north London.[12] Ambushed by a policeman, Glenville was ultimately charged but, being considered of weak mind and ultimately harmless, was let go. The press did make frequent mention of potentially genuine culprits being rounded up, albeit without any successful conviction. In several accounts it was said that the monster had been encountered in Lincoln's Inn Fields, and even as far as Brighton on the south coast, as well as Margate and Ramsgate on the Kent coast, the latter claim being described as an 'idle report'.[13] For the residents of east London, however, there was no frivolity; as early as the Alsop incident, the press noted the impact on women who, it reported, were 'afraid to move a yard from their dwellings after dusk, unless they are very well protected'.[14]

Nonetheless, despite all the supposed supernatural attributes of 'the suburban ghost',[15] only the naïve considered him anything other than the product of a few men's semi-malicious mischief, perhaps fuelled by alcohol or a thirst for quick thrills. The acts of this 'Terror of London' were arguably criminal, for in the above cases in the East End alone, had the culprit – or culprits – been apprehended for the Alsop and Scales incidents, they would have been charged with assault, wounding and breaking the peace. Like all enigmatic and mysterious characters, Spring-heeled Jack became the stuff of urban folklore, penny dreadfuls and comic books; during the 1838 scare he became a household name in the most unlikely of ways, even being used as a rather tasteless advertisement of ostensibly useful products:

SPRING-HEEL'D JACK DEFEATED!
This miscreant's pranks in the lonely vicinities of the Metropolis have created a visible panic, more especially among the fair and

unprotected part of the creation. His recent attack on a beautiful young female, whose arms and bosom he tore with his 'iron claws' is fresh in the memory of every one:– but little reason will he have to triumph henceforth, since with the application of HOLLOWAY'S UNIVERSAL FAMILY OINTMENT, the severest wound is speedily healed – and, of course, the monstrous cruelty of even a 'Spring-Heel'd Jack' defeated![16]

The East End in descent

By the beginning of the 1840s, semi-isolated neighbourhoods like Old Ford and Bow were becoming few and far between. A rapidly swelling population had seen to it that many of the open spaces found themselves quickly claimed by developers as the surge in new residents demanded more housing. In the first four decades of the nineteenth century, the population of the Tower Hamlets had almost trebled;[17] the population of Bethnal Green alone, boosted by a progressive influx of migrant weavers from Spitalfields, had more than doubled from 1801 to 1821 and trebled within the following decade.[18] The arrival of the Eastern Counties Railway in 1839 had cut a swathe through Bow, Bethnal Green and Shoreditch; the following year saw the opening of the London and Blackwall Railway, snaking through the Isle of Dogs, Limehouse, Shadwell and Whitechapel on its route to Fenchurch Street. The construction of the railways, along with the canals, may have made the East End an important transport hub, benefiting the flourishing docks which had sprung up in the early decades of the nineteenth century, but it did little to alleviate the housing situation in the affected neighbourhoods. The demolition of over 1,250 homes to make way for St Katharine's Dock in the 1820s displaced up to 11,000 people,[19] all of whom needed to find accommodation in the surrounding, already overcrowded, districts. A similar situation arose after the arrival of the railway infrastructure, which meant that assigned areas had to deposit their populations elsewhere, and truncated thoroughfares were created which became hidden and forbidding. They would quickly become perfect breeding grounds for crime and squalor. Related to the carving up of communities by Victorian developments, Gareth Stedman Jones writes, 'One great effect of railway, canals and docks in cutting into human communities was a psychological one... East Londoners showed a tendency to become decivilised when their back streets were cut off from main roads by railway embankments.'[20]

Economic depression in the early 1840s had also hit London hard, and the once prosperous yet turbulent area of Spitalfields struggled through the terrible winter of 1841–42 and beyond. 'Distress in Spitalfields' became a frequent headline in the press, with many observers commenting on 'the distress, suffering, and unparalleled misery ... which must be daily on the increase from the severity of the winter'.[21] Adding to the difficulties was the sudden upsurge in the arrival of Irish immigrants fleeing the devastating Potato Famine, which continued throughout the 1840s and 1850s. There had been an Irish presence in the East End since the turbulent days of the labour disputes of the 1700s, but this renewed influx of the most desperately poor certainly compounded the existing issues. They crowded into the cheapest and most squalid dwellings and their desperation led to antisocial behaviour; Angel Alley, a tiny narrow passage off Whitechapel High Street, was known for its tight enclave of Irish families who belligerently kept rent collectors at bay for prolonged periods of time with threats of violence.[22] One landlord felt powerless when he had 'his tenements violently forced open and taken possession of by sturdy Irish poor, who persisted in harbouring large hordes of nightly lodgers, without his being able to prevent it'.[23] As it had been 100 years before, the willingness to work for less remuneration than others saw the Irish pushing out the local labour force, particularly by the river, and local workers knew 'they could get no engagement at the docks in consequence of the immense numbers of Irish employed there.'[24]

The year 1855 was a turbulent one, and a steep rise in the price of bread instigated a number of disturbances around the country, further agitated by proposals to ban trading on Sundays. The East End, as was perhaps to be expected, was an early instigator of dissent when 'bread riots' broke out in Whitechapel on 21 and 22 February that year. Various bread and provision shops were attacked by mobs, often comprising 200 to 300 people, who smashed windows and helped themselves to whatever they could. One incident on Mile End Road saw up to 600 people take part in an organised display of looting which was led by a man holding aloft a flag.[25]

Describing the poverty and overcrowding that had become standard by this time, one writer, Mile End resident H.R. Williams, told of visiting twenty-six houses around King Edward Street, Whitechapel, to find that even though only half were fully occupied, they were home to forty-eight families. In one particular property, he recorded, one room was occupied by two extended families, a total of eleven individuals, and this was not an unusual discovery for the shocked observer.

Some families had gone into the much-maligned workhouse, where the very poor and helpless could find shelter and food in return for menial labour. The work offered was often hard and monotonous, such as picking oakum or breaking rocks, and since the introduction of the Poor Law Amendment Act of 1834, was deliberately intended to discourage the able-bodied, who by rights should have had no physical impediment to finding legitimate work, from taking advantage of the system: 'Into such a house none will enter voluntarily; work, confinement, and discipline, will deter the indolent and vicious; and nothing but extreme necessity will induce any to accept the comfort which must be obtained by the surrender of their free agency, and the sacrifice of their accustomed habits and gratifications.'[26]

For many it would become the only way to avoid starvation and a life on the street. And so it was that only the very desperate would willingly enter 'the spike', as it was colloquially known; the unmarried mothers (who were given less relief), the mentally ill and the 'indolent and vicious', effectively put off by the draconian rules and harsh expectations of the workhouse, would remain at large. For them, the common lodging house, at a small price, would provide shelter and camaraderie without the burden of excessive toil.

Such an establishment, also known as a 'doss-house' or 'kip-house' by those who used it, was officially defined as 'a house in which persons are harboured or lodged for hire for a single night or for less than a week at a time, or any part of which is let for any term less than a week'.[27] A few pence would be paid up front for a bed – in some cases little more than a wooden box big enough for a person to lay in – in a room where the occupants would share space and each other's personal peccadilloes. A communal kitchen with rudimentary utensils would usually be found on the first floor or in the basement, providing the sense of community, albeit a dysfunctional one, that the workhouse apparently lacked. With an increasingly poor population, many of whom were transient, whether gainfully employed or otherwise, the East End became a thriving district for those willing to provide for, and thus benefit financially from, the needy citizenry. Such lodging houses had been a standard fixture in the riverside districts for a considerable time, often in the guise of sailors' homes, but the now overcrowded and poverty-stricken areas of Whitechapel and Spitalfields gave property owners a licence to print money by opening cheap lodging houses.

The rookery

Certain areas stood out for their overabundance of doss-houses. In Whitechapel, George Yard, a narrow, grimy alleyway which ran between

Whitechapel High Street and Wentworth Street, contained ten such establishments along its short length; almost every property on the even shorter stretch of Wentworth Street between Brick Lane and the junction with Essex Street was a lodging house; tiny Osborn Place off Old Montague Street was also entirely made up of doss-houses.[28] But for sheer density of common lodging houses, the streets either side of Rose Lane and Red Lion Street could not be beaten, and names such as Dorset Street, Fashion Street and particularly Flower and Dean Street and the adjacent thoroughfares would become synonymous with all the problems that high numbers of cheap lodging houses would produce.

As early as 1838, a parliamentary report made clear how low Spitalfields had sunk, describing the area around Red Lion Street as harbouring 'an extremely immoral population; women of the lowest character, receivers of stolen goods, thieves and the most atrocious offenders'; this presented 'serious obstacles to the efficient action even of the best constituted police'. Improvements were deemed urgent, and the result was the laying out of Commercial Street between Whitechapel High Street and Christ Church, a project that served a number of purposes: importantly, its construction would improve drainage and sanitation in the fever-ridden district, and its employment as a new trade route to the north would later become effective with a northward extension to Shoreditch in 1846. The initial section, built between 1843 and 1845, necessitated the removal of over 250 substandard properties, serving to wipe out the slum neighbourhood and, in the interests of public safety, 'open it to public observation'.[29]

In that latter aim, the construction of Commercial Street partly failed. Certainly, the loss of Essex Street, Rose Lane and Red Lion Street, along with their numerous grim alleys and courts, cleaned up and simplified the area, but the many displaced inhabitants simply began to pile into the outlying streets. Thus the 'rookeries' to the east and west of the new road, gorged with new tenants, absorbed the existent problems and the doss-houses accordingly flourished. At one time, Flower and Dean Street, Keate Street, Lower Keate Street, Thrawl Street and George Street, with yards such as Wilson's Place and Keate Court, as well as nearby Wentworth Street, contained over 100 lodging houses.[30] According to the rector of Christ Church, W. Stone, 'Many of the houses in the streets have actually communications with each other . . . [and there is] a sort of boarding partition, in which persons of all sexes are sleeping together, through a range of two or three houses, and sometimes more.'[31]

As these streets were associated with depravity and lax morals, they were avoided by those wishing to ensure their own safety and that of their belongings. Flower and Dean Street was deemed to be the worst of all, 'for there is no street in any other part of this great Metropolis that has for its inhabitants a like number of the dangerous class.'[32] During the 1840s, the problems generated by the occupants of the overcrowded tenements began to manifest themselves in earnest. In 1846, William Thompson, described as a beggar, entered into a drunken quarrel with his wife, abusing and beating her, before obtaining more drink and passing out in a doss-house in Keate Street. He was later found dead with his head resting on a windowsill, having apparently died of suffocation.[33] The same year, Anne Sinner, who kept a cook's shop in Flower and Dean Street, stabbed a customer, Daniel Crawley, in the chest over a disagreement over payment for a portion of meat. As she plunged the meat knife into Crawley she was heard to say, 'Take that you bastard'. The injured man staggered out of the shop, exclaiming to a passing police officer, 'I am stabbed, I am stabbed to the heart; oh, save me, save me!' Sinner, who already had a conviction for felony, gave herself up willingly to the officer, and Crawley, who was taken to the London Hospital for treatment, died six days later. Surgeon William Holman concluded, 'I have no doubt his death was caused by that wound.' Anne Sinner was convicted of manslaughter and transported for ten years.[34]

A most extraordinary incident was reported in 1847 when Michael Sweeney, newly arrived from Cork, took a night's lodgings in a Flower and Dean Street doss-house, only to be awoken during the night by four men. One of the men was heard to say, 'I think he has got "rhino" [ready money] about him, and now's the time to cut his throat.' Unable to get out of the room, Sweeney fell to his knees and pleaded with the strangers not to kill him. They ignored his entreaties, and the desperate man ran to the upper-storey window and threw himself out of it; he was taken to the London Hospital with lacerations to the head and face, and a fractured thigh and kneecap, injuries which put his life temporarily in danger.[35]

Theft in the street and in private dwellings was also prevalent. Richard Bailey and Thomas Sawl, both criminals known to the police, appeared at Worship Street for breaking into a Thrawl Street storeroom and stealing 'thirteen dozen prepared skins', the property of Mr Arnold.[36] In fact Thrawl Street was arguably a contender for the mantle of most dangerous street in the district: it often proved perilous even to pass through it. Cecilia Young, a married woman from Clapham, foolishly walked alone along Thrawl Street and had a considerable amount of money stolen from her purse (a total of £13 – almost £800 in today's money) by Thomas Welsh. She chased Welsh, but was stopped by a group of men who were obviously working in tandem with him.[37] The violent robbery of John Byland in 1849 demonstrated how arrogant and fearless some of these street robbers could be, in that they sometimes had little regard for the repercussions of their actions. Two young women, Margaret M'Carthy and Ann Wood, having lured Byland down George Street, were joined by George Davis and all three proceeded to beat Byland to the ground and relieve him of his money and watch. As the victim struggled, Davis cried out, 'Let us murder the bastard', before Byland managed to flee. What was peculiar was that after Byland had found a police officer, only minutes afterwards, they easily located

Wood and M'Carthy standing in a nearby doorway. Davis was found soon after in Wentworth Street, not too far away. The thieves hadn't even felt the need to make haste from the area after committing the crime. All three were found guilty and transported for seven years.[38]

Prostitution was also rife in the unmonitored lodging houses as some allowed men and women to share beds, making them little more than sanctioned brothels; shockingly, Henry Mayhew mentioned that some may have even been child-brothels.[39] Often the prostitutes would lure unsuspecting clients to their beds with the sole intention of stealing from them. One such was Anne Williams, a woman of 'revolting aspect', who took one Mr Phillips to her squalid lodgings in Thrawl Street. Within moments of their arrival her hand was in his pockets, emptying them out. As Phillips attempted to wrestle back a gold coin and two gold earrings from her grasp, the woman swallowed the lot.[40]

In November 1850, Josiah Blanchflower, a silk manufacturer from Bethnal Green, was accosted by a young prostitute, Johanne Driscoll, in Osborn Street, and was persuaded to escort her home. On the way they stopped by a public house to buy a quartern of gin, which the woman poured for them. After finishing it, they left, at which point Blanchflower was overcome by 'an indescribable feeling of giddiness' which was so powerful that he lost all resistance and fell to his knees.[41] Before he knew it he was lying on a bed in a house in Thrawl Street, and Driscoll and a companion were removing his trousers. The insensible victim was aware of the sound of a bag of money, which had been in his trouser pocket, hitting the floor: it was soon picked up by the two women, who walked out with it. The bag contained £32 in gold and silver. It would later transpire that before Blanchflower had taken his half of the drink earlier that evening, Driscoll had managed to slip a quantity of chloroform into it, enabling her and her accomplices to easily overwhelm their drugged quarry, drag him back to the lodging house, and relieve him of a considerably quantity of cash. Driscoll was caught, charged and convicted of the robbery, and sentenced to six months' hard labour. Earlier the previous year, Frederick Hardy Jewett had also been robbed under similar circumstances, by Margaret Higgins and Elizabeth Smith, having woken from a drugged stupor to find himself stark naked on a bed in a Thrawl Street lodging house, with all of his valuables missing.[42]

Undoubtedly, such incidents as those recounted above were merely the tip of the iceberg, and concern over the conditions in the common lodging houses, particularly regarding public health, led to the passing of the Common Lodging House Acts of 1851 and 1853, whereby all such establishments were required to be registered by the Metropolitan Police and regularly inspected. The general rules, however, mainly being concerned with improving hygiene and reducing overcrowding, did not alter the nature and circumstances of those who needed to use lodging houses in the first place, and the problem of criminality remained. Henry Mayhew's observations in the 1850s revealed that in these dwellings there was 'tacitly established an arrangement as to what character of lodgers shall resort thither; the thieves, the prostitutes, and the better class of street-sellers or traders, usually resorting to the houses where they will meet the same class of persons'.[43]

The character of doss-house owners was not exactly spotless either. Many had once been travellers themselves and, through various means, had come into enough money to be able to invest in such properties. This would sometimes be from gambling at the races, from a 'run of luck', and even from the proceeds of robbery.[44] The surviving Metropolitan Police registers from 1852 onwards also provide a revealing insight into the proprietors themselves, namely how dominant some of them were in the lodging-house business.[45] Mayhew spoke of one owner (actually George Wilmott) who owned six lodging houses in Thrawl Street alone, grossing enough income to keep a country house in Hampstead.[46] John Cooney, another ubiquitous landlord, had apparently once been as poor as those who relied on his services, but in time came to be 'worth thousands'.[47]

85

Wilmott and Cooney were but two men who would join the ranks of the 'Lords of Spitalfields' through their sheer dominance of the district's lodging houses. In the registers relating to the 'Flowery Dean' enclave, names like Wildermuth, Smith, Lewis and Cooney repeatedly appear, families who owned houses for decades at a time, passing them down to sons and daughters who would sometimes marry into the families of other lodging-house-keepers. One of James Smith's houses at 56 Flower and Dean Street, the White House, was known to allow men and women to cohabit, raising suspicions that it was little more than a brothel.[48] To say that these dynasties were profiting from the misfortune of others is putting it mildly; the owners' ability to turn a blind eye to the squalor in which their often desperate tenants were expected to live, along with their ability to ignore the preponderance of thieving, child neglect, drunken violence and prostitution that took place under their roofs, made them as good as criminals themselves. Mayhew politely described these landlords as 'capitalists', which was in effect true, but their methods came at a price.

The language of the street

It was during this period that a most durable aspect of London life is believed to have originated in the fractious district of the East End (and other dubious locations such as Seven Dials in Covent Garden): cockney rhyming slang. It was essentially a contemporary form of 'thieves' cant', a lexicon used by criminals since the sixteenth century 'to the end that their cozening, knaveries and villainies might not so easily be perceived and known'.[49] Thieves' cant, also known as 'rogues' cant' or 'pedlars' French', was a now all-but-extinct secret language, preserved in many examples of Elizabethan theatre; but the rhyming slang of the nineteenth century has persevered, evolved and is still in colloquial use today, although perhaps not always for its original purposes.

The vocabulary may have been developed by specific communities to maintain some form of unity, or may be a linguistic accident that was seized upon to add a little colour to the English tongue, but it would invariably be used to intentionally disguise the true meaning of something in the presence of an outsider who was unfamiliar with the dialect. Street traders could speak to each other in the presence of potential customers, who would be none the wiser to the dubious deals being cooked up for them. Such nefarious usage was also the preserve of the criminal classes, whose secret words and phrases could be used to outwit the unsuspecting, or to warn fellow criminals of impending danger without raising alarm or suspicion elsewhere. Not all slang used by the criminally disposed rhymed with the original word intended, but such terms were still used to identify one criminal to another and to affirm a sense of community. 'Classic' cockney rhyming slang can still be heard today, though it is more often used for comedic effect than for disreputable purposes. For example, 'whistle', the shortened form of 'whistle and flute', still refers to a suit; and 'syrup', short for 'syrup of figs', means wig. Modern forms of slang, sometimes referred to as 'mockney', have given us 'going out for a ruby', meaning eating at an Indian restaurant (from the Irish singer Ruby Murray, rhyming with curry), and 'lionels' (referring to the British actor, choreographer and television presenter Lionel Blair) meaning flared trousers. The latter became 'tonys' in the 1990s, after Tony Blair became prime minister, proving that this historic East End idiolect is continually evolving.

Pity the innocent

In January 1861, the *Clerkenwell News* reported a meeting of the Clerkenwell medical officers which broached the subject of a worrying trend that was seemingly afflicting the country at large, namely the increasing instances of child desertion and infanticide. The report mentioned a case which took place in Baker's Row, Whitechapel, the previous year, of a woman who spontaneously put a one-month-old baby into the arms of a young girl and simply walked away. A reward of 2 guineas was offered for the apprehension of 'the inhuman mother', but the woman was never found. Discussion moved on to the desire for a national inquiry to be commissioned to determine the causes of such tragic occurrences, although it was felt that it was predominantly 'the inability of mothers to support their infants'.[50] Another cause, often cited by correspondents to the press, was that of the stigma of illegitimacy and the country's 'bastardy laws', whereby any unmarried mother, invariably abandoned, was alone accountable for the support of the child. The problem appeared to be widespread: figures compiled for the years 1858–65 regarding child-related offences in the Metropolitan Police district of London as a whole revealed a small decrease in the late 1850s before a gradual increase led to a sudden upsurge in 1863 when such cases doubled.[51] The impoverished East End, with all its other difficulties, saw a spate of occurrences which predated the sudden rise and became a major concern to the local press.

The *East London Observer* reported in March 1861 on the desertion of a one-hour-old baby girl in Canal Road, Stepney. The child was found crying and bitterly cold behind a gateway and 'had a piece of barege dress twisted four times round the neck, but not sufficiently tight to cause strangulation', which suggested an attempted infanticide. The infant died soon after of inflammation of the lungs due to exposure. The same report spoke of the discovery of the corpse of a child in a garden in Poplar, who had died many hours prior to discovery; on this occasion the cause of death was suffocation. In both cases, the perpetrators were not caught, leading the newspaper to decry the 'inefficiency of [the district's] boasted detective system'.[52]

The case of Emma Papworth, aged only seventeen, received a considerable amount of coverage in the national press, as it was one of the rare cases that went to trial. Miss Papworth, of Wells Street, Mile End New Town (part of today's Hanbury Street), was accused of hiding the corpse of her newborn baby daughter in a box, and although the child had been born alive, the subsequent death was deemed to have been caused by suffocation, 'the result of interference with the organs of breathing, as the mouth and nose were flattened as if by some pressure.'[53] During the magistrates' hearings, the girl was obviously distressed and fainted on several occasions as the tragic story unfolded. The court was told that, for a short time, Papworth, in service to a local publican, had been taken advantage of by a man who lodged at the pub and had become pregnant.[54] She kept her condition secret for as long as she could; even her mother claimed that 'I did not know that my daughter was in the family way – I never had a suspicion of it – I wish I had known it.'[55] After giving birth, Papworth put the child into the airtight box and left it amongst other boxes of belongings in her room; the after-birth was apparently disposed of down the toilet. Although spared the charge of manslaughter, Emma Papworth was convicted at the Old Bailey of unlawfully concealing a birth and sentenced to two months' imprisonment.

Throughout this period, John Humphreys, coroner for east Middlesex, was regularly called upon to hold inquests into cases of infanticide and child desertion in east London. As well as the Papworth case, he had presided over inquests concerning cases discovered in short order in Shoreditch, Spitalfields, Stepney, Hackney and Whitechapel. In one incident, a baby boy was found abandoned on the steps of a tenement in Mount Terrace, close to the London Hospital; upon his ragged clothing was pinned a note which read, 'Whoever may find this child, pray be kind to it. The few things it has were given to me by a kind lady. I have been seduced; and have lately come from Australia.'[56] The child died from the effects of cold some days later. In Bromley, a baby boy was found in a fish basket which had been thrown over a wall into the garden of a house in Archibald Street; the child was already dead and had apparently been suffocated.[57] On another occasion, a child, with umbilical cord still present, was found dead, wrapped in a piece of calico, floating down the Regent's Canal at Hoxton.[58] A baby girl was found in the churchyard of St Leonard's church, the umbilical cord having been torn and not treated with a ligature; thus had the child bled to death.[59] The case of Emma Papworth was unusual in that the parent of the deceased child was known and the perpetrator of the crime brought to some form of justice, but amongst almost all of the melancholy events witnessed by the East End, this was the exception, not the rule; Humphreys or his deputies were thus invariably called upon to declare a verdict of 'found dead' or 'wilful murder against persons unknown'. Regarding the final case described above, Humphreys commented 'that notwithstanding the vigilance of the police, they very rarely detected the perpetrator of the crime, which he was very sorry to say, was alarmingly on the increase'.[60]

Two other bizarre cases emanate from Whitechapel around this period. The first, in August 1863, was the discovery of a child's coffin, standing on its end, in the belfry of St Mary's church. Further examination of this part of the building revealed the body of a child in a shroud and no fewer than eleven skulls; in another chamber were found a coffin holding the skeleton of a child wearing a cap, and other remains placed amongst some beams. Fourteen bodies of children were found in all, many of them shrivelled or mummified, and some observers suggested (owing to the condition of the remains and the coffins, a few of which had begun to fall apart) that some of these corpses might have been there for up to thirty or forty years.[61] It was believed the bodies had been dropped through an opening into the space and it was remarkable that they had not been discovered earlier; in May that year, the bells had been thoroughly refurbished to mark the birthday of the Prince of Wales. The mother of one of the dead children was located thanks to an inscription on one of the coffins, and she confirmed the child's identity by some calico which was present with the body. Sarah Allen admitted to having disposed of several stillborn children, only one of whom was legitimate; the bodies had been handed to a Mr Canham for burial. The cost of this was put at 3s 6d, and Miss Allen was charged 7s in all;[62] it appeared that the interments never happened as they should have, and that the money had been creamed off.

A year later, Whitechapel was 'thrown into a considerable state of alarm' with the discovery of the bodies of eighteen children piled up in an old shed adjoining St Mary's church.[63] Some of the bodies were 'shockingly mutilated and deprived of their heads', and appeared to have been placed there comparatively recently.[64] It was immediately concluded that this terrible discovery was in some way connected with that made at St Mary's the previous year, and that 'the parties concerned in the sacrilegious transaction [had] placed those fragments of humanity where they were found with a view to ulterior removal'.[65] Despite the initial outrage, an explanation for this incident was soon forthcoming; apparently the bodies had been dug up during renovation work to the area around the 'bone-house', and had been placed in the shed covertly to avoid attracting public attention. All were later re-interred.[66]

By 1862, the media had been constantly commenting on the now nationwide increase in infanticide, with correspondents repeatedly calling for a revision of the bastardy laws. It was clear that many of the cases were a direct result of illegitimate births, with some undoubtedly the product of rape. Analysis of the reported cases of infanticide conducted by W. Cox, MP for Finsbury, based on figures from coroners' inquests, revealed that in London in 1861 there had been over 1,100 deaths of children under the age of two.[67] In the eastern Middlesex division, within which the East End of the time sat, 421 inquests were held, the highest tally of all, of which seventeen returned a successful verdict of murder. Compare this to Westminster, where only ninety-one inquests were held, or the City of London and Southwark divisions, which held only eighty-four,[68] and it is evident that child mortality, for whatever reason, was a burning issue in troubled east London. In 1871, a correspondent to the *East London Observer* brought to light the statistical work of Edwin Lankester, coroner for central Middlesex, who since the early 1860s had been analysing child-death figures within his jurisdiction. His findings declared that there were five reasons for the 'destruction of infant life': ignorance, carelessness, overcrowding, overwork and drunkenness,[69] attributes which by this time were strongly associated by many with the people of the East End.

CHAPTER 6

Cruel Beasts

There is nothing picturesque in such misery; it is but one painful and monotonous round of vice, filth, and poverty, huddled in dark cellars, ruined garrets, bare and blackened rooms, teeming with disease and death, and without the means, even if there were the inclination, for the most ordinary observations of decency or cleanliness.

'Dwellings of the Poor in Bethnal Green',
Illustrated London News (1863)[1]

In the early 1860s, Poplar, Limehouse and the Commercial Road were the haunts of a rather singular burglar named Joseph Francisco, a Spanish-speaker from Cape Verde. His agility as a cat-burglar earned him no small amount of notoriety when, for several nights, he worked the streets around Queen Street in Stepney, 'flitting past windows, passing through bedrooms, and climbing over walls, until he became an object of terror to the inhabitants of the neighbourhood, and the "black man" and the "black ghost" were universally talked of . . .' Despite such

93

obvious physical talents, he sometimes showed a degree of ineptitude; on one occasion, he ransacked a house in Limehouse and stole objects of trifling value while leaving behind others worth considerable sums. On another occasion, during his brief terrorising of the Stepney area, he broke open the back window of a house, climbed through and promptly trod on the face of a woman in bed. With the alarm raised, Francisco executed a most athletic escape, suggestive of the exploits of 'Spring-heeled Jack' a few decades previously: 'He displayed all the activity and agility of a monkey, leaped over water-butts, scaled walls, and ran up and down water-spouts, until he fairly baffled his pursuers and disappeared.'[2]

Francisco had previously been on trial at the Old Bailey for burglary, but was deemed of unsound mind and acquitted, allowing him to continue his criminal activities. In late January 1863, after exasperating the authorities with his superhuman feats of escape, he was apprehended again and charged with four burglaries. Leaving the dock at the magistrates' court, he bit the jailer and exhibited such violence against the officers who attempted to restrain him that he was detained in a lock-up cell. Later, he attacked police officers in an onslaught that lasted a good hour, knocking down seven men and yelling in broken English that, before his trial was over, he would murder someone. One imagines that Joseph Francisco, who from that moment appears to vanish from the historical record, met his fate either in prison or, more likely, an asylum.

The Nichol

The evidently unhinged Joseph Francisco may have worked alone, but burglaries and the successful distribution of stolen goods were often carried out by organised collectives. In March 1863, the police smashed a major operation after arresting Benjamin Everett of Sale Street, Bethnal Green, along with four others for a range of robberies executed in Bow, Dalston, Shoreditch, the City and as far afield as Islington and Dulwich.

Other members of the gang who were associated with the thefts were already serving prison sentences for other crimes, and the five arrested men were convicted felons, known by dubious nicknames such as 'Sixtoes', 'Velveteen', 'Scotch Dick' and 'Jack the Flat'. The scope and audacity of the gang were considerable: they had netted large amounts of cash and valuables including furniture, carpeting, jewellery, silver-ware and clothing, and upon his arrest, Benjamin Everett, the prime receiver, was believed to have been worth £4,000.[3] A press report on the conviction of the individual members of the gang concluded that 'one of the most numerous and desperate gangs of thieves and receivers in London has been broken up and dispersed'.[4]

In December 1863, a police raid on a house in Old Nichol Street, Bethnal Green, revealed a large cache of stolen goods received from a number of burglaries throughout the district. Joseph and Mary Ann Hacker ran a 'leaving shop', or illegal pawnbrokers, from the premises, and they were arrested, along with their tenants Edward Humphreys and Elizabeth Lyons, for being in possession of stolen property. The items found were numerous: a number of chairs, stolen along with a length of green baize and a harmonium from Bethnal Green Mission Church, were confiscated; police also found a picklock key, two half-crowns and a set of fire irons stolen previously from a neighbouring public house; and more chairs, eight bed quilts of good quality, a number of framed photographs and a bag of raw silk had all been stolen over the previous few months. This was a major find for the police, and with the arrest of William Brown (who was known by several aliases) and William Butcher in connection with the burglary of the Mission Church, another major burglary gang had been quashed.[5]

The Hackers' 'leaving shop' was situated in one of the most promi-nent slums of the era, that of 'the Nichol', a dense enclave of squalid streets tucked behind St Leonard's church just to the north of Bethnal

Green Road. In 1866 it was reported that the parish of Bethnal Green, an area of 760 acres, had a population of around 120,000, and that Old Nichol Street, New Nichol Street and Half Nichol Street together had a population of 7,000.[6]

The heart of this district was known as Friar's Mount. An 1863 report describes its inhabitants:

> Bandbox and lucifer-box makers, cane workers, clothespeg makers, shoemakers, and tailors, mostly earning only just enough to keep them from absolute starvation, swarm from roof to basement; and, as the owners of such houses have frequently bought the leases cheaply and spend nothing for repairs, the profits to the landlords are greater in proportion than those on a middle-class dwelling.[7]

Perhaps the real crime inherent to the Nichol was that much of the property in the area was owned by comfortably-off individuals unwilling to fork out the required revenue to maintain the houses to anywhere near a decent standard, and who allowed their tenants, the poorest of the parish, to live (in many cases literally) in filth. Mortality rates were up to four times higher than in the rest of London; in one house, it was recorded that there were forty-five occupants, the water supply coming from an 18-gallon cask situated by an open privy and an uncovered rubbish bin.[8] Death from disease was shockingly common, with newborn babies in some cases dying from the effects of suffocation brought about by the acrid fumes of open drains and sewage present in the airless basement rooms which their destitute families were resigned to inhabiting. Such conditions were, sadly, the norm.[9]

Half the properties were run by solicitors to maintain the estates of previous owners who were deceased, and many houses were managed on behalf of phantom landlords. During one investigation into the conditions in the Nichol, it was found that many tenants had little idea who their landlords were, despite paying more in rent per cubic foot than those living in the better conditions of the West End.[10] The 'vampyres of the poor', as these owners were once called, were conveniently disconnected from the squalor which they helped to sustain, their rent collected by bullying agent's clerks, unaware of how their tenements were being used by their occupants, and safe from the dangers in the streets.

Life in the tenements was cruel, and the overcrowded, harsh conditions meant that domestic violence – often fuelled by drink (the small area contained seventeen pubs) – was common. Caroline Burgins was asleep in her room when her common-law husband, Joseph Hodges, came in and without warning twice hit her so hard that she was rendered unconscious. One blow to the head had ruptured the temporal artery, and when Dr Howard Dilworth arrived from his surgery in Spital Square he recalled that 'blood was pumping out in a jet as thick as my little finger . . . in fact had I been a few minutes later she must have bled to death'.[11] In another serious case, John Norris was charged with throwing his wife out of a second-storey window. In her deposition, taken as she lay at death's door in the London Hospital, Mrs Norris claimed that her husband had done no such thing and that she had sat on the window ledge before throwing herself off of her own volition. This seems bizarre until one learns that she also claimed that before the incident her husband had beaten her with his fists, hit her round the head with a kettle and thrown boiling water at her.[12] Women of the Nichol could also be brutal: Margaret Cacus, Mary Framey and Mary Seymour, three 'stalwart women . . . well known to the police',[13] were charged with an assault on Ellen Murray in Old Nichol Street which left the injured woman with three laceration wounds to the scalp, four stab wounds to the right arm, and five to the fingers, some of which had gone down to the bone.[14]

However much the Nichol was witness to violent crime, it was perhaps more notorious for its desperate living conditions, grinding poverty, dirt and disease. Isolated from the wider community as a whole, in this regard the Nichol had much in common with the Flower and Dean Street area of Spitalfields, which as well as having a reputation for poor standards of living in its doss-houses, was known even more for its criminality. The Spitalfields rookery essentially had very few entrance points: from Commercial Street led narrow Keate Court, and a much-constricted entrance to Flower and Dean Street; George Street was the only way in from Wentworth Street, and both entrances from Brick Lane, namely the eastern end of Flower and Dean and Thrawl Streets, were also narrow. In the Nichol the only way in from Shoreditch High Street was via a couple of tight alleyways; three streets led in from Church Street (modern Redchurch Street), and access from the north was through a veritable maze of slim thoroughfares stretching south from Columbia Road. Equally, the narrow courts and alleys that branched off from those hidden streets, many culminating in dead-ends, increased the sense of isolation. The urban historian Harold James Dyos pointed out 'how often these introspective places were seized by the "criminal classes", whose professional requirements were isolation, an entrance that could be watched and a back exit kept exclusively for the getaway'.[15]

Tiger Bay

Between the accommodating thoroughfares of Berner Street and Christian Street in St George-in-the-East lay Tiger Bay, another dangerous enclave known for its predatory prostitutes and the robbers and thieves who targeted the unsuspecting sailors who went there in search of base pleasures:

It is true that the unsuspecting wayfarer going through some of these dark alleys might be suddenly pounced upon by a couple of ruffians and there and then be robbed and half stifled, but it is not this sort of crime which gives its name to Tiger Bay. The tigers are, for the most part, quiet in their lairs; slinking, watchful, crouching, cruel beasts, who wait there, sharpening their claws, and looking with hungry eyes for the prey that their treacherous she-cats bring down.[16]

Frederick Street, which along with Brunswick Street contained the nucleus of the worst vice, was not riddled with tiny alleys and courts, but was rather 'simply a once respectable street, which has by some means or another fallen into the tenancy of a number of low brothel-keepers, who harbour several of the worst characters of both sexes, and who are rapidly deteriorating the morale and feelings of the surrounding neighbourhood'.[17]

Incidents of robbery, assault and brothel-keeping in Tiger Bay were consistently reported in the press and its reputation was known far and wide, even beyond London. Indeed, the very name Tiger Bay would come to denote any rough neighbourhood: a district close to the London Docks was also known by that soubriquet, the densely packed area close to the church of St George-in-the-East known as Bluegate Fields, rightly considered to be another of the East End's most dangerous slums. In 1869, the journalist, novelist and biographer Blanchard Jerrold set out across London with the artist Gustave Doré to collect a series of observations which would become his acclaimed *London: A Pilgrimage*. On their journeys through the extremes of the capital, the two intrepid investigators did not shy away from the East End's less respectable quarters, and covered, often accompanied by an experienced police officer, the squalid districts of Whitechapel, the docks, Petticoat Lane and, in one memorable account, 'this weird and horrible Bluegate Fields':

We plunge into a maze of courts and narrow streets of low houses – nearly all the doors of which are open, showing kitchen fires blazing

99

far in the interior, and strange figures moving about. Whistles, shouts, oaths, growls, and the brazen laughter of tipsy women: sullen 'good nights' to the police escort; frequent recognition of notorious rogues by the superintendent and his men; black pools of water under our feet – only a riband of violet-grey sky overhead![18]

One colourful Bluegate Fields character was Mary Ann Bennett, also known as 'Cast-iron Poll', a woman of fifty years who was described as 'The Queen or Chieftaness' of this 'abominable locality'.[19] She had apparently barely spent more than a month out of prison, having been convicted of various crimes, usually theft, no less than fifty-three times, and was so used to life in the cells that, invariably, after one of her sprees in the East End, she would do anything to get back to it. If she was given no charge, she would apparently say, 'Well, I'll soon make one', before going outside and attacking the first person she came across, or deliberately smashing the windows of the nearest public house. When brought back to the police station, she would merely ask why she hadn't been locked up when she first asked, when it was known full well that she would end up doing something that would get her arrested.[20] 'Cast-iron Poll' would become a character in William Travers's play *The Watercress Girl*, one of several popular melodramas which dramatised the world of the poor as described by Henry Mayhew and others, and which was widely lauded by audiences and critics for its 'powerful cast, beautiful scenery and stupendous effects' when first performed at the City of London Theatre in 1865.[21]

Dead drunk with opium

For journalists like James Greenwood, Thomas Archer and Blanchard Jerrold, the numerous 'Tiger Bays' were living freak shows. Jerrold, in his descent into the gloom of Bluegate Fields, was very aware of another activity which some felt had become a scourge of the riverside districts – that of smoking opium. Charles Dickens himself visited an opium den in Limehouse run by one Chi Ki in 1869, and immortalised the establishment in his final work, the unfinished *Mystery of Edwin Drood*, first published in instalments in 1870:

> Shaking from head to foot, the man whose scattered consciousness has thus fantastically pieced itself together, at length rises, supports his trembling frame upon his arms, and looks around. He is in the meanest and closest of small rooms. Through the ragged window-curtain, the light of early day steals in from a miserable court. He lies, dressed, across a large unseemly bed, upon a bedstead that has indeed given way under the weight upon it. Lying, also dressed and also across the bed, not longwise, are a Chinaman, a Lascar, and a haggard woman. The two first are in a sleep or stupor; the last is blowing at a kind of pipe, to kindle it.[22]

Anglo-Chinese trade disputes in the nineteenth century had resulted in the two Opium Wars – the first from 1839 to 1842, the second from 1856 to 1860 – which weakened China's sovereignty and forced it to trade freely with the rest of the world. The British capture of Calcutta in 1756 had meant that the cultivation of Indian opium poppies became a major source of potential profit. Once trade was open with China, and with the active encouragement of the British, Calcutta's ports became a major conduit for exports of opium to the west. The opium trade thus formed an important part of the regional economy and therefore that of the all-powerful East India Company.

The link between the Chinese immigrants around the London Docks and the importing of opium from the east was considered a given, and elicited much suspicion and prejudice. The Chinese population in London was nowhere near as large as many were led to believe, yet the small concentration of East Asian immigrants in the East End, usually sailors employed by the East India Company, drew considerable attention, laced with xenophobia. The *East London Observer* noted that, for the Chinese, 'opium-smoking represents the indulgence which spirit drinking does to the British seaman', drawing similar associations to unproductive languor and sloth from the 'scores of Chinese and Lascars, whose sallow, corpse-like complexions, bleared eyes, and relaxed look indicate the effects of their indulgence'.[23] The opium habit was thus thought to be the preserve of 'wretched Lascars, Malays, Chinese and one or two debauched Europeans' – 'opium debauchees are nearly all of foreign birth'.[24] Nonetheless, there was also a certain glamour associated with the drug, attracting 'earls and princes', as well as artists; it was often assumed that 'any man might become a poet, or at least a writer of flowing and flowery prose, if he only possessed courage sufficient to avail himself of this convenient picklock of the gates of paradise'.[25]

Although the use of opium was not illegal, those who partook of it were frowned upon and regarded as low life. One journalist, writing in *London Society*, believed that to experience the full benefits of opium, one had to be of a 'particular type', and a 'degenerate one' at that.[26] Numerous reported deaths from opium poisoning and concerns regarding the regulation of other potentially dangerous drugs led to the passing of the 1868 Pharmacy Act, which limited the sale of such substances to registered chemists. This brought the death toll from opium misuse down from six to four per million population within the space of a year. But throughout the 1870s, the opium dens of east London continued to flourish, despite the controls, and the narcotic still claimed its casualties. It would be later, in the early twentieth century, that a more exaggerated sense of depravity was presented to the reading public in the fictional works of authors such as Arthur Ward, who wrote under the name Sax Rohmer, the creator of the super-villain Fu Manchu. First appearing in print in 1911, Fu Manchu's murderous plots emanated from his headquarters in a seedy Limehouse opium den. It was an area Ward knew from his days as a reporter, but he received much criticism for his portrayal of East Asians. In an attempt to fend off accusations of demonising them, as well as Limehouse itself, Ward answered his critics (but probably failed to calm them):

Of course, not the whole Chinese population of Limehouse was criminal. But it contained a large number of persons who had left their own country for the most urgent of reasons. These people knew no way of making a living other than the criminal activities that had made China too hot for them. They brought their crimes with them.[27]

Opium dens had already featured in other works of fiction as a focus of criminal activity; in Arthur Conan Doyle's Sherlock Holmes story *The Man with the Twisted Lip*, first published in 1891, Holmes investigates the case of a missing man, Mr Neville St Clare, who is believed to have been seen in the window of an opium den in the fictional Upper Swandam Lane, described as 'a vile alley lurking behind the high wharves which line the north side of the river to the east of London Bridge'.[28] In *The Picture of Dorian Gray* (1891), Oscar Wilde evocatively delineated the slum quarters of London and depicted the opium dens as places 'where one could buy oblivion, dens of horror where the memory of old sins could be destroyed by the madness of sins that were new'.[29]

More recently, the criminality of Limehouse and its Victorian drug dens has been referenced in the graphic novels of Alan Moore, namely *From Hell* and *The League of Extraordinary Gentlemen*.

The philanthropists

A key indicator of the depths to which the East End was perceived to have sunk by the second half of the nineteenth century was the arrival of William Booth in Whitechapel in 1865.

It was the ideal place for Booth, who had been preaching to the poor and wanton of his native Nottingham for many years, to begin his Christian Mission in London. The meetings, understood today as the germinating seeds of the Salvation Army – the name given by Booth to the organisation in 1878 – were initially held in the open air along Mile End Waste, but these were difficult beginnings: the gatherings were often 'surrounded by blaspheming infidels and boisterous drunkards; the processions down Whitechapel Road pelted with garbage'.[30] Nevertheless, Booth held firm in his faith and to the task ahead of him, and found enough converts to his cause and enough supporters amongst local missioners to be offered a new venue, a tent pitched on a former Quaker burial ground in Thomas Street.[31] One night, the tent allegedly blew down in a storm, although it was said that a gang of roughs sabotaged it by cutting the ropes, as Booth's public sermonising was not popular with the irreligious masses, 'for the atheism of East London in those days was a fierce and oppugnant atheism, an atheism which hated the very name of God, and to which Jesus appeared as the arch deceiver of the human race'.[32]

Temperance was a principle insisted upon by the Salvation Army, and all members were required to practise total abstinence from alcohol. Booth's wife Catherine had a lifelong interest in the temperance movement, partly owing to her father's problems with drink, and early in her relationship with her husband she persuaded him to stop consuming alcohol, which he had occasionally imbibed for medicinal purposes. Catherine Booth became proactive as a campaigner for temperance, encouraging drunkards to attend reform meetings, and such direct public action became an integral part of the Salvation Army's outreach work, as it continues to be today. But such principles in action would not have sat well with the 'fierce and oppugnant atheism' of east London.

Drink was considered by many reformers as a root evil: the poor indulged enthusiastically and the East End offered an enviable quantity of public houses and beer shops for the enjoyment of this frequently destructive pastime. By the beginning of the 1870s, the main road between Aldgate and Mile End, the site of Booth's initial concern, had over thirty-five premises licensed to sell liquor; the Ratcliffe Highway, part of which had been renamed St George's Street in the 1840s, had thirteen; Brick Lane, which today has no surviving public houses, had eleven. The prevalence of breweries in east London, originally the result of such 'stink-industries' being located there to allow prevailing winds to blow unpleasant manufacturing smells away from the City, resulted in the presence of a large number of attendant drinking establishments. The oldest, Truman, Hanbury and Buxton, had been established on Brick Lane as early as 1666 and by the mid-nineteenth century was the largest brewing concern in London, producing over 400,000 barrels of beer a year.[33] On the Whitechapel Road stood the formidable Albion Brewery of Mann, Crossman and Paulin, and a little farther east, on Mile End Road, was Charrington's Anchor Brewery. Founded in Bethnal Green by Robert Westfield in the early eighteenth century, the brewery had come under the auspices of the Charrington dynasty in 1776 when John Charrington became a partner, and from then on, successive generations of Charringtons had taken over from their predecessors.

By the 1860s, the young Frederick Charrington was heir to a fortune worth £1,250,000. Having converted to evangelism in 1869, the following year, with financial help from his father, he set up a school and mission room with accommodation for over 100 boys, many of whom came from poverty-stricken homes or who were already living a life of crime, including members of the Mile End Gang, a group of lads who had often been in trouble with the police. On one occasion, a rival gang of youths from the Kate Street Gang, also known as the Forty Thieves, descended upon the mission, sticks hidden up their sleeves, ready for a confrontation with the boys living there. Incredibly, although these young roughs were all convicted thieves, Charrington later proudly claimed that 'after gaining their confidence, and assuring them that we

105

were not in connection with the police, they were induced to enter the building and join in the boys' Sunday evening service'.[34]

But it was in 1870 that he had the experience that would alter the course of his life. One evening, as he walked from the brewery to the school, he passed the Rising Sun public house in Bethnal Green, 'about as hideous an erection as can be found anywhere in England':

> As I approached the public-house, a poor woman, with two or three children dragging at her skirts, went up to the swing doors, and calling out to her husband inside, she said, 'Oh, Tom, do give me some money, the children are crying out for bread.' At that the man came through the doorway. He made no reply in words. He looked at her for a moment, and then he knocked her down into the gutter. Just then I looked up and saw my own name, CHARRINGTON, in huge gilt letters on the top of the public house, and it suddenly flashed into my mind that that was only one case of dreadful misery and fiendish brutality in one of the several hundred public houses that our firm possessed. I realised that there were probably numbers of cases arising from this one public-house alone ... And then and there, without hesitation, I said to myself – in reference to the sodden brute who had knocked his wife into the gutter – 'Well, you have knocked your wife down, and with the same blow you have knocked me out of the brewery business.'[35]

Frederick Charrington thus abandoned the brewing industry and his considerable wealth and devoted his life to helping the poor of east London: 'Then and there I pledged to God that not another penny of that money should come to me.'[36] Charrington's later achievements would include his crusade to eradicate brothels in the East End, in which he was considerably successful, being instrumental in the closing of up to 200 such establishments. One side effect of this was to force prostitutes out onto the streets, where they were more vulnerable, but Charrington persevered in his efforts.[37] It was said that some houses displayed a portrait of him so that they would recognise him when he turned up unannounced, for they 'feared Frederick Charrington as they feared no policeman, no inspector, no other living thing'.[38]

'A disease approaching insanity'

Charrington was also, perhaps unsurprisingly, a vociferous supporter of the temperance movement. The disruptive effects of alcohol abuse, alarmingly prevalent in the East End, were the source of innumerable reports in the press, some of them tragic. Alfred Webb, proprietor of the Cannon in Cannon Street Road, was summoned to Thames Police Court to face two charges, one of allowing prostitutes to convene on his premises and another of allowing drunkenness and other disorderly conduct. The Cannon's potman had also been seen to throw a drunken woman from the pub with great violence after she had delivered a volley of abuse when she was refused service, being already intoxicated.[39] Another report described how John Mullett, a 'weather beaten, sun-dried mariner', had accosted PC Christopher Ginn in Bancroft Place, Mile End, in the early hours of the morning while extremely drunk from the previous evening's revelry. He asked PC Ginn where he could find more beer, and when he was told there was none to be had (the pubs having now closed), he grew furious, beating the officer around the face, throwing him to the ground and attempting to strangle him.[40]

Children were often victims of their parents' drunken habits. Two horrific cases, both reported in 1867, told how in one incident, a father drunkenly threw his young son against a wall and 'dashed his brains out', whilst in the other a dead child had been tipped out of its coffin by the father, who then sold the casket simply to buy drink.[41] Mary Ann Herring, a confirmed drunkard for twenty-five years, appeared at

Worship Street Police Court on a charge of assaulting her two daughters at her home in Cleveland Street, Mile End; the girls, who were by now adult, were apparently happy to support their mother financially providing she committed no nuisance, but her drunken ways meant that if they refused her drink money, she would steal from the household to pay for it. On one occasion, Mrs Herring was challenged by her daughters over her behaviour and she punched both of them in the face before biting one of them, all the while keeping up a tirade of foul language. Sometime after, one of the girls had dislocated her shoulder at work and had had it treated, only for Mrs Herring, in a drunken state, to knock the daughter about and dislocate the joint again. Mr Cooke, the magistrate, commented that it was 'a most lamentable case: a woman cannot stand before a court of justice in a more degraded condition than when her children are compelled for their own protection to appear against her and give testimony, however unwillingly, of her utter worthlessness from abandoned habits'. Mrs Herring was sent to the house of correction for six weeks.[42]

In May 1870, Henry Parker appeared at the Old Bailey on a charge of murdering his brother-in-law, James Rutter, in Bacon Street, Shoreditch. Apparently, Rutter had remonstrated with Parker (who had been drinking during the day) over an earlier argument he had had with his sister, punching him in the face outside the Ship pub. A second blow sent Parker to the floor; he pleaded with his assailant to see reason, but to no avail. As Parker got up and ran down the street, Rutter followed him, threw another punch and bashed his head against a wall. Suddenly, Rutter moved away, clutching his chest and declaring that he had been stabbed. He was led back to the Ship, and there he died, for Parker had indeed stabbed him in the chest, the blade passing between his ribs and entering his heart. Henry Parker went on the run and was found three weeks later in a lodging house in Rotherhithe. At the trial, he was convicted of manslaughter and sentenced to six months' imprisonment on account of the provocation he had received.[43] The original altercation between brother and sister was a relatively minor one over money, but the drinking of alcohol on the part of Parker undoubtedly caused the situation to spiral out of control, with tragic consequences.

Misuse of alcohol also caused problems at the docks, particularly the London Docks at Wapping, where hundreds of stored barrels of spirits such as rum and brandy, as well as wine, were a constant temptation. However, the large casks would have been almost impossible to smuggle out of the secure, manned gates of the docks without immediate detection by the dock constables, and so an alternative method of nefariously acquiring the drink was devised, known rather vulgarly as 'sucking the monkey' (the 'monkey' in this case being the barrel within which the liquor was held). At sea, this act was also known as 'bleeding the monkey' or 'tapping the admiral', but wherever it was enacted, it entailed the insertion of a small tube or straw in the bung-hole of the barrel through which the contents could be rapidly imbibed. It was highly illegal, of course, and apprehension of the guilty party was not uncommon owing to the suspicions raised as they left the docks in an obvious state of inebriation. One man, John Barrett, was caught by a dock constable in the act of sucking wine from a barrel and promptly assaulted the officer. At the court hearing, the tube used to commit the deed was produced, but Barrett, who had not drunk enough to be inebriated at the time, was convicted of the more serious charge of assaulting a constable.[44]

'Sucking the monkey' was also extremely dangerous, for the relatively narrow aperture of the straw often led to the intake of high levels of alcohol without the drinker being immediately aware of it: 'The spirit thus drank has a greater and more instantaneous effect upon the brain of the drinker than liquor taken in the normal way. It is stated that if a pint of strong ale be sucked through a straw it will produce immediate insensibility.'[45] Thomas Smith, a labourer at the London Docks, drank so much brandy in this way that he was found in a stupor at the scene and conveyed to the London Hospital, where, despite the use of a stomach pump, he died of alcohol poisoning.[46] Similarly, four men, after 'sucking the monkey' at the London Docks, made their way to the Three Cranes pub in Whitechapel, boasting about how much drink they had managed to get through. One of the men, Philip Godfrey, very soon became insensible and was taken to Leman Street police station, where the divisional surgeon, Dr George Bagster Phillips, pumped nearly a pint and a half of brandy from his stomach. It was not enough, for Godfrey later died in a police cell.[47]

For some, the scourge of drink, particularly amongst the working classes, was a major cause for concern. In a lecture at the People's Mission Hall in Mile End in 1870, Mr John Hilton proclaimed that 'large expenditure in public-houses caused national impoverishment, not only by the dead waste of capital, but on account of the pauperism, vice, and crime which spring from drinking'.[48] Numerous presentations on the subject of temperance throughout the 1870s further emphasised the growing worry about overindulgence in alcohol: a correspondent to the *London Daily News* firmly believed that the love of drinking was 'itself a disease approaching insanity, inasmuch as its victims are unable to resist the temptation to indulge it, however injurious or immoral they know such indulgence under the circumstances to be'.[49]

The bishop of Guildford, in an address on 'The Drink Question' at St Mary's Schoolrooms in Whitechapel, turned his attention to the perceived lust for drink exhibited by the poorer working classes, stating that 'upon the whole there was no finer specimen of humanity than the working man, but he had an enemy, and that enemy was drink'.[50] The East End, being predominantly working class, and poor working class at that, appeared to be exhibiting all the most unsavoury characteristics to which the ready availability of alcohol could lead. At one Monday morning session at Worship Street Police Court in September 1874 there were no less than twenty cases of drunkenness or drunken and disorderly conduct.[51] The area appeared to have a firmly rooted drinking culture, for another issue brought to light by such proclamations was the increase of drinking amongst young people; at a lecture held at St Saviour's School in Poplar, Mr J. Ford expressed how 'he had often been informed that education would stop drunkenness but notwithstanding the rapid progress of education during the last few years, drunkenness was on the increase'.[52]

Drink was thus blamed for reducing the poor to destitution, causing insanity, encouraging criminal activity, violence and, in some cases, incidents of manslaughter and homicide. Poverty and squalor became the perceived cause of child neglect, abandonment and infanticide. For many observers, the East End was entering its most infamous period, presenting problems that were simply too big to solve outright even with the help of philanthropists such as Booth, Charrington and latterly, Dr Thomas Barnardo.[53]

CHAPTER 7

'Vulgarity, Rudeness and Immorality'

We have on the highest authority of Shakespeare, the dictum that murder will always out, but even that great master of human nature had not quite plumbed the extreme depths to which our basest nature can sometimes reach . . .

Illustrated Police News (1890)[1]

The Whitechapel tragedy

At about 4.30 p.m. on Saturday, 11 September 1875, a brush-maker named Alfred Stokes was asked by Henry Wainwright, his co-manager at Edward Martin's corn merchants in New Road, to help him move some parcels from a warehouse on Whitechapel Road. Stokes had formerly worked under Wainwright at the latter's own mat and brush-making shop at 84 Whitechapel Road, and the pair were now reunited as employees of Mr Martin following the dissolution of Wainwright's business. The warehouse, which Wainwright had once owned and for which he had retained the keys, was at the rear of 215 Whitechapel Road, and was accessed via Vine Court.

Stokes, holding Wainwright in high regard, was more than happy to help; however, when he arrived at the warehouse and took possession of the heavy parcels, which were wrapped in black American cloth and tied with rope, he could not help but notice a foul smell emanating from them. The two men walked with the burdensome parcels to St Mary's church and as Wainwright walked off to fetch a cab from a nearby cab-rank, Stokes felt compelled to look inside one of them: to his horror he caught sight of a human head and an arm and hand, all of which were greatly decomposed. Despite his obvious shock, and believing the worst of his former employer, Stokes kept his counsel when Wainwright returned, and said nothing as the parcels were loaded onto a cab, after which Wainwright got in and told the driver to head to Commercial Road. Stokes then took it upon himself to follow the cab and watched as it stopped at the corner of Greenfield Street, whereupon Wainwright got out and met a young lady on the corner. The woman was Alice Day, a ballet girl from the nearby Pavilion Theatre,[2] who was at that time Wainwright's paramour. It was noted that Wainwright was smoking a cigar, probably in an attempt to hide the smell.

Miss Day got into the cab with Wainwright and the vehicle moved off, with Stokes following as it began to travel west. Along the way, Stokes alerted two police officers to what he had seen, but they merely laughed at him and said he was mad; nonetheless, he maintained his pursuit across London Bridge to Borough, where the cab finally stopped outside an empty building on Borough High Street known as Hen and Chickens. Wainwright, carrying one of the parcels, got out and let himself into the empty property, at which point two other police officers, this time successfully alerted by Stokes, went to the cab and found Alice Day there. They asked her what was in the remaining parcel that sat on the seat opposite but she refused to entertain them, saying, 'The idea of your interfering with me! I am waiting for my husband.' Wainwright came out to collect the other parcel and was questioned by the police as to its contents and what his purpose was with the empty Hen and Chickens building. Taken back inside the property, Wainwright coolly offered both officers £50 to ask no further questions and to keep silent on the matter, but when PC Turner said he was going to see what was in one of the parcels, Wainwright lost his composure, declaring, 'Don't, for goodness sake, don't touch it', and as the officer picked up the parcel, he again said, 'Don't touch it; let me go; I will give you £200 and produce the money in 20 minutes.'[3] But it was too late – the officer was already examining the wrapped objects and immediately realised he was looking at parts of a dismembered body. Wainwright was put back into the cab and, with Alice Day, taken to Stone's End police station.

With Wainwright and Day in police custody, a concerted examination of the contents of the two parcels could begin. It turned out to be the dismembered body of a young woman:

> The pieces were in a very decomposed condition . . . they had been subject to the influence of quicklime, and death had taken place at least two months ago. The trunk of the body alone was in one of the parcels; the head, legs, feet, arms and hands in the other. Every limb had been disjointed and the right thigh bore indications of a severe blow thereon.[4]

As the investigation into this most bizarre incident picked up steam, it was not long before the identity of the body, as well as Wainwright's part in this grisly story, were ascertained. Contrary to the medical findings, the woman had been dead for a year: she was Harriett Lane, described as a good-looking auburn-haired woman of about twenty-four years of age,[5] who had gone missing a year before, in September 1874. Importantly, in 1871 she had become Henry Wainwright's mistress; under the name Percy

King – he already had a wife and children – he had married her on 22 February the following year.[6] The birth of two children followed. The much-respected pillar of the community was soon in trouble financially, and his business was faltering. His brother Thomas, with whom he shared the mat and brush-making business on Whitechapel Road, dissolved their partnership in 1874, being owed considerable sums of money. Wainwright, who had set up his second family in the pleasant Tredegar Square in Bow, was reduced to pawning valuables, as was Harriett, the secret wife. The oldest of their two daughters was now being looked after by Ellen Wilmore of Sidney Square, and the situation was putting a strain on the relationship between Harriett and her husband. The money that Wainwright had been giving Harriett in the past as maintenance was gradually diminishing, and soon the anxious woman was turning up at inopportune moments to castigate her floundering husband, often demanding money. This not only caused him tremendous embarrassment, but also raised the risk of his secret marriage being exposed to the community at large. On Friday, 11 September 1874, Harriett told Mrs Wilmore that she was off to meet Wainwright at Whitechapel. She was never seen again.

That evening, three men working by the warehouse at 215 Whitechapel Road reportedly heard three distinct gunshots. Wainwright had shot Harriett in the head and, after cutting her throat, buried her body in chloride of lime beneath the wooden floor of the warehouse. The chloride of lime was believed by Wainwright to speed up decomposition of the body, so that before long, there would be very little of it left. Unfortunately for him, it only served to preserve the corpse. When Wainwright was ultimately declared bankrupt in June 1875 and the premises at 215 Whitechapel Road were repossessed, he must have realised that the final resting place of his former mistress was no longer secure; a peculiar smell in the building had already been noticed by some people, as well as by a curious dog, which soon went missing. Wainwright still had keys (he would often visit the premises to collect mail), and on 10 September 1875, he and his brother Thomas, who by then held a lease on the empty Hen and Chickens in Borough High Street, bought a spade, a chopper, some rope and some cloth and, that day, exhumed Harriett's body, crudely divided it up, placed the pieces in the parcels, and left them in the warehouse until they were picked up the following day by Henry Wainwright and the unwitting Alfred Stokes. And thus that most peculiar of journeys through London began, and the affair of the 'Whitechapel tragedy' (as it became known) came to light.

In the aftermath of Wainwright's execution for murder on 21 December 1875,[7] the press commented on the sorry story with regret:

> Shakespeare had long ago told the world that a man might 'smile and smile and be a villain,' but it was something unusual in the annals of murder to find a genial gentleman like Henry Wainwright behaving so coolly with such a terrible secret in his breast, with such terrible evidences of his guilt at hand.[8]

This most exceptional criminal case certainly drew national attention to the environs of east London, but on this occasion it had very little to do with the district's numerous problems. In fact, it could have happened anywhere at any time, and in the descriptions of the man Wainwright, it also became apparent that not all denizens of the East End were squalid and poverty-stricken, although crime, and in this case a crime of passion, could strike anywhere.

Wainwright might have been cool, sober and premeditated when he took Harriett Lane's life, but not all tragic cases were executed with such forethought. A number of incidents from the East End from this period were reported with great relish by the *Illustrated Police News*, which continued the traditions of the *Newgate Calendar* and the 'penny dreadfuls', a forerunner of the sensationalist tabloids.[9]

One article reported how Joseph Millward, a wire worker from the borough, on discovering that his wife was living with another man, Robert Wales, in Whitechapel, had gone to Wales's lodgings in Crown Court, Wentworth Street, broken down the door and attacked Wales with a knife, plunging the blade into his face. In the ensuing struggle, Wales fought back with a poker, but was stabbed several times about the body. After the weapon was wrestled from Wales's grasp, his furious assailant threatened to murder both Wales and his own wife, making a failed lunge at her with a pair of scissors.[10] On his arrest, Millward exclaimed to his targets, 'I ain't settled you, but I mean to settle you; and I am only very sorry I did not serve her the same.'[11] At the resulting trial, the defence claimed provocation, in that Mrs Millward had been lured away from her husband by Wales some time before, an appeal which saw Millward's conviction for unlawfully wounding reduced to six months' imprisonment.

Not unexpectedly, when the desire for drink or the effects of drink were present, some incidents could be extremely unpleasant, as in the case of Henry Hill, who apparently awoke one afternoon at his home in Brady Street to find a fellow lodger, Henry Snelgrove, cutting his throat with a broken table knife. Defending himself, the bleeding Hill attacked Snelgrove with a chisel, inflicting several wounds to his face and wrist. Both men were conveyed by a police officer to the London Hospital where, while undergoing treatment, Hill suddenly picked up a spoon and thrust it into his wounded throat, 'tearing the edges apart, and causing fresh hemorrhage'.[12] Hill was put into a straitjacket, and when asked why he had exacerbated his already terrible injury, merely replied that it was because he could get nothing to drink. It would transpire that Hill's initial story was an attempt to cover for the fact that, having been drinking 'freely all the week', he had actually cut his own throat before attacking Snelgrove.

In another case, Amelia Green was brutally set upon by her husband for refusing to give him both the money their son had recently earned, and beer. She was kicked and beaten so badly that her abdominal injuries threatened her life, and it was considered urgent to get her deposition before she passed away.[13] Meanwhile, two entire families living in Nelson Court, off Whitechapel Road, were affected so much by a whole day's heavy drinking that they entered into an argument with each other and ended up fighting with sticks and pokers. One stick was used so violently against Jane Grayburn that it broke with the force, and John Grayburn later died of severe head injuries in the London Hospital. The press claimed in the aftermath of the murderous affray that Nelson Court had 'the appearance of a "slaughter-house" in the morning light'.[14]

Vulgarity, rudeness and immorality

To the Editor of the East London Observer.

SIR – I should feel much obliged if you would make public a little adventure I had whilst walking down the Bow-road (also I believe, called the Monkey Parade) on Sunday evening last. I am a foreigner, but still I can speak and understand English. Whilst I was taking a stroll I was very much disgusted at the manner in which boys and girls push and insult people. I had not been in the road two minutes when a female evidently taking a fancy to a rose I had in my coat, took a snatch at it, and walked off with it as coolly as if it belonged to her . . .[15]

'Monkey parade' was a term originating in the 1870s, meaning 'an informal but regular event, in some public place, in which (generally) young people, intent on meeting and flirting with the opposite sex, stroll in couples and groups of friends to advertise themselves to others similarly engaged'.[16] In rougher quarters, that could also extend to the kind of mischief and unpleasant behaviour witnessed by Mr Alfred Brookens in the correspondence above; the letter appeared to suggest that the particular section of the Bow Road described had acquired that nickname through the regularity of such gatherings, in much the same way that on every Sunday Middlesex Street, on account of its market, became Petticoat Lane to one and all. Later, the name 'monkey parade' would be used to signify an actual gang of youths who would saunter down a street with disruption and mischief in mind, much to the discomfort of the local residents. These roughs would make their unpleasant presence felt by marching 'along the pavements several abreast, jostling and insulting pedestrians on their way to and from places of worship'.[17]

Recent research has shown four main factors which lead to the formation of gangs: the need and/or desire to make money; seeking protection against victimisation; gaining a sense of belonging or connectedness with others; and the achieving of status and respect.[18] All these factors were found in abundance within the melting pot of cultural, ethnic, religious and social diversity that was the East End towards the end of the nineteenth century. Gatherings of youths such as the monkey parade certainly manifested themselves out of a sense of belonging, but soon developed into groups dedicated to achieving some form of standing over the nervous citizenry. Other organised groups seemed to exist 'for the purposes of civil warfare and private revenge', gaining their names from the areas they so aggressively defended, such as the Old Street Gang or the Dove Row Gang.[19]

In his 1959 book about the Jack the Ripper murders, the journalist Donald McCormick speaks of the Old Nichol Gang, a notorious mob based in the equally notorious Bethnal Green slum district.[20] It has never been ascertained whether a gang of that name ever existed, for there is no mention of it in any contemporary press or police documentation; but despite McCormick's reputation as something of a storyteller, prone to fabrication, the name of the Old Nichol Gang is still dragged out in many studies of the East End underworld. That is not to say that gangs

119

did not exist in this troublesome slum; throughout the 1870s and up to the 1890s, several Nichol 'clans' would notoriously 'pit themselves against each other, armed with knives and staves, unmolested by the local constabulary unless a serious injury occurred'.[21] When confronted by any threat from a gang from outside the Nichol, these groups could be relied upon to cast any differences aside and unite against the common foe, often positioning themselves in an abandoned house and hurling tiles, bricks and other improvised missiles down upon the intruders.[22]

Naturally, forming a collective of like-minded villains was a more reliable way of making money, and accounts in the magistrates' courts and local press of multi-participant street robberies were rife. Sadly, some of these gangs consisted of youngsters, the new generation of Ikey Solomon's thieving apprentices, who, being brought up in an environment where criminality was often a means of survival, took the lead from their elders. The common lodging houses were particularly looked upon as breeding grounds for crime and vice amongst the very young, with destitute youths living there being exposed to all manner of depravity from an early age or, in some cases, from birth. From these rough dwellings would come reinforcements 'to the overwhelmingly large army of thieves and harlots'.[23] Children raised in lodging houses where prostitution was present were also exposed to a dangerous immorality: 'What future can be expected for a girl ... who is taught day by day, by precept and example, to see little or no harm in a career which, when, as often happens, work is slack or food scarce, is frequently adopted without hesitation or compunction, and in many cases without even the knowledge of sin'.[24]

'The Maiden Tribute'

By the turn of the 1880s, child prostitution, and particularly the illicit procurement of young girls for the purposes of prostitution, was a shockingly common undertaking. In the early part of the decade, several newspapers spoke of the increase in such incidents, and many of the girls involved were barely past the age of consent, which was then thirteen. In some cases, 'there were to be found too many little girls of eight years old and upwards who were plying the same horrible trade'.[25] Virgins were in particularly high demand on the Continent, and money would change hands between procurers and their clients, usually impoverished parents who were desperate enough to sell their daughters into the sex trade for a good price. By the time the girls realised what was happening to them, it was too late. According to one brothel-keeper on the Mile End Road,

The getting of fresh girls takes time, but it is simple and easy enough when, once you are in it . . . How is it done? Why, after courting my girl for a time, I propose to bring her to London to see the sights. I bring her up, take her here and there, giving her plenty to eat and drink – especially drink. I take her to the theatre, and then I contrive it so that she loses her last train. By this time she is very tired, a little dazed with the drink and excitement, and very frightened at being left in town with no friends. I offer her nice lodgings for the night: she goes to bed in my house, and then the affair is managed. My client gets his maid, I get my £10 or £20 commission, and in the morning the girl, who has lost her character, and dare not go home, in all probability will do as the others do, and become one of my 'marks' – that is, she will make her living in the streets, to the advantage of my house.[26]

The impoverished East End was a significant focus of such degradation, where 'vice is much more natural than in the west'.[27] Although the girls proffered for prostitution there were not as young as those taken elsewhere, suggesting that even this deprived district had some moral compass, it was said that 'In the East-end, you can always pick up as many fresh girls as you want. In one street in Dalston you might buy a dozen. Sometimes the supply is in excess of the demand.'[28] This market for unwitting virgins would be exposed in a series of articles in the *Pall Mall Gazette* in July 1885, entitled 'The Maiden Tribute of Modern Babylon' and written by its then editor, William Stead, producing an exposé which was considered truly shocking for its time and which even today retains its power to appal. Stead uncovered the rampant trade in young girls through confidential interviews with brothel-keepers and other connected characters, producing page after page of depressing reportage, and then, perhaps unwisely, he demonstrated how easy it was to buy a 'maid'.

Assisted by Bramwell Booth (son of William, of Salvation Army fame), Josephine Butler and others, Stead and his co-conspirators managed to buy a 13-year-old girl named Eliza Armstrong from a procuress in Lisson Grove, northwest London. Armstrong's mother, an alcoholic in dire need of money, let her daughter go for £5, the approximate equivalent of £580 today. Mrs Armstrong was told that Eliza was going into service as a maid, although it was felt she fully understood what was happening to her daughter. Eliza was taken to a brothel to meet her new master, namely Stead, who behaved as a libertine to add to the reality of the situation, drinking a whole bottle of champagne before entering the girl's room. Eliza, who had been drugged with chloroform, came out of her stupor and screamed aloud at the sight of Stead, who let her cry out to suggest that he had used her, before simply walking out of the room. Bramwell Booth took the girl to France where she was delivered safely to a Salvation Army family. This done, Stead set to work on his highly controversial articles.

'The Maiden Tribute of Modern Babylon' threw Victorian Britain into a moralistic fever, but as an example of 'government by journalism' it was successful in instigating legislation to raise the age of consent to sixteen: the relevant revisions in the Criminal Law Amendment Act of 1885 would become known colloquially as 'Stead's Act'. The ramifications for William Stead and his co-partners was less positive, as all were charged with kidnapping and tried at the Old Bailey. Stead was found guilty on a technicality, in that he had not sought permission for the transaction from Eliza Armstrong's father, and he was given a three-month prison sentence in October 1885.[29] On release, he returned to edit the *Pall Mall Gazette*. The newspaper would continue to be a firebrand of what had become known as 'New Journalism', regularly highlighting social injustice throughout the 1880s, and often focusing on the plight of the poor in the East End, particularly during the infamous Whitechapel murders of 1888, when the newspaper became a vociferous critic of the police and other authorities. Stead would go on to become one of the 815 passengers who lost their lives in the sinking of RMS *Titanic* on 15 April 1912, apparently having given his lifejacket away in an act 'typical of his generosity, courage, and humanity'.[30]

CHAPTER 8

'The Social Cancer Spreading in our Midst'

The Polish Jew comes as an unskilled worker to an already over-stocked market, where he undersells native labour. This, it is true, may be more his misfortune than his fault, but the English workman who is made to suffer does not stop to draw nice distinctions between the two.

Pall Mall Gazette (1885)[1]

Throughout the 1880s, the East End of London found itself the home of the outsider yet again with a major influx of Eastern European Jewish refugees, which only served to squeeze the already limited resources of the area. On 13 March 1881, Tsar Alexander II of Russia was assassinated by representatives of the revolutionary Narodnaya Volya organisation, marking the end of what was seen as a more progressive and tolerant regime. The *Jewish Chronicle* in London had grave misgivings about the repercussions for Russian Jewry: 'God help them if but the faintest shadow of suspicion rests upon any Jews for complicity in the Regicide conspiracy. When we reflect that the fate of the majority of existing Jews is thus hanging in the balance, we cannot but follow the course of events in Russia with breathless anxiety.'[2]

Only one of the ringleaders, and a minor one at that, was Jewish, but with the erroneous speculation by two newspapers, *Vilenskii Vestnik* and *Novoye Vremya*, that Jews were responsible for the assassination,[3] a wave of pogroms tore through Russia. In towns like Elisavetgrad, Kiev and Odessa, anti-Jewish rioting erupted in earnest; homes and businesses were ransacked, synagogues wrecked and religious texts destroyed. People were thrown into the street and subjected to horrifying acts of violence and, in the case of women, rape. One observer noted that he had 'seen things that sickened him to think of'.[4] The resultant denigration of the Jewish peoples of Eastern Europe led to a colossal flight, a spate of migration which spread outwards to other more sympathetic nations. The East End became the first point of entry for those desperate and often bitterly impoverished refugees who settled in London or used it as a springboard to immigrate to the United States. It has been said that between April 1881 and June 1882, as many as 225,000 families left Russia,[5] with thousands descending upon the East End in a steady stream that would continue for decades as further unrest in Eastern Europe drove more Jews out.

The East End already had an established Jewish presence and a significant number of places of worship to cater for them; along with such notables as at Duke's Place and Bevis Marks by the edge of the City, by 1881 there were synagogues in Adler Street, Old Castle Street, Artillery Lane, Dunk Street, Goulston Street, Sandy's Row and Spital Square, among others. As the 1880s progressed, the new arrivals began to find their feet within self-imposed communities: 'The newcomers have gradually replaced the English population in whole districts which were formerly outside the Jewish quarter . . . Now the Jews have flowed across that line; Hanbury Street, Fashion Street, Pelham Street, Booth Street,

125

Old Montague Street, and many streets and lanes and alleys have fallen before them.'[6]

As with prior influxes of immigrants, the Russian Jews, soon followed by Jews from Poland, Germany and Hungary, attracted disdain from the indigenous population of the East End, and for the same reasons as before: they were seen to be overcrowding an already struggling labour market, and to be willing to work for significantly lower wages. 'It suffices that the Polish Jew will labour patiently till midnight, accepts starvation wages, and depreciates the trade, for him to become an unwelcome guest in the East End, and these exiles from Russia already number close upon 30,000 men, women and children', opined one newspaper report.[7]

The resentment of many in the East End was aimed at the recently arrived Jews of the area, but this tended to be in the form of verbal insults as opposed to physical violence: the *Poilishe Yidl*, an early Polish newspaper published in Britain, spoke of groups of English workers sitting in doorways who would call out 'Bloody Jew!' every time a Jewish person walked past. The same article also warned that the looks in English eyes were 'already half indicative of a pogrom . . . a more bloody and terrible affair than one in the Baltic'.[8] For the moment at least, such rising resentment fell far short of the direct racially motivated violence that was being seen in other Jewish immigrant enclaves in places such as Limerick and Constantinople, but it was a precarious situation that threatened to erupt at any moment.

This may have had much to do with the tendency of the Jewish immigrants of east London to keep themselves to their distinct communities, where they looked out for each other, ultimately creating self-contained organisations for the relief of their poorest fellow countrymen, of whom there were many. They were also noted in the early days for not being particularly disposed towards serious criminal activity:

Regarding Jews from the social standpoint, no difference is observable between the highly-educated, accomplished, and well-born Jewish lady and gentleman and the highly-educated, accomplished and well-bred Christian lady and gentleman ... From wife-kicking, assassination, and other unnatural crimes it is shown by the published records of crime that the Jews are happily free. Drunkenness is not a Jewish vice. Conjugal infidelity is a most rare Jewish crime.[9]

Prostitution amongst the poorest Jewish women, on the other hand, was seen as a growing problem from the perspective of London Jewry, despite the opinion of the outside world that 'there was something about Jewesses which would not let them abandon themselves to a life of immorality'.[10] The chief rabbi, Dr Hermann Adler, bemoaned the fact that it appeared to be on the increase, arguing that 'The extension of the social evil to my community may be directly traced to the overstocked labour market and to the Russian persecutions continuing to this day which cause thousands of Jewish girls to arrive at these shores without any means of sustenance.'[11]

Religion and morality collided dramatically in August 1885, although not with regard to the growing population of East End Jews; on this occasion it centred on the relatively minor Mormon community, who for some weeks had been meeting at Clifton Hall on Mile End Road. Rumours had been circulating that the Mormons, who had recently developed a more public profile, were inducing young girls to migrate to Utah 'to lead polygamous and immoral lives'.[12] In light of W.T. Stead's exposés in the *Pall Mall Gazette* the previous month, great indignation was raised within the local community, a meeting was stormed by a noisy mob and several Mormon elders were forced to evacuate the hall. They were chased down the Mile End Road by the mob, pelted with all manner of refuse, and their clothes torn, until they found refuge in a house on Stepney Green.

The Batty Street murder

Local opinion of the Eastern European settlers was not improved by a high-profile murder case which occurred in 1887, and which involved a self-employed Polish umbrella-maker by the name of Israel Lipski. On 28 June, Miriam Angel, a young Jewish woman who lodged with her husband Isaac at 16 Batty Street, Commercial Road, was found dead in her bed, apparently having consumed nitric acid. She was six months pregnant at the time. Lipski, who had been lodging in the upstairs room for around two years, was found under her bed with acid burns around his mouth, having consumed a quantity of acid himself. In a bad state, Lipski was arrested and sent to the London Hospital to recover, before being charged with the murder of Miriam Angel. Perhaps unsurprisingly, Lipski denied everything, claiming that he had discovered two men who had previously asked him for work in the room, and on challenging them had been restrained while they poured a liquid, which they claimed was brandy, down his throat.[13] He also believed they were responsible for doing likewise to Angel; what he could not explain was how the room was seemingly locked from the inside.

In the trial that took place following Lipski's recovery, two theories were entertained: one was the claims of the accused, which never changed over frequent retelling; the other that he had 'suddenly determined to enter the room for an immoral purpose'[14] and, when Mrs Angel resisted, had become furious, beaten her insensible with his fists and then poured nitric acid down her throat, before drinking acid himself in order to commit suicide. It was a troubled trial, with enough doubt regarding Lipski's guilt to cause major debate in the national press. One question was whether he had actually bought the bottle of acid that was found close by him that fateful day; there was a connection in that Lipski's assistant, the young Richard Pittman, had bought some 'aqua-fortis' for the purpose of staining walking sticks, but it was not a sufficient connection to definitively link Lipski to the bottle found. Another concern was the condition of the door to Angel's room and whether it had been locked from the inside, or was merely faulty, thus giving the appearance of being locked. The jury, however, felt that the evidence was enough to prove guilt and on 25 July 1887, Israel Lipski was sentenced to death for the murder of Miriam Angel.[15] Despite the verdict of the jury, there was much worry in the press over the decision to hang a man on what was felt to be uncertain evidence. The *Pall Mall Gazette* ran the headline, 'Dare We Hang Lipski?' and published the names of thirty-one members of Parliament who had signed a memorial objecting to the execution.[16] Such was the public concern over a possible miscarriage of justice that Lipski's execution was delayed whilst his case was reconsidered, but during this reprieve he broke down and apparently made a full confession.

Israel Lipski was hanged at Newgate on 21 August. According to one observer, the huge crowds outside the prison were in a state of great excitement; 'never, since the abolition of public executions, has the neighbourhood of Newgate presented such an appearance.'[17] The case of Israel Lipski generated a spike in anti-Semitism in the area. The *Evening News* stated that 'The low class of Polish Jews which Lipski belonged to are the pariahs of modern European life . . . In the districts blighted by their presence the standard of living and morality alike is lowered . . . For the man one may feel sorrow, but one cannot look with equanimity on this social cancer which is spreading in our midst, and is so baneful to all human progress.'[18]

The trouble between the Angels and the Lipskis did not end with the latter's death, either. Isaac Angel, Miriam's widower, along with his two brothers, attacked Leah Lipski, the landlady of 16 Batty Street, despite her being no relation to the hanged man. (Israel Lipski's surname was actually Lobulsk.) During the assault, Angel yelled out, 'I'll do for you the same as you done for my wife!' His brothers had also visited the street previously and smashed the windows and shutters of no. 16, shouting 'Lipski, Lipski!'[19] That surname, which Leah Lipski had the misfortune to bear, would quickly become a derogatory byword in the East End, 'used by persons as a mere ejaculation by way of endeavouring to insult the Jew to whom it has been addressed'.[20]

Crimes of passion

A few days after Christmas 1887, Henry Blaming, employed as a potman and barman at the small Two Brewers pub on Brick Lane, was accused of raping the 14-year-old daughter of manager Robert Matthews. The case went to trial at the Old Bailey on 30 January 1888 and although Blaming was acquitted the following day, he unsurprisingly lost his job at the pub where he had been gainfully employed for five months without prior incident.[21] Perhaps imprudently, the evening after the trial, Blaming went to the Two Brewers with some other men, despite knowing that his presence would not be welcome. Strangely, Matthews, who was tending the bar at the time, served Blaming, but when the latter began laughing at a private joke between himself and one of his companions, the atmosphere changed. 'Who are you laughing at?' asked Matthews. Blaming replied, 'I have nothing to cry for', and at that Matthews pulled out a revolver from behind the bar and shot Blaming in the stomach.

The wounded man fled as Matthews fired again, hitting Blaming in the buttocks. Later, in the London Hospital, the house surgeon was unable to remove the bullet from the abdomen, resulting in a three-month stay in hospital until Blaming was deemed out of danger. Matthews was arrested and was totally unrepentant; he admitted to shooting the man twice, and wished, he said, that he had shot him a third time. When the arresting officer, Walter Dew, told him how serious the incident was, Matthews exclaimed, 'What! I wish I had killed him, there would be an end to the bastard then.'[22] The subsequent trial saw leniency towards Matthews owing to the provocation involved; nonetheless, he received six weeks' hard labour for wounding.

On the same day, another crime of passion was tried at the Old Bailey, this time the trial of Elizabeth Williams for wounding Matilda Lacey. The incident happened in the disreputable enclave of Spitalfields streets that surround Great Pearl Street; Lacey was first punched by Williams, who then proceeded to slash Lacey across the face with a clasp knife. The alleged reason for the assault was that Lacey had apparently offered to give Williams's husband 6 shillings to sleep with her, and the understandable anger resulting from this offer boiled over into drunken violence with a blade outside a pub. Williams was found guilty and received fifteen months' hard labour.[23]

It is interesting to note the differing verdicts in these two cases; Robert Matthews's punishment was small in comparison to Elizabeth Williams's, and yet the repercussions of being shot in the stomach are far more serious than a slash across the face. The court obviously took into account the unfortunate events which led up to the shooting of Henry Blaming by an otherwise respectable publican, who kept a loaded revolver in case of burglary. With the Lacey case, tougher sentences on random, drink-induced violence, for whatever reason, appear to have been the order of the day, particularly as the Great Pearl Street neighbourhood was a noted den of criminals and prostitutes; Lacey herself said that she was single, and would 'do anything' to earn a living.[24]

It was still not uncommon for women to be the instigators of violence against other women and men. A number of incidents were played out in the early part of 1888, such as the assault on Mary Ann Scully by Mary Kennedy in the Victory pub in Watney Street, Shadwell. Kennedy, Scully and another woman had recently robbed a sailor on Devonshire Street and Scully had helped herself to the majority of the spoils. In the pub, Kennedy hit Scully around the head several times with a pint pot, resulting in serious injuries which had to be dressed at the police station.[25] Another incident involving women spilled over into violence against uninvolved parties when 40-year-old Catherine Dooley, described as a 'rare virago' and a 'pest in the neighbourhood', attacked Catherine Sullivan and her daughter with an iron poker. Sullivan was attempting to protect her daughter from the assault, but Dooley set about them wildly and also attacked another woman when she tried to intervene, giving all three serious injuries. Dooley was given four months' hard labour.[26]

For the common rogue, the knife was still the weapon of choice. Easily concealed and easy to acquire, it was said that they were so readily available in the East End markets that old knives and even discarded bayonets could be found being used as 'playthings for the gutter children of the street'.[27] A demonstration of how quickly knives could be used to terrible effect came in February 1888 when a woman named Annie Millwood returned to her lodging house in White's Row, Spitalfields, suffering from a number of stab wounds to her legs and lower abdomen.[28] Millwood, who probably earned her living as a casual prostitute, claimed not to have known her attacker, a man who had produced the knife from his pocket quickly and without warning, and it is still unclear how many wounds were inflicted. Millwood made a complete recovery before dying of natural causes in the South Grove workhouse several weeks later.[29]

In March, Ada Wilson was attacked in her own home in Maidman Street, Mile End, by a man who called at the door and forced his way in. He demanded money from her and when she refused, he stabbed her several times in the throat before making his escape. Fortunately, despite being left for dead by her assailant, Wilson made a full recovery.[30] But within the space of a few months, the East End of London would fall under even more intense scrutiny, and thus into the world's gaze, producing outrage after outrage which would reverberate through the late nineteenth-century consciousness and beyond.

The gathering storm

For some, the brutal assault and subsequent death of Emma Smith, a 45-year-old widow and prostitute, in April 1888 was merely a continuation of the violence inherent in the East End that had seemingly gone unchecked for too long; soon, it would be seen as the beginning of the most infamous series of murders in criminal history.

Emma Smith was a regular inhabitant of the Spitalfields doss-houses and, like many in her position, her earlier life was something of a mystery. Former detective Walter Dew, reminiscing in his memoirs half a century later, made a touching reference to this East End 'unfortunate':

> There was something about Emma Smith which suggested that there had been a time when the comforts of life had not been denied her. There was a touch of culture in her speech unusual in her class.
>
> Once when Emma was asked why she had broken away so completely from her old life she replied, a little wistfully: 'They would not understand now any more than they understood then. I must live somehow.'[31]

But that particular way of life, that of the prostitute, meant walking the mean streets of the district and taking the attendant risks. On the evening of Easter Monday, 2 April 1888, Smith had made her way to Poplar, perhaps to take advantage of the potential custom around the populous thoroughfares and pubs close to the London Docks, which would undoubtedly have been busy on a bank holiday evening. Already that night, one of Smith's fellow lodgers, Margaret Hayes, had been punched in the face[32] by a man and had decided to call it a night and return to her George Street lodging house[33] where both she and Smith had been staying. She recalled seeing Smith at the corner of Farrance Street and Burdett Road in Poplar with a man at about 12.15 a.m. as she made her way home.

Emma Smith herself returned to George Street between 4 and 5 a.m. in great distress; her face was bloodied and her ear was badly cut. She also complained of severe pain in the lower abdomen, but despite these injuries, she was reluctant to say what had happened to her. Taken to the London Hospital on Whitechapel Road by two fellow lodgers, and pointing out the scene of the incident near the junction with Brick Lane and Wentworth Street on the way, Smith was seen by house surgeon Dr George Haslip, who listened to Emma's version of what had happened to her that morning. She said that she had been on her way back to her George Street lodgings when she had turned up Osborn Street and noticed three men who had begun to follow her. Passing St Mary's church on Whitechapel Road at around 1.30 a.m., she crossed the street to avoid them. The men caught up with her near the junction with Brick Lane and Wentworth Street, assaulted her, robbed her of whatever money she had on her person and concluded the attack by thrusting a blunt instrument into her vagina with great force, before running off.[34] In the hospital, Smith contracted peritonitis as a result of the injury, slipped into a coma and died early on the morning of 4 April. Violent assault had become murder.

Questions regarding the veracity of Emma Smith's story have arisen over the years. If she was assaulted around 1.30 a.m., what had she been doing until, at the earliest, four in the morning, when she finally stumbled into the lodging house only a minute's walk away? If she was lying in agony in the street where she claimed to have been assaulted, why did nobody, particularly passing police officers, find her? It is quite possible that her story was a fabrication, perhaps created to deflect from her activities as a prostitute, and that she may have been attacked by a violent client somewhere, or even by a vicious pimp who was unhappy about Emma's lack of financial success that night. Such deliberate obfuscation, if it indeed existed in this case, would not necessarily have been unexpected. But Emma Smith's assertion that she was attacked by three men, one of them no more than nineteen years of age,[35] obviously suggested, to the authorities at least, a continuing alarming trend in mob violence. Coroner Wynne Baxter, who presided over Smith's inquest, made his feelings clear about the severity of the incident, saying 'it was impossible to imagine a more brutal case'.[36] By the summer of 1888, the death of yet another East End prostitute would set alarm bells ringing for sure.

In the early hours of 7 August 1888, Martha Tabram, a 39-year-old hawker and casual prostitute, was found brutally stabbed to death on the first-floor landing of a tenement block in Whitechapel. Situated in George Yard, a dingy, narrow thoroughfare running off Whitechapel High Street, George Yard Buildings, for all its insalubrious setting, was inhabited by predominantly respectable people, 'the poorest of the poor, but very honest', as one observer described them.[37] A hard-working waterman, John Reeves, leaving his rooms at the early hour of 4.45 a.m. to seek work by the London Docks, found Martha Tabram's body on the dimly lit stairwell lying in a pool of blood, for she, as was discovered later, had been stabbed thirty-nine times, apparently with two different implements. In the opinion of Dr Timothy Killeen, who examined her body and conducted the post-mortem, one weapon, perhaps resembling a clasp knife, had caused thirty-eight injuries, puncturing numerous vital organs; a second knife, more in keeping with the proportions of a large dagger or bayonet, had punctured the breast bone. Killeen was also of the opinion that all the injuries had been inflicted while Tabram was still alive.[38]

Again, confusion over the nature of the murder prevailed, for the only person who would have had anything significant to say about the last hours of Martha Tabram's life was her drinking companion on the previous night, a rather masculine and ruddy-faced prostitute named Mary Ann Connelly, also known as 'Pearly Poll'. Connelly led the police a merry dance. When she was eventually traced, she claimed that she and Tabram had spent much of the previous night drinking in various local pubs in the company of two soldiers, a private and a corporal, and that the night ended at about 11.45 p.m. with Connelly going up Angel Alley with the corporal and Tabram going with the private through the archway leading into George Yard, presumably for paid sex. A police officer, PC Thomas Barrett, also claimed to have met a soldier loitering at the junction with George Yard and Wentworth Street, apparently waiting for a friend who had gone off with a woman, a few hours before the murder was discovered.[39] These revelations led to Connelly and Barrett being asked to attend identification parades where they would view lines of soldiers who had been off duty on the fateful night. Barrett unfortunately picked out two men with impeccable alibis, and Connelly, after failing or refusing to pick anybody at one parade, was invited to another and there, like Barrett, picked out two soldiers who could easily prove their innocence. The failure of PC Barrett and 'Pearly Poll' to find their men led Inspector Edmund Reid to declare later that 'they could not be trusted again as their evidence would be worthless'.[40]

Once more, it was all a frustrating mystery and, as with the murder of Emma Smith four months earlier, the coroner's inquest (this time presided over by Wynne Baxter's deputy, George Collier) reached the unsatisfactory verdict of 'wilful murder against some person or persons unknown'. Like Baxter before him, Collier expressed his revulsion at this most awful of crimes, describing it as 'one of the most brutal that had occurred for some years. For a poor defenceless woman to be outraged and stabbed in the manner which this woman had been was almost beyond belief.'[41]

But whereas the media response to Emma Smith's murder had been limited, Martha Tabram's passing invited much more investigation and comment. An interesting article appeared in the press which demonstrated the lawless nature of that particular neighbourhood – this was an interview with John Reeves and his wife, who were apparently awoken during the night of the murder by serious disturbances nearby:

These two rows, Mr. and Mrs. Reeves say, were of a very noisy and quarrelsome character. The crowds round surged backwards and forwards a great deal. At last the police came and dispersed the crowd. This did not conclude the riotous proceedings of the night. About 2 o'clock Mr. and Mrs. Reeves heard more screams, they were this time very piercing. Only a few roughs seemed to constitute this crowd, which seemed to be moving in the direction of George Yard. However, the noise soon lessened in volume, and Mr. and Mrs. Reeves then retired for the night.[42]

Mrs Reeves, in a further interview, perhaps unselfconsciously demonstrated a reaction to such disturbances which suggested that such a thing was not uncommon. Referring to that night, she told a reporter from the *Echo*, 'I knew something would happen out of the ordinary, for me and my old man were never so much disturbed before, though we almost nightly hear cries of "Murder!" and "Police!" we pay no attention to them whatever.'[43] Tellingly, another resident of George Yard Buildings, superintendent's wife Amy Hewitt, also claimed to have heard a cry of murder that night, which emanated from outside but echoed around the tenement's stone stairwells: 'But the district round here is rather rough, and cries of "Murder!" are of frequent, if not nightly, occurrence in the district', she explained.[44]

Accounts like these demonstrate the volatile nature of the area in which the two murders occurred, and the almost casual manner with which those exposed to local antisocial behaviour dealt with it all. The tight East End enclaves of Whitechapel and Spitalfields came under fire as dens of vice and violence, a criticism which the local press, perhaps unsurprisingly, were quick to reject:

Now a murder in Whitechapel or Bethnal Green is regarded by the public altogether differently from a similar occurrence in Belgravia

137

or Mayfair . . . Indeed, some fearful-minded persons think the inhabitants of particular parts of our district are all ruffians and viragoes, who acquired a taste for thieving and violence in their mother's arms . . . Such opinions and sentiments are so ridiculous that were it not for the harm they do it would not be worth while to notice them. What are the facts? The statistics or returns of criminal offences show that, in proportion, there is really no more crime, either of a greater or lesser degree, in East London than in any other part of the metropolis, or, for the matter of that, in Great Britain.[45]

The two unsolved murders of 'fallen women' in Whitechapel appeared unconnected and merely, to some at least, to be the by-product of an area corrupted by poverty and vice. Both investigations, to the chagrin of the police, sputtered to a halt, but all the skills of Whitechapel's H-Division would be put to the test when matters quickly and violently escalated.

CHAPTER 9

The Nemesis of Neglect

All England was murmuring his name with bated breath . . .

'Dagonet', *Sunday Referee* (1888)[1]

On 31 August 1888, with the memory of Martha Tabram's demise still floating on the slum's haze, another woman, Mary Ann Nichols, was found murdered in a narrow, gloomy thoroughfare named Buck's Row.[2] Nichols's downslide into the anonymity of the East End's poor was perhaps not much different from that of many of the other women who plied their trade on the streets – her marriage, which produced five children,[3] had been blighted by alcohol abuse until it fell apart for good in about 1881, leaving Mary Ann to survive as best she could on the streets of London and to earn her living by casual prostitution.

If Martha Tabram's death had been shocking enough, Mary Ann Nichols's assailant had dispatched her in a way that struck a nerve with an already edgy East End populace: her throat had been cut through to the spine and an examination of her body in the mortuary revealed that she had been disembowelled. Once again, the police investigation turned up little of any use in terms of finding the perpetrator, although by now some were beginning to link this crime with the previous two. Soon after the discovery in Buck's Row, several newspapers hinted at the direction the police were taking:

> The officers engaged in the case are pushing their inquiries in the neighbourhood as to the doings of certain gangs known to frequent the locality, and an opinion is gaining ground amongst them that the murderers are the same who committed the two previous murders near the same spot . . . [The gangs] have been under the observation of the police for some time past, and it is believed that, with the prospect of a reward and a free pardon, some of them might be persuaded to turn Queen's evidence, when some startling revelations might be expected.[4]

One story, syndicated across a number of publications, made more of the 'gang' idea when it reported the assault on a woman, possibly a prostitute, who had met a man outside Forrester's Music Hall on Cambridge Heath Road and had agreed to go back to his lodgings, only to be pulled down a darkened passageway near Buck's Row and assaulted and robbed by a small gang comprising both men and women. When she attempted to cry for help, one of the men raised a large knife to her throat and said, with obvious reference to the recent murders, 'We will serve you as we did the others.'[5] Typically, more sensationalist newspapers like the *Star* took a different tack, quickly suggesting that the murderer in all three cases was likely to be the same man, a maniac to boot, who worked alone.[6] From here on in, the press would play a significant role in shaping the image of the crimes, of the supposed perpetrator and, with the East End now coming under more negative scrutiny than ever, all the evils that had for too long been festering away in this troublesome district.

'A noiseless midnight terror'

What was most unusual about these crimes was the public's reaction to them. Undoubtedly bolstered by the police's lack of success in apprehending what was quickly looking like the sole perpetrator of three awful murders, the confused citizens of the East End were now looking for a scapegoat, and the press were about to give them one.

'[T]here is a man who goes by the name of the "Leather Apron"', the *Sheffield and Rotherham Independent* declared, 'who has more than once attacked unfortunate and defenceless women. His dodge is, it is asserted, to get them in to a house on the pretence of offering them money. He then takes whatever little they have and "half kills" them in addition.'[7] Although the name 'Leather Apron' – from the garment the man was always said to wear – first appeared in a northern provincial newspaper, within days it was on everyone's lips. The press, as well as the women who described being assaulted by 'Leather Apron', undoubtedly felt that this was the man the police should be looking for in connection with the murders in Whitechapel. Before long, he was being portrayed as 'a noiseless midnight terror', whose expression was 'excessively repellent' and whose appearance was of 'a marked Hebrew type'.[8] It was this latter description that became caught up in a sudden explosion of panic and criminality when, on 8 September, another East End unfortunate, Annie Chapman, was found brutally mutilated in the backyard of an overcrowded house in Hanbury Street, Spitalfields.[9] The savagery of this crime – the murderer had removed much of the poor woman's sexual organs – brought out the very worst in the now bewildered, horrified and angry public as the news quickly spread. Hanbury Street and the neighbouring thoroughfares were besieged by great crowds, and it was 'outsiders', particularly the Jewish 'newcomers', who bore the brunt of the suspicion, for now the bottled-up resentment over the immigration question had reached breaking point:

Bodies of young roughs raised cries against the Jews, and many of the disreputable and jabbering women sided with them. This state of things caused several stand-up fights, thus putting a further and serious strain on the police, many of whom began to express their fears of rioting.[10]

The police were stretched, to say the least. Aggravation became the order of the day and one local villain, George Cullen, also known as 'Squibby', discovered much to his horror how far the crowds were prepared to go. A notorious street-gambler, Cullen had been involved in an altercation with a police officer the previous week, throwing a stone which accidentally hit a young woman, Betsy Goldstein. Having escaped arrest, he was seen in Commercial Street on the morning of the Annie Chapman murder and Detective Constable Walter Dew gave chase, soon to be joined by several other officers. The excitable crowds quickly became aware of this, and, according to one press report, came to the mass conclusion that the pursued man was the murderer, whereupon 'some thousands of persons gathered in a state of the greatest excitement'.[11] An aggressive mob joined the chase, and Cullen was then more than happy to forgo his usual struggle against arrest and give himself up to the safety of police custody in Flower and Dean Street.[12]

But this incident was one of many. That same day, the *Star* reported that two men were detained by police for no other reason than to protect them from a 'hue and cry' which had resulted from suspicions levelled at them by the excitable crowds in Whitechapel Road. The same edition mentioned other stories which suggest that on that day, 8 September 1888, the East End had begun to lose control of its senses:

The excitement in Spitalfields is now rendering the people almost frantic . . .

A man for whom there has been a warrant out for some time was arrested. In an instant the news spread like wild-fire. From every street, from every court, from the market stands, from the public-houses, rushed forth men and women, all trying to get at the unfortunate captive, declaring he was 'one of the gang,' and they meant to lynch him. Thousands gathered, and the police and a private detective had all their work to prevent the man being torn to pieces.[13]

The press seemed quick to report on any violent incident, particularly against women, often with one eye to the murders, but also serving, intentionally or otherwise, to show its readership the evident lawlessness of the East End. A woman was assaulted in Key Street, also near Buck's Row, by the man she had been living with, and much was made of the fact that he also struck her with a knife.[14] The name 'Leather Apron' was mentioned in one report about a woman being attacked in Green Street, Bethnal Green, particularly when local gossip insisted that the victim had died in the London Hospital of her injuries, which was later found to be untrue.[15]

In effect, the mysterious 'Leather Apron' had become a catch-all appellation for any unpleasant character disposed to assaulting women, with one newspaper suggesting that the individual whom other papers were calling a 'half crazy creature, with fiendish black eyes,'[16] and 'unquestionably mad,'[17] was little more than 'a mythical outgrowth of the reporter's fancy'.[18] Nonetheless, the murders in the East End were inspiring crime and disorder. Behind the scenes, the police had identified a man named John Pizer as 'Leather Apron' and within a few days had arrested him at his home in Whitechapel.[19] Nothing came of this, however; although taken by the experienced arresting officer, Detective Sergeant William Thick, Pizer had iron-clad alibis as to his whereabouts on the nights Mary Ann Nichols and Annie Chapman had been killed, and thus this sudden ray of light amidst a seemingly chaotic and desperate police investigation had quickly dwindled.

Before the unknown assassin struck again on 30 September, in what was seen as the shocking and audacious double murder of Elizabeth Stride and Catherine Eddowes – the former found with her throat cut in Dutfield's Yard, Berner Street, and, forty-five minutes later, Eddowes discovered horrifically mutilated in Mitre Square, just within the boundary of the City of London – much comment was already forthcoming about the dire circumstances in which these crimes occurred. The London correspondent of the *Irish Times* noted that

The newspapers have awakened to the fact that our city is infected with plague spots which breed moral diseases owing to the overcrowding and want of proper sanitary arrangements. A wholesale excision of these centres of immorality and crime is advocated, but as usual the means suggested to bring about the much needed reform are somewhat visionary.[20]

Sweeping statements such as this again elicited defensive responses from the East End press, who were undoubtedly better equipped to see the bigger picture. Responding to claims that the area was 'a plague spot', one local paper declared that

We must admit that the recent crimes have done us considerable harm; they are blots on our fame, which will take some time to erase. But they are not a justification for a hundredth part of the exaggerated rubbish which, although fit for no higher place than the wastepaper basket, has been given the dignity of type.[21]

It was the satirical magazine *Punch* which delivered the most durable metaphor for the East End's problems, linking the criminality and horrors of murder with the general state of the area. Illustrated by artist John Tenniel in a sinister engraving of 'Crime' personified as an open-mouthed

144

1. 'A Pirate Hanged at Execution Dock', an eighteenth-century engraving by Richard Dodd. In use for more than 400 years, the last executions took place there in 1830.

2. 'The Poor-Whores Petition' was a satirical swipe at the licentiousness of the royal court of Charles II following the Bawdy House Riots of 1668.

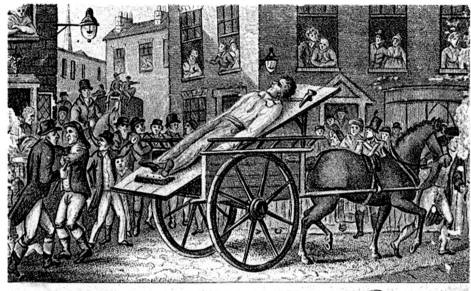

The public Exhibition of the Body of Williams

3. A contemporary engraving depicting the burial of John Williams. Suspected of the Ratcliffe Highway murders, Williams committed suicide in prison and was buried at the crossroads of Cable Street and Cannon Street Road.

4. Isaac 'Ikey' Solomon, an early East End anti-hero. His exploits were published in several pamphlets, much to the enjoyment of the reading public.

5. 'Spring-heeled Jack', the 'Terror of London', defies the police in one of the many depictions of this quasi-supernatural menace which graced the pages of the penny dreadfuls in the mid-nineteenth century and beyond.

6. The urban and rural characteristics of the developing East End can be clearly seen in Langley and Belche's map of 1822. The open spaces were often the haunts of highwaymen and footpads.

7. Gustave Doré's evocative engraving of a Limehouse opium den, from Blanchard Jerrold's 1872 study *London: A Pilgrimage.*

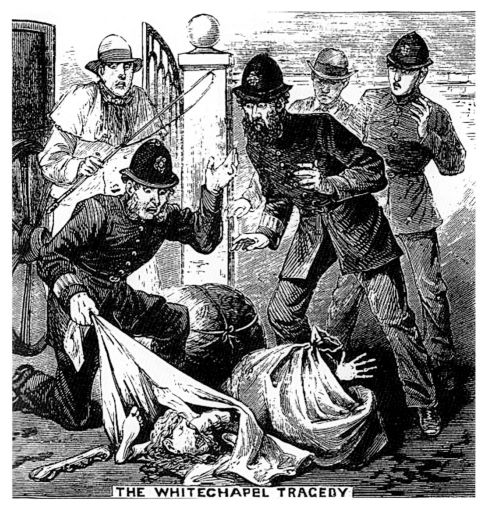

THE WHITECHAPEL TRAGEDY

8. A lurid illustration from the *Illustrated Police News* of the discovery of the dismembered body of Harriett Lane, murdered by Henry Wainwright in 1874.

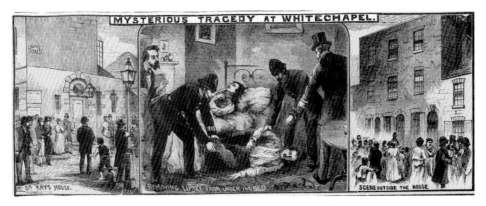

MYSTERIOUS TRAGEDY AT WHITECHAPEL.

9. The *Illustrated Police News*'s depiction of events surrounding the discovery of the body of Miriam Angel, allegedly murdered by Israel Lipski in her room in Batty Street, June 1887.

10. 'The Nemesis of Neglect', the ghoulish metaphor for crime and decay in London, illustrated in *Punch*, 29 September 1888, at the height of the Whitechapel murders.

11. Detective Inspector Frederick Abberline, the enigmatic officer who has since become synonymous with the investigation into the Ripper murders. Despite a long career, no confirmed photograph of him has been found. This portrait is from *Toby* magazine, September 1888.

12. Mary Jane Kelly leading 'Jack the Ripper' into her room in Miller's Court, Dorset Street. Published in November 1888 in the *Penny Illustrated Paper*, this illustration is the first depiction of the 'gentleman Jack' so prevalent in the media today.

13. A lone police officer copes with East End disorder in a press illustration from 1890. Commercial Street police station can be seen in the background.

14. The respected and reviled Inspector Frederick Wensley takes charge: an undated photograph from Wensley's scrapbook.

THE VICTIM CONSTABLE THOMPSON.

THE ACCUSED

"HOLD HIM — 'I'M DONE.'

HE DIES ON THE WAY TO THE HOSPITAL.

15. The *Illustrated Police News*'s portrayal of the dramatic death of PC Ernest Thompson in December 1900.

16. The dramatic closing scenes of the Siege of Sidney Street, as fire services struggle to contain the blaze in the house containing the anarchist fugitives.

17. Anti-German feeling in the East End during the first years of the Great War gave way to violence, criminal damage and looting across the area in May 1915.

18. Oswald Mosley in full militaristic pomp, surrounded by saluting supporters, in east London on 3 October 1936. The following day, the people of the East End would take their stance against him.

19. Behind the barricades: the Battle of Cable Street in full swing, 4 October 1936. Graffiti on the shutters of one shop front pleads, 'Don't touch, worker's shop'.

20. Jack Spot, one-time 'king of the underworld', parading a knife injury inflicted upon him in 1956.

21. A women-only doss-house at 56 Flower and Dean Street in the 1930s. No. 56 had formerly been known as the 'White House' and had once allowed men and women to cohabit, making it little more than a brothel.

22. Children at play around the slums of Wapping in the 1950s.

23. Two dock-workers take a peaceful break at the London Docks in the 1950s. During this period, labour on the river was often controlled by gangs like the Watney Streeters, a situation that often resulted in confrontation and violence.

24. Reginald and Ronald Kray with Judy Garland and her husband Mark Heron at a London club in 1963. The Kray twins' courtship of celebrity made them prominent media figures throughout the 1960s.

25. The Carpenter's Arms in Cheshire Street, Bethnal Green, commandeered by the Kray twins in 1967. On the pavement to the right, Tommy 'Ginger' Marks was gunned down in January 1965.

26. The *East London Advertiser* devotes its front page to the release of George Davis in May 1976, following the lengthy and often dramatic campaign to prove his innocence.

27. Bangladeshi shopkeepers examine damage to their property following a night of racist vandalism in Brick Lane, June 1978.

28. Thousands of Bangladeshis took to the East End streets in protest at the increase in racial violence after Altab Ali was murdered in May 1978.

29. Following the 'poor doors' and anti-Ripper Museum protests in 2014, Class War took their fight against the gentrification of the East End to Shoreditch.

ghoul brandishing a knife, 'The Nemesis of Neglect' echoed the public's fear of an untouchable wraith, born of the slums, with murder in mind:

Dank roofs, dark entries, closely-clustered walls,
Murder-inviting nooks, death-reeking gutters,
A boding voice from your foul chaos calls,
When will men heed the warning that it utters?
There floats a phantom on the slum's foul air,
Shaping, to eyes which have the gift of seeing,
Into the Spectre of that loathly lair.
Face it – for vain is fleeing!
Red-handed, ruthless, furtive, unerect,
'Tis murderous Crime – the Nemesis of Neglect![22]

The day after the publication of *Punch*'s piece, the double murder of Stride and Eddowes also recalled the recent case of Israel Lipski: Israel Schwartz, who may have seen Stride being attacked close to the scene of her death only about ten minutes before her body was found, claimed that the assailant shouted 'Lipski!', possibly at Schwartz himself, which brought up the name's use as anti-Semitic slang in a subsequent police report.[23] Anti-Semitism also impinged on the investigation into the Eddowes case: a piece of blood-soaked cloth, cut from the victim's apron, was found in a doorway in Goulston Street, Whitechapel, which led to the staircase of a tenement block housing many Jewish families. When graffiti reading 'The Juwes are the men that will not be blamed for nothing' was discovered on the brickwork above where the cloth was found, Metropolitan Police Commissioner Sir Charles Warren ordered its removal lest it create a riot. When later called to qualify his decision, Warren exclaimed:

after taking into consideration the excited state of the population of London generally at the time, the strong feeling which had been

145

excited against the Jews, and the fact that in a short time there would be a large concourse of people on the streets and having before me the Report that if it was left there the house was likely to be wrecked . . . I considered it desirable to obliterate the writing at once . . .[24]

'Yours truly, Jack the Ripper'

The double event would also prompt the police to release a letter, received a few days previously by the Central News Agency in London. Written in red ink, supposedly by the murderer himself, and filled with threatening verbiage and arrogant taunts aimed at the police, its author claimed to be 'down on whores and I shan't quit ripping them until I do get buckled', as well as promising to cut off his next victim's ears and send them to the police, 'just for jolly'. This significant missive, famously (and rather politely) signed 'Yours truly, Jack the Ripper', and in all probability penned by a deceitful journalist with one eye on newspaper sales, would ensure that this mysterious monster of the East End would be endowed with a name far more durable than 'Leather Apron', and seal these unsolved murders in history and legend for evermore.[25] The publication of the letter caused such a sensation that from that moment on, the receipt of bogus letters, supposedly from the Whitechapel murderer and invariably bearing that infamous soubriquet, would become commonplace. Many would attempt to replicate the quirky arrogance of the original; the following was typical of the sort of nonsense the authorities had to deal with on a continual basis:

I come from Boston you spanking ass. Glad you prented my last letter. Having no more of the right sort I wright with red ink Yo will hear of another murder before the month is out. Yes, you'll hear of

Saucy Jacky very soon Will send next ears I clip to Charly Warren Nice work isnt it. Ye damned fool are the police.

Jack the Ripper[26]

Maria Coroner, described as 'good-looking, respectably dressed, and in regular work at one of the leading drapery establishments in Bradford', was arrested for sending such missives, apparently because 'she wanted to make a sensation'.[27] After a prolonged legal argument as to whether she had committed a breach of the peace, she was bound over for six months at a cost of £20, being told that if she again transgressed she would go to prison.[28]

The five-week hiatus between the 'double event' and the truly barbaric murder of Mary Jane Kelly in her squalid room in Miller's Court, Dorset Street, on 9 November allowed both press and public to fully vent their consternation at the perceived evils of the East End. The inability of the authorities to apprehend the Whitechapel murderer invited accusations of incompetence against a beleaguered police, particularly the Metropolitan force and its unpopular figurehead, Chief Commissioner Warren. Some, like Canon Samuel Barnett, the vicar of St Jude's, Whitechapel,[29] felt that the situation did not warrant such denunciations as ultimately the real problems could be found in the very areas where the crimes had occurred. In a letter to *The Times*, he wrote:

I am appalled more 'by the disorderly and depraved lives' of our neighbours than by the actual murders. The acts of a madman are not matters for horror, and his escape is not sufficient reason for wholesale condemnation of the police. A series of courts such as Miller's-court, where rooms unfit for stables are let at 4s. a week, where the cries of murder are too common to arouse notice, where vice is the staple trade and drunkenness the chief resource – this fact should arouse horror, and ought to be remedied.[30]

Canon Barnett's sentiments about the vice-ridden slums, although effectively true and of course echoed by others, did not take into account a local sea-change in opinions about East End unfortunates. With each murder committed by 'Jack the Ripper' came an increasing show of sympathy and unity in the community, amply demonstrated by the reactions to the victims' funerals. Emma Smith and Martha Tabram appear to have been buried without fanfare or any press coverage of note; however, when Mary Ann Nichols was buried in the City of London cemetery at Manor Park on 6 September,[31] a number of people assembled at various points in Whitechapel to view the modest funeral cortege, and although much of this was perhaps as much down to natural curiosity as anything else, it was enough to require a police presence. Some residents along the route had closed their curtains out of respect for the dead woman.[32] By the time Catherine Eddowes was buried, close to where Nichols had been interred a month previously,[33] public interest had increased significantly. Large knots of people congregated along the early part of the funeral route, with sizeable crowds gathered in Old Street and Commercial Street, and by the time the coffin had reached the cemetery, the small entourage of seven mourners had been joined by a crowd estimated at 500.[34] And the funeral of Mary Kelly on 19 November provoked a tremendous outpouring of not only sympathy, but grief. Several thousand people congregated outside St Leonard's church in Shoreditch to witness the coffin being taken from the nearby mortuary; it was an orderly crowd by East End standards, but the emotion reserved for one of the area's forgotten souls was truly remarkable, with a local paper commenting on the 'natural and unconstrained' emotion it aroused. [35]

The 'Jack the Ripper' murders, for all their uncertainty and mystery, would become a 'whodunnit?' without equal. Much has been said elsewhere about these shocking crimes, with an exhaustive media output analysing every aspect, particularly regarding the motives and identity of the killer himself. But it is remarkable how much criminality and tragedy was inspired directly by these particular homicides. As well as mob violence, there were individual instances such as the case of Elizabeth Sodo, the wife of a weaver, who committed suicide by hanging herself from the stairwell of her home in Hanbury Street. Since the murders began, she had been showing signs of great distress and a few days before her death had been found with a razor in her hand, contemplating ending it all.[36] Another woman, fearful that her two daughters, aged three years and seven months respectively, would 'perhaps go wrong and fall into the hands of "Jack the Ripper"', attempted to strangle them both with the intention of saving them from an even more horrific end.[37]

The day after Mary Kelly's funeral, Annie Farmer, a prostitute, took a man back to her lodging house in George Street after spending some time with him in various local pubs. A few hours later, a scream was heard and the man ran out, cursing the woman and pointing out a scratch and some blood on his face to bystanders before he ran off. Farmer followed soon after, badly wounded in the throat. Even as the injury was being dressed at the lodging house, word began to circulate that 'another Whitechapel horror'[38] had been committed, and before long, excitable crowds had gathered in the George Street neighbourhood; early rumours spoke of another murder, and that the Ripper had struck again. These were seemingly confirmed by an initial press release by the Central News Agency which erroneously spoke of mutilations 'of a most shocking character'.[39] When Annie Farmer was taken to Commercial Street police station, it was discovered that she had some coins hidden in her mouth, suggesting that she had attempted to rob the client, only to be found out and to suffer the consequences of the man's anger, an attack from which she would make a full recovery.

The *Daily News* made the observation that some of the latter murders could have been the 'outcome of man's perverted imitativeness',[40] suggesting a ghoulish copy-cat, as well as referring to the proliferation of

149

incidents where men appeared to be using the Ripper's name and notoriety as a means to cause mischief or worse. The newspapers had become full of reports of men wishing to do away with their wives or partners in the 'Whitechapel way', with one man even offering a fee of 10 shillings to anybody who would rid him of his wife using the 'Whitechapel process'. Practical jokers found great amusement in brandishing knives as they jumped out at lone women, proclaiming themselves to be 'Jack the Ripper'; one incident apparently caused a woman to die of shock.[41] Later murders of prostitutes, particularly those of Alice McKenzie in Castle Alley, Whitechapel, and the shocking discovery of a headless torso under a railway arch in Pinchin Street,[42] St George-in-the-East (both in 1889), along with the discovery of Frances Coles in Swallow Gardens in 1891, reignited fears of the Ripper's return, but the police and medical experts were not entirely convinced. Interestingly, given the anti-Semitic response to the earlier murders, when the Pinchin Street torso was discovered, a close examination of the area around the crime scene revealed one word scrawled in chalk on a fence opposite the arch where the remains were discovered: 'LIPSKI'. As one reporter exclaimed, 'Whether done before the discovery or after no one seems to know, but the name was there.'[43]

CHAPTER 10

Black on the Map

The vast majority of these foreign Jews are Nihilists, Socialists and Anarchists of the very worst type. They have no nationality, and know nothing whatever of patriotism or allegiance.

St James's Gazette (1887)[1]

The shadow of the Ripper would linger over the East End in perpetuity, and the endless accounts of the poverty and vice which the crimes exposed would remain an almost indelible stain on the area's reputation. But there were other concerns, perhaps of a less pressing nature, such as the rise in popularity of illegal gaming throughout the 1880s, described by one newspaper as an 'insidious gambling germ' propagated in 'unwholesome dens'.[2] A number of parliamentary acts – particularly the Betting Act of 1853 – had made it intentionally difficult for the working classes and the poor to indulge in this popular pastime, favouring licensed betting on racecourses, invariably the preserve of the wealthy. The act made it illegal 'to keep or use any house, office, room, or other place, for the purpose of the owner or occupier a) betting with persons

151

resorting thereto, or b) receiving money in advance in respect of bets'.[3] In 1889, the *Pall Mall Gazette* compared the rise of betting amongst the poor to other social evils:

> Among the working classes the mania has reached a pitch of which only those who associate with them can form a proper conception. It is not only on horse racing, pedestrianism, and athletics that men gamble; they bet about everything! . . .
>
> In the nature of gambling, by the hopes it inspires, it tends to its own perpetuation; gambling drives to drink: drink encourages gambling; there is a network of evils, and the issue from them is dark.[4]

The poor of the East End were frequently observed risking their earthly possessions in the optimistic pursuit of betting, with the impoverished Jewish immigrants being particularly affected by 'The Curse of Gambling':

> In the wretched rooms of the East-end, evening after evening, may be seen gathered round rickety tables poor Polish tailors and boot finishers who, out of work, and utterly incapable of supporting their wives and children, have just succeeded in raising a few shillings by pawning actual necessities which they are staking at cards . . .
>
> And the little children are looking on, and imbibing a love for the vice that is ruining their parents.[5]

Violence resulting from disputes over money was common, and raids on known gambling dens became a frequent element in the Metropolitan Police's continual battle against crime in east London, often in response to disturbances taking place in them. The disputed sum of 6 shillings was the cause of a ferocious brawl at a coffee house in Commercial Street (which had been doubling as a gambling house for some time) involving two men, John Sampson and Abraham Rosenthal, and their wives; Mrs Rosenthal clawed at Mr Sampson, scratching his face, while her husband attempted to hit him with a glass dish. Sampson head-butted Rosenthal 'like a bull', knocking out several teeth and sending him over a table, but despite the violence, the case was thrown out of Thames Magistrates' Court due to conflicting testimony.[6]

The popularity of such establishments was confirmed by the presence of thirty individuals at the house at the time of the raid. Similarly, during a police raid by Superintendent Thomas Arnold of H-Division on a house in Little Alie Street, two men, James Carthy and James Weissbaum, were arrested for keeping a gaming house and a further twenty-seven individuals, a mix of Jewish and Gentile gamblers, were also taken into custody. On being charged, Carthy pleaded with the arresting officers, claiming that, 'I am not the keeper, I only assist, as I must do something for a living.'[7] Another of Superintendent Arnold's raids, this time at the Tower Hamlets Club on Whitechapel High Street, saw the arrest of nearly forty men, predominantly Eastern Europeans, for using the club 'for the purposes of gambling'.[8]

The 'Jewish problem'

By the end of the nineteenth century, the question over Jewish immigration in the East End was coming to the fore, and concerns vented by the press often stepped over the line into outright xenophobia. One particularly disturbing commentary was given by the *St James's Gazette*:

Now the presence in East London of a colony of 30,000 to 40,000 Jews, steeped to the lips in every form of moral and physical degradation, having no sympathy with the surrounding population,

153

carrying things with a high hand whenever the chance arises, exacting to the utmost the privileges which the law confers upon Englishmen, underselling English workmen in the labour market by sheer force of their ability to live as he could not possibly live – the presence of such a colony constitutes a very serious and social economic evil.[9]

The murder of Elizabeth Stride – one of the unfortunates allegedly slain by 'Jack the Ripper' – in the narrow Dutfield's Yard in Berner Street, St George-in-the-East, brought much negative attention to the neighbouring International Working Men's Educational Club. In fact, the *Church Times*, as a result of the proximity of the murder to the club, even suggested that the murderer was a Russian Jewish anarchist.[10] The club was considered a favoured centre for anarchists and social democrats of all nationalities, and despite offering a whole range of activities and events for its predominantly Jewish membership, including English lessons for new arrivals, it was generally frowned upon by more orthodox Jews, who felt that its members were unruly and brought disrepute upon the local Jewish community. Again, the *St James's Gazette*, continuing its attack on the Jews, made more of members' politics, demonstrating how, in the minds of the commentators at least, anarchism and socialism were becoming conveniently interchangeable:

When they come as refugees to England they are saturated with Anarchist ideas; and, although they find here a political freedom such as they have never known before, they fall at once under the tyranny of the British sweater, and feel the pressure of laws directed against the improvident and shiftless classes of the community. All this naturally drives them into modes of thought and habits of life which otherwise they might have left behind them; and thus they develop into a very active centre of the Socialistic propaganda.[11]

154

Indeed, this period was certainly a political time for the working classes of the East End. Several incidents demonstrated that the down-at-heel labourers of London, particularly those sweating it out in the east, were ready to make their voices heard. In February 1886, a number of serious disturbances in the West End, targeting the wealthy neighbourhoods around Pall Mall and Piccadilly, and involving criminal damage and looting, were bolstered by angry mobs from the east. The crowds, fresh from a public meeting held in Trafalgar Square to 'ventilate the grievances of the unemployed', wreaked havoc, and it was said that the most disruptive elements 'were not genuine industrious working men, but members of the "rough" class, largely recruited from the East End; rowdies and desperadoes . . .'[12] A further disturbance at Trafalgar Square in November 1887, now famously known as 'Bloody Sunday', which resulted in many injuries to both protesters and members of the police and military who were called in to quell the rioting, involved up to 5,000 protesters from east London.[13] Such disturbances were followed by the famous match girls' strike of 1888 and the highly disruptive dock strike the following year,[14] important events which led to a more organised unionisation of labour. It appeared that the East End, with all its issues, was becoming a problem for those who for so long had been happy to brush its inconvenient issues under the carpet. No longer was it, in the words of the anarchist writer John Henry Mackay, 'a world in itself, separated from the West as the servant is separated from his master. Now and then one hears about it, but only as of something far off, somewhat as one hears about a foreign land inhabited by other people with other manners and customs . . .'[15]

The International Working Men's Educational Club in Berner Street experienced its own little disturbance in March 1889, which centred on Louis Diemschitz, the club steward, who had been in the news less than a year before after he discovered the dead body of Ripper victim Elizabeth Stride in Dutfield's Yard. It all began with a demonstration by

155

the Jewish unemployed which set off from the club and marched, with the accompaniment of a band, to the Great Synagogue on Duke's Street. The chief rabbi refused the gathering an audience and thus, accompanied by nine constables, the march made its way to a piece of waste ground on Mile End Road where a meeting was held. After the demonstrators' return to the Berner Street club, a boisterous crowd gathered round the building; one of the club members came outside in his shirtsleeves and in the ensuing disturbance struck a boy. Some thirty or so individuals rushed out of the club and attacked people with sticks and other weapons, including a saucepan. Louis Diemschitz, Isaac Kozebrodski and Samuel Freidman were seen as being the ringleaders, and Freidman was heard to say, 'I will do for someone to night, and don't care if I get twelve months for it.'[16] Diemschitz, Kozebrodski and Freidman launched themselves into the throng and 'struck out right and left among the crowd'; in the fracas, PC James Frost was hit and dragged into Dutfield's Yard where Kozebrodski beat him with a stick several times. The incident escalated:

> The people were throwing stones and creating a great disturbance. The door of the club was broken open, and Frost struck Diemschitz, and rushed into the club. The police ran after Diemschitz; and two of the crowd struck him on the back... On the way to the police-station Diemschitz was kicked and handled by the police.[17]

The accused men alleged police brutality, and a number of witnesses were called for the defence, giving evidence to the effect that the police had made an entirely unprovoked attack on the defendants and their companions. At a hearing at the Clerkenwell Sessions House, the evidence of members of the crowd who had claimed to have been assaulted by the accused had to be disregarded as unreliable, 'for they were in such a state of excitement that they hardly knew what did take place'.[18] The three men, however, were judged guilty of assault: Diemschitz received a three-month prison sentence with hard labour and Kozebrodski was sentenced to pay a fine of £4 or face a month's imprisonment.

Change for the better?

Whilst we conventional Social Democrats were wasting our time on education, agitation, and organisation, some independent genius has taken the matter in hand, and by simply murdering and disembowelling four women, converted the proprietary press to an inept sort of communism.[19]

It is an oft-repeated suggestion – first sarcastically mooted in September 1888 by George Bernard Shaw in the above letter to the *Star* – that the Ripper's deeds were born of a desire for the advancement of social reform in the East End, in order to finally give the authorities the shock they needed to instigate real change for the better. Those who practised and benefited from crime and vice in the district, then, perhaps found their first truly formidable enemy in the form of an unknown proto-serial killer, albeit indirectly.

The Ripper's legacy – a final concerted effort for improvement – threatened to sweep away the breeding grounds of lawlessness: George Yard Buildings would receive better lighting for its dark stairwells; the notorious Castle Alley would soon be widened and made into an altogether more agreeable and safe public thoroughfare.[20] But generally, such change was slow: a reporter in 1890, exploring the Ripper sites, observed how little some places had improved:

It was rare, even before the murder, to find any pedestrians in Buck's-row after midnight . . . After the tragedy even the unfortunates fled from it . . . But now the unfortunates have forgotten the fate of their 'pal', the police patrol has been withdrawn, and passers-by at night are rarer than ever ... At about one o'clock on one morning I happened to be near Buck's-row, when my attention was attracted by violent screaming, evidently proceeding from that locality ... It was only a drunken woman, you say? True. But it might have been a victim screaming in her last agonies, and eight minutes to get two policemen together on the very scene of a former murder is a big start to give the quick heeled Ripper. It would make all the difference between his capture and his getting safely off with another murder added to his long record.[21]

The most notorious district associated with the victims of the Whitechapel murders, the Flower and Dean Street rookery, would meet its fate in a wholesale demolition of its lodging houses and slum courts. Prior redevelopment had already taken place with the destruction of a large area between Wentworth Street and Flower and Dean Street in 1883, as part of the Artisans' and Labourers' Dwellings Improvement Act of 1875, instigated by Home Secretary Richard Cross to allow local authorities to buy up slum properties and replace them with worthier tenements in the ensuing years. The lofty, almost barrack-like Lolesworth Buildings and Charlotte De Rothschild Dwellings, populated by the more respectable working classes, would, for a while, continue to look down upon the surviving squalor and criminality of the surrounding area until joined by Nathaniel Dwellings in 1892.[22] Final and decisive demolition began soon after: as the historian Jerry White would later conclude, 'Within six years, then, Jack the Ripper had done more to destroy the Flower and Dean St rookery than fifty years of road building, slum clearance and unabated pressure by the police, Poor Law Guardians, vestries and sanitary officers.'[23]

But the 'Flowery Dean' still had a few more surprises, even after its demolition. In October 1892, as excavation work was being carried out on the site of a former lodging house in readiness for the construction of new model dwellings, three skeletons were discovered in what would previously have been a cellar or cesspit. Two of the skeletons were contained in the same box, placed end to end, and one of them had a damaged skull.[24] When the scene was examined more thoroughly, a further four bodies were exhumed. During the inquest, the suggestion was made that these may have had something to do with the outrages perpetrated on the weavers in the late seventeenth century, and comment was made on the many disturbances and deaths at the time of the Spitalfields riots, but this was mere speculation. Interviews with a number of former residents of the demolished lodging house, including an elderly woman who had known the establishment eighty years previously, drew no definitive answer, although foul play was definitely considered.

Ultimately, it was declared that the bodies had been in the ground for between seventy-five and one hundred years, although there was no evidence 'to show who the deceased were, nor how they came by their death'.[25]

'The Worst Street in London'

Despite the redevelopments, places like Dorset Street remained untouched by such concerns, upholding their foul reputations and enduring as some of the most dangerous thoroughfares in the metropolis.

Prior to 1888, Charles Booth, the pioneering social reformer, had been working with a team of researchers looking into the extent of poverty in London. Unsatisfied with existing data, Booth had instigated a more thorough investigation of the people, beginning with the East End; he and his researchers examined places of work and working conditions, people's homes and the surrounding urban environments, and gathered data, where possible, of average earnings. Trade union representatives and ministers of religion were also consulted, and often the researchers were accompanied on their endeavours by policemen endowed with excellent local knowledge. It was the latter partnership that allowed Booth and his team, although chiefly concerned with poverty, to sketch out the criminal life of the East End. The resulting study[26] was accompanied by Booth's best-known and most accessible achievement, the *Descriptive Map of London Poverty*, wherein the streets on an Ordnance Survey map of east London had been carefully inked with different colours representing the conditions of the people living in any particular enclave. The most affluent category, upper class, represented by the colour yellow, unsurprisingly did not exist in the East End, although the colour red, used to denote the 'well to do, middle class', was surprisingly abundant, albeit largely confined to the main thoroughfares where predominantly solvent shopkeepers and publicans operated.

But for our purposes, the colour black, denoting the lowest class, that of 'vicious, semi-criminal' residents, is of most interest. In his book, Booth expanded on this simple definition: 'The lowest class . . . consists of some occasional labourers, street sellers, loafers, criminals and semi-criminals. Their life is the life of savages, with vicissitudes of extreme hardship and their only luxury is drink.'[27] From Shoreditch north to the River Thames to the south, the City to the west and Bow to the east, a number of prominent black scabs stood out within Booth's colourful philanthropic masterpiece. To the south of Cable Street were a number of tiny thoroughfares which lay in the shadow of the walls of the London Docks on Pennington Street, St George-in-the-East. One of Booth's investigators, George Duckworth, surveyed this tightly knit enclave of filthy slums, accompanied by Detective Inspector Edmund Reid; on Pennington Street itself he found thieves, cockney-Irish roughs and a good number of prostitutes, 'but the prostitution is of a sturdy kind and there are no bullies who live off the earnings of the women', Reid assured his readers. The worst street was John's Hill, containing dirty properties with broken windows, where lived a number of German prostitutes and characters who made 'much trouble to the police'.[28]

In Spitalfields, Duckworth and Sergeant French found a district worthy of its black colouring around Great Pearl Street, which was notable for its 'common lodging houses with double beds, thieves, bullies, prostitutes'. The claustrophobic Corbet's Court had brothels on both sides, Lotus Court was full of rough characters and Crown Court, according to Duckworth, was 'as black as you can make it'.[29] On Wentworth Street in Whitechapel, Wildermuth's lodging house, described as one of the largest in London, was apparently home to over 800 lodgers of the poorest type which, added to the brothels on neighbouring George Yard, painted this small section black on the map.[30] There was also much to comment on regarding the neighbourhood around Star Street off Commercial Road, the claustrophobic Nichol in Bethnal Green, the tight collection of slums in Mile End New Town around Brady Street and, of course, the last vestiges of Flower and Dean and Thrawl Streets. Dorset Street and its tributaries unsurprisingly appeared as a patch of black amongst the otherwise respectable poor.

In 1898, ten years after the original survey, George Duckworth described Dorset Street in his notebook as

Black in map – still black – the worst street I have seen so far, thieves, prostitutes, bullies all common lodging houses. Some called doubles with double beds for married couples but merely another name for brothels; women, draggled torn skirts, dirty, unkempt, square jaws standing about in street or on doorsteps.[31]

He also made reference to three stabbings and one murder which had taken place on the street within the few months prior to his visit.[32] One of the stabbings resulted in the death of John Meady, who paid with his life for acting the Good Samaritan after stopping a boot-hand

161

named Louis Lewinsky from harassing some elderly people outside a lodging house. A scuffle ensued and Lewinsky produced a clasp knife, the threat of which appeared to stop the conflict, but the quarrel flared up again later and Meady was stabbed in the side with the knife.[33] Lewinsky was arrested for cutting and wounding, but the charge became murder when Meady succumbed to haemorrhaging at the London Hospital a few days later. The murder charge against Lewinsky was changed to manslaughter, but he was ultimately acquitted at the resulting trial at the Old Bailey.[34]

The murder noted by Duckworth, which garnered considerable press coverage, took place on 26 November in Miller's Court, where Mary Kelly had been killed at the hands of the Ripper a year previously. The victim this time was Elizabeth Roberts, who died of stab wounds inflicted by her sister, Kate Marshall. What had begun as a drunken argument about work, with punching and hair-pulling, followed by the smashing of windows, rapidly turned into murder when Marshall, who later admitted to having several convictions for stabbing, set about her sister with a knife. Roberts died of her injuries within fifteen minutes.[35] Marshall was sentenced to death at the Central Criminal Court on 12 January 1899; however, the home secretary advised that the sentence be commuted to penal servitude for life on the grounds that the jury felt that the murder was not premeditated and thus would constitute manslaughter.[36] The appeal was successful and Kate Marshall was sent to Holloway prison before being moved to Wormwood Scrubs, apparently in a poor state of health.[37]

As late as 1901, Dorset Street was being described as 'The Worst Street in London' by one national newspaper.[38] Another stated that its inhabitants were all 'Thieves, Murderers and Burglars' and that 'the criminals of London, were trained in this street and that it was the home of prostitutes and *everything that was bad*'.[39] In a letter to *The Times*, one correspondent painted a disturbing picture:

One alley is known among some of the older residents as 'Blood Alley,' on account of the amount of human blood that has been shed there. There are few houses in Dorset Street which have not seen at least one murder, and one house is often declared to have had a murder in every room. How true that is I cannot say, but I do know that the same house has had a history which for sheer horror surpasses almost everything in the criminal annals of this country.[40]

This letter, and the renewed media attention surrounding the street, were prompted by the murder, on 27 May 1901, of Mary Ann Austin in Crossingham's lodging house, a low 'doss-house' of disreputable character; it was another prominent case which brought Dorset Street's already tattered reputation to the fore. On the night of her death, Austin had apparently hired a double bed with an unidentified man whom the authorities were keen to trace, and there was the obvious suggestion that this had been done for immoral purposes. Alas, the man and assassin, if indeed they were the same person, was never apprehended and the standard verdict of 'wilful murder against some person or persons unknown' was given. At the coroner's inquest, attention was paid to the lodging house's stance on permitting men and women to share the same beds, as it strongly suggested the tacit advocacy of prostitution on the premises; William Crossingham, the owner, when challenged regarding his apparent disregard for morality, said, 'What are we to do? We do not ask them if they are married; we should get insulted.' And when the coroner cross-examined Crossingham on the number of women who had reportedly died in his numerous houses, he replied, chillingly, 'They come to the lodging houses to die, rather than go to the workhouse. Men have brought their wives to the lodging houses to die.'[41]

Dorset Street would be most notorious for its murders, but all manner of crimes took place there. Assault and wounding were common, often involving intoxicated parties. One of the more remarkable incidents was

163

perpetrated by John Collins, who in 1894 cut his wife's hand with a knife so violently that bone was exposed; when the case came to trial, however, Collins, who in any case claimed his wife was violent, said he did not remember anything about the incident as he was too drunk.[42] Violence was not necessarily the preserve of adults either; in February 1903, groups of Jewish and Gentile children fought each other in Dorset Street with such aggression that many had to be treated for injuries received from stones and bottles. One man who attempted to intervene found himself in the London Hospital as a result.[43]

The street was certainly a go-to location in any attempt to locate goods stolen from anywhere in the capital; on one occasion, following the theft of £78-worth of equipment from an optician's in High Holborn, the thieves and the property were found that same night in Dorset Street, suggesting that the police quickly, and correctly, assumed that the stolen items would be there. One of the detectives who raided the suspects' house was set upon by two bull-terriers, who obediently held the officer down while his quarry fled.[44] The risks taken by the police were significant and the suggestion that they walk down Dorset Street 'in pairs' for their own safety as much as anything else is a legend which has prevailed in East End lore. One officer, having broken up a fight, was returning to his fixed point when a man, George Cullen, possibly the same man who was chased by crowds during the 1888 'Leather Apron' scare (see page 142 above), ran out of a lodging house and threw a can of boiling liquid over him.[45] Another officer, PC Mitchell, was attacked by seven men, including one Jack Bond who was already wanted by the police.[46]

Dorset Street would later be renamed Duval Street, probably in an attempt to remove the stigma associated with its former title, although it would take many decades for redevelopment to ultimately wipe away the notoriety and lawlessness.[47] Soon after its 1904 renaming, coroner Wynne Baxter, presiding over one of his many inquests relating to criminal activity in the street, was moved to mention the frequency of incidents there which had come to his attention; one of his jurors exclaimed that it was 'a new friend with an old face', a comment that was met with great amusement.[48]

Legends of H-Division

The late nineteenth and early twentieth centuries represented the era of the celebrity detective, and a number of them cut their teeth in the challenging H-Division of London's East End. Indeed, it was once said by Superintendent Thomas Arnold that the division possessed 'some of the smartest men attached to its criminal investigation department'.[49]

Walter Dew was stationed in Whitechapel from 1887 and would go on to achieve fame in 1910 as the officer who arrested the murderer Hawley Harvey Crippen, for which he effectively became Scotland Yard's first 'superstar' detective.[50] But perhaps H-Division's most famous alumnus was Frederick Abberline, the former Dorset watchmaker who joined the Metropolitan Police in 1863 before being promoted to inspector and sent to the East End ten years later. Abberline carved out a notable career in east London, gaining himself an encyclopaedic knowledge of the area and its criminal fraternity, where he frequently dealt with cases of dog stealing, disorderly drunkenness and the problem of gambling dens;[51] he was highly active in investigations into Fenian 'dynamitards', and received many commendations and awards. Despite being portrayed in the modern media – mainly in film – as everything from a rough-and-ready cockney alcoholic to a drug-addicted psychic aesthete,[52] this careful and efficient officer was anything but, being once described as 'portly and gentle speaking. The type of police officer – and there have been many – who might easily have been mistaken for the manager of a bank or a solicitor.'[53] His move to Whitehall's A-Division put him on the general staff of the Metropolitan Police's Scotland Yard headquarters and took him away from fieldwork, but this proved short-lived: his considerable experience of the East End saw to it that he was drafted back to his former division at the onset of the Jack the Ripper murders. Abberline coordinated the individual investigations on the ground, although he was not actually in charge of the Ripper case as a whole (as many erroneously claim – the officer with that role was Chief Inspector Donald Swanson). It is preconceptions such as these which have continually put the man in the public eye, and which have only served to lead to the misrepresentation of his true character.

Another prominent East End detective, though not as universally famous as Abberline or Dew, was William Thick. Apart from brief service with B-Division (Chelsea) and P-Division (Camberwell), Thick spent the majority of his police career from 1868 to 1893 in the East End, and as a detective sergeant was highly active during the Whitechapel murders investigation, most notably when he arrested John Pizer on suspicion of being 'Leather Apron'. He was known as an 'unholy terror to the local lawbreakers'; his nickname, 'Johnny Upright', had allegedly been bestowed upon him by a criminal in the dock, seemingly 'because he was very upright, both in his walk and his manners'.[54] Thick was apparently rather proud of this soubriquet, a fact noted by a journalist writing in the *Pall Mall Gazette* in 1891, because it indicated

> a generous appreciation of the fair and square dealing which has been his motto all through his long years of detective work, and by which he has gained a perfectly unique status in Whitechapel... with the result that he can walk, with his hands in his pockets, into the lowest and roughest dens in the district without a thought of precaution, and can be sure that if some ill-starred ruffian should attack him the very men against whom he plays with all his energies – but without loaded dice – would be the first to protect him.[55]

It has also been suggested that 'upright' could be a shortening of the expression 'upright man', meaning 'one who has been bought by a criminal or criminals, so that a blind eye is turned'.[56] One incident from 1882 does suggest that William Thick may not have been quite as upstanding as people made out.

In March that year, the prominent Dorset Street property owner and businessman, John McCarthy, was involved with several other men in a confrontation with police over an illegal prize-fight they had organised in St Andrew's Hall, Tavistock Place. Among the men involved was Richard Smith, a member of the large family who owned numerous lodging houses in the Brick Lane and Flower and Dean Street areas, and several others who were also notable doss-house keepers. When police officers raided the event, a fight broke out and several officers were assaulted, leading to charges of a more serious nature than merely organising an illicit boxing match. When the accused men appeared at the Middlesex Sessions House in Clerkenwell, Smith's brother Jimmy had managed to persuade Sergeant Thick to give the men good character references, which resulted in them avoiding imprisonment, their punishments being reduced to fines.[57] This incident suggests that, perhaps not unexpectedly, some of the more prominent characters of the East End had the police in their pockets, and it has been suggested that Thick, 'enjoying a financially beneficial relationship with the lords of Spitalfields',[58] took a bribe, as it was very unlikely that a police officer would give such assistance to anybody who had assaulted a brother constable without some form of sweetener. Despite such doubts, it was the retired William Thick whom the American journalist Jack London turned to for advice about acquiring lodgings when he came to London in 1902 to research his landmark book *People of the Abyss*, visiting him at his modest home in Dempsey Street, Stepney. Thick, clearly a formidable character, was described by London as having 'shades of Old Sleuth and Sherlock Holmes!'[59]

The death of PC Ernest Thompson in Whitechapel in December 1900 elicited a tremendous outpouring of respect for an unsung hero of H-Division. Thompson, described as 'one of the most intelligent members of the force',[60] had, on his first solo beat as a new police officer on 13 February 1891, discovered prostitute Frances Coles lying under a gloomy railway arch between Royal Mint Street and Chamber Street, Whitechapel, which went under the inappropriately pretty name of Swallow Gardens. The woman's throat had been cut severely, and though she was not dead at the time of her discovery, she soon passed away on her way to the hospital. Thompson recalled that as he approached the archway, he heard footsteps running in the opposite direction, leading him to believe that Coles's killer had made a last-minute escape. Frances Coles would quickly be seen by some as a further victim of Jack the Ripper, and consequently it was said that PC Thompson had always felt that he had been frustratingly close to catching the infamous murderer. In fact, by sticking to police procedure and staying with the body, he found himself unfairly criticised for not giving chase, and was believed to have reproached himself for the rest of his life for missing this significant opportunity.[61]

That life was cut short early on 1 December 1900 when Thompson was attracted to a disturbance outside a coffee stall at the junction of Commercial Road and Union Street (today's Adler Street). As he attempted to arrest Barnett Abrahams for his involvement, Abrahams stabbed Thompson in the neck, puncturing the artery; still holding on to his quarry, Thompson began bleeding profusely. The intervention of other officers saw to it that the injured man was swiftly sent to the London Hospital, but he died en route. The comments of one witness who lived in Morrison's Buildings, which overlooked the scene, demonstrated once again the often casual disregard for such incidents shown by local inhabitants. 'There is frequently a row going on here', the neighbour said, 'so I just took no notice. There was then a shuffling of feet on the pavement and shouting, but I did not take much notice of that . . . Well, next I heard a policeman's whistle, but we are used to that too; so I did not get up.'[62]

Barnett Abrahams was himself badly injured, apparently by a mob as he fled the scene, and by the time he was arrested 'both his eyes were closed, his nose was broken, one of his ears was almost torn away, and generally his face horribly cut'.[63] Regardless, he was clearly guilty of attacking, and killing, PC Thompson, and was charged with murder at Leman Street police station. Facing trial at the Old Bailey in February 1901, Abrahams was sentenced to twenty years' imprisonment for manslaughter.[64] The death of PC Thompson was seen as a major incident in the East End and the well-attended funeral, with over 3,000 officers present, brought forth much sympathy:

All along the line of the route the streets were packed with sympathising spectators. The blinds of the houses were drawn, and in some cases the shopkeepers closed their establishments entirely whilst the procession proceeded solemnly along. At the cemetery, an impressive service was held. Hundreds of beautiful wreaths were sent to the residence and the coffin was covered with costly emblems.[65]

Hooliganism rampant

The popular reaction to the death of PC Thompson demonstrates how much respect popular police officers could garner from the ordinary citizens of the East End. Still, the media, as a result of the murder, were focusing on what was described as 'hooliganism rampant'[66] and the 'reign of the hooligan'[67] in the district. On the same weekend as PC Thompson's death, which *Reynolds's Newspaper* described as adding to 'the long and fearful record of crime among the Hooligan class of the

East-end', other outrages were noted by the press. A woman named Harriet Ficker, after remonstrating with a group of roughs who were causing a disturbance outside her house in Elsa Street, Limehouse, was shot in the hand by one of the mob.[68] The same weekend, Simon Sekone, a wood-carver, was hospitalised with a large, deep stab wound to the back after being attacked by three men in a street in Whitechapel. Sekone was set upon simply for telling one of the men – who had bumped into him – to be careful.[69]

Richard Free, a resident of Millwall on the Isle of Dogs, was keen to speak out about 'rowdyism' in his neighbourhood; in a letter to the press, he spoke of how 'crime, in the accepted sense of the word, is, indeed, practically unknown among us, and even ladies are far safer from molestation here than they would be in the West-end'.[70] Despite such claims, he also wrote that 'street fights, gambling, and other evils are the order of the day, and go on practically unchecked'. Mr Free went on:

> On a certain Saturday night, from 11.20 p.m. to 1.30 a.m., as timed by me, there were four furious rows, with accompanying language of the unprintable kind, going on within fifty yards of my house; and during the whole of those two long hours not a single policeman was visible, although calls for help were made from time to time by the friends of battered men and injured women.[71]

Mr Free's grievance was obviously with the lack of visible policing in his district of St Cuthbert's, Millwall, and it is fortunate that he suffered such a low crime rate in his area; the sort of misdemeanours that happened on a regular basis in other East End locales, which usually elicited little in the way of alarm from the locals, seemed to have appeared more disturbing to him.

The year of 1888 would see Frederick Wensley begin his long tenure as a detective in the East End; he would make a significant mark on policing in the area. He first came to prominence in April 1896 for his energetic pursuit of double-murderer William Seaman after the killings of John Levy and Sarah Gale at 31 Turner Street, Whitechapel. Wensley, on discovering that Seaman was hiding out on the roof of the house, went up to a top-floor room and proceeded to remove his coat and belt, enabling him to squeeze through a small hole in the ceiling before crawling along the rafters in search of the wanted man. In an act of desperation, Seaman threw himself off the roof into the large crowd that had assembled in the street below, sustaining several injuries. Wensley found a bloodstained hammer on the roof, which proved to have been used in the shocking murders of Levy and Gale; a similarly bloodstained knife, which had been used to cut the victims' throats, was found later in a back room.

Like Abberline, Thick and Dew, Wensley's extended service in the East End gave him comprehensive knowledge of its criminality, and undoubtedly made him ready for anything the lawbreaking community of east London could throw at him. When he was first posted to H-Division, he was under no illusions that it would be an easy ride:

> Most of the inhabitants of my new division considered that they had a natural right to get fighting drunk and knock a policeman about whenever the spirit moved them. Bruises and worse were our routine lot. Gangs of hooligans infested the streets and levied blackmail on timorous shopkeepers . . . The maze of narrow ill-lighted alleyways offered easy ways of escape after a man had been knocked down and his watch and money stolen.[72]

Like many prominent detectives, Wensley earned himself a nickname – 'Weasel' – from the local criminals, an appellation of which he was rather proud. He was far from being universally respected in the underworld, however; many lawbreakers hated him as they suspected him of

171

corruption. Arthur Harding, a Shoreditch villain through and through, thought as much: he disliked Wensley immensely, and the feeling was mutual. Harding regarded him as a 'vain, bullying type of detective',[73] and spoke distastefully of his enthusiasm for promotion and occasional inclination to influence witnesses and tamper with evidence to secure a conviction. Harding's first encounter with Wensley took place during an identity parade, and it was hardly an auspicious start. While waiting for proceedings to commence, Harding lit a cigarette on a gas lamp; Wensley immediately told him to put it out, to which the recalcitrant Harding responded by telling Wensley to 'piss off'. Then, after the witness failed to pick out Harding in the parade, Wensley quipped, 'Well, Harding, we will have you for another offence.' The result of that offhand remark was the East End hard man having the prominent detective brought up before the Royal Commission on the Metropolitan Police for attempting to fix the identity parade. 'And he always hated me after', Harding later recalled.[74]

Despite the gripes of local criminals, Frederick Wensley would go on to enjoy a distinguished career: in 1924 he was appointed chief constable of the Metropolitan Police CID, the first person to attain the position via a steady promotion through the force, rather than by being selected from the ranks of the military or other professional 'gentlemen'.

CHAPTER 11

Gangs and Guns

Any reader of the daily papers these days might come to the conclusion that Chicago is the only place in which organised bands of desperate criminals ever existed. The public have a short memory.

Frederick Wensley, *Detective Days* (1931)[1]

Immigrant gangs

In the early part of the twentieth century, street gangs had become a major concern in the East End. With the continued arrival of Eastern European immigrants and their gradual absorption into the community, it was inevitable that they too would fall into the ways of criminality, forming close-knit and greatly feared gangs in the process, the most prominent – and most maligned – being the Bessarabians of Whitechapel. Known also as the Bessarabian Tigers or the 'Stop at Nothing Gang', the forty-strong group lived a life of violence, intimidation and extortion, even amongst their own fellow immigrants. 'They levied a protection toll on timid alien shopkeepers, proprietors of coffee stalls and so on,'

173

ex-Chief Inspector George Cornish later recalled. 'The faintest shadow of protest on their part at this blackmail and the gang descended on them with force armed with guns, knives, and such weapons as broken bottles.'[2]

One potential victim, a man named Weinstein, proprietor of the Odessa café, had successfully fought off the gang with an iron bar when they attempted to extract protection money from him, and another local gang, named the Odessians in his honour, became the Bessarabians' rivals. Tit-for-tat reprisals were common between the two sides, and resulted in a case of murder in 1902. On 4 October, a member of the Bessarabians, Samuel Oreman, picked a fight in a cookshop with a man named Cooksey Lewis; there had been bad blood between the two for some time, but on this occasion, Lewis was rather reluctant to take the bait. The situation, however, was inflamed by another man present, Henry Brodovitz, who expressed his intention to challenge Oreman in any ensuing fight; Oreman threatened to kill him if he did. The incident came to nothing, but hours later, Brodovitz went to the York Minster Music Hall in Philpot Street accompanied by brothers Israel and Hyman Coleman, and in the foyer they were spotted by Oreman, who had been at a performance there with fellow Bessarabians Max Moses and Barnett Brozishewski. The three men approached Brodovitz and his two companions and attacked them. The fight spilled out into the street and grew in size as more men joined in; apparently, a gang of Bessarabians had been trawling the Commercial Road looking for Odessians for much of the evening and word of the fight must have spread quickly. Before long, up to 200 individuals were involved in a rapidly escalating fracas. Oreman and Moses were armed with knives and bottles were being thrown, but there was little the sole policeman at the scene, PC Arthur Pryor, could do to disperse the violent mob. In the tumult, Moses stabbed Brodovitz, and the injured man fled to the nearby White Hart public house in Turner Street, where he died of his wounds

174

soon after. The trial at the Old Bailey in November declared Moses, Oreman and Brozishewski guilty of manslaughter: Moses was given ten years' imprisonment, Oreman received five and Brozishewski, who was recommended mercy by the jury, received six months' hard labour.[3]

The trial of the Bessarabians brought to light 'the existence of a state of things in the East-end of London which was no less lamentable than surprising in a civilized city', and brought attention to the existence of 'a gang of persons who employed themselves in creating turbulences and promoting lawlessness'.[4] The first decade of the new century was revealing not only that gangs were becoming a growing menace to the district, but also that criminals were now often working as a cohesive unit – it was the beginning of organised crime. Newspapers of the period reveal numerous gang names, many of them merely based on the neighbourhood or street to which they were attached, such as the Bow Mob, the Bethnal Green Boys, the Watney Streeters and the Blind Beggar Gang. The latter, named after the public house at Mile End Gate, were known as 'a gang of expert London pickpockets'[5] who roamed further afield than just the East End; their exploits were reported far and wide, whether it be at the racecourses at Ascot or football matches in Tottenham.[6] One member of the gang, James Hawkins, prior to being arrested and imprisoned for theft in 1907, was revealed to have moved on after the notorious Blind Beggar Gang and joined 'a gang of expert thieves who operated on the racecourses, at railway stations, in crowded salerooms, etc', whose speciality was 'the robbing of old gentlemen of their pocket books'.[7] Another member of the gang, Harry Hall, was described as 'a most dangerous man . . . many times convicted for violent assaults and other offences'.[8]

David Robinson, with several others going under the peculiar name of the Indiarubber Gang, attacked Israel Woolf and his lady friend, Ellen Murley, as they walked home one evening. The gang were apparently armed with sticks and hammers, and Miss Murley valiantly defended herself by punching Robinson in the face. At Thames Magistrates' Court, Woolf was asked for a possible reason why Robinson had attacked him, to which he replied, 'I don't know of any; but he is a member of the Indiarubber Gang. The king of the Indiarubber Gang intends killing everyone in the world'[9] – an answer that was as mysterious as the origins of the gang's odd name. Another oddly titled mob was The Titanic, based in the Hoxton–Shoreditch area around Nile Street, a pickpocket collective whose members generally worked Petticoat Lane market, but who, like the Blind Beggar Gang, were more than willing to venture out to racecourses, as well as targeting the crowded trains that travelled to them on race days. Although they concentrated on picking pockets, they could look after themselves when provoked, and were known for being violent when the need arose.[10]

About fifty young men, all members of local gangs around Stepney and Limehouse – the A1 Gang, the Duckett Street Gang and the Carr Street Gang – were involved in a major disturbance in June 1906 involving around a dozen firearms, which were fired off to the obvious distress of passers-by. An elderly man and woman were knocked down in the affray and missiles were thrown as the mob made its way up Ocean Street. Two years later, the Duckett Street Gang were part of another disturbance involving guns when they had a confrontation with the Bow Boys and the Globe Gang of Bethnal Green. One of the latter gang, 17-year-old George Askew, had previously bought a pistol for 3 shillings and, on seeing the approaching rivals, had fired it into the ground as a deterrent. The ricocheting bullets injured two bystanders,[11] resulting in Askew being sentenced to fifteen months in borstal.[12] In September 1907 there had also been three separate incidents of shooting in the East End, invariably by mere teenagers; one youth, 19-year-old Robert Wannell, apparently 'belonged to a gang of youths who had a mania for arming themselves with revolvers, which they discharged in the public streets'.[13] If gangs, particularly relatively chaotic youth gangs, were becoming local pariahs with their love of firearms, then more organised armed gangs, driven by a common ethical purpose, were about to become an even more disturbing development.

The Houndsditch murders

At about 10 p.m. on 16 December 1910, Max Weil returned to his home at 120 Houndsditch and became immediately aware of peculiar noises emanating from the property next door at no. 119, a jeweller's shop owned by Henry Harris. Weil informed a police constable he found in the street, PC Walter Piper, and the officer duly attempted to check the neighbouring properties before walking round the corner into Cutler Street and then into Exchange Buildings. Aware of the noise of what sounded like 'drilling and the breaking away of brickwork',[14] PC Piper knocked at the door of 11 Exchange Buildings, the only property in the cul-de-sac which appeared to have a light on inside; almost immediately the door opened. Piper, not wishing to excite suspicion, asked the man before him if his wife was in, to which he received a furtive, negative reply, heightening suspicions straight away, as it appeared that the man was keen to get rid of the officer as quickly as possible. Saying that he would call back later, Piper went out into Houndsditch where he found PCs Walter Choate and Ernest Woodhams and directed them to Exchange Buildings while he went to Bishopsgate police station to file a report, now convinced that all was not as it should be.

On his way to the station, Piper encountered Sergeant Robert Bentley accompanied by two plainclothes officers. Piper introduced Bentley to Max Weil, who took the sergeant to his house in Houndsditch to listen to the noises, which were still ongoing. Two other sergeants, William Bryant and Charles Tucker, sent from Bishopsgate to convey the news that there were already suspicions that some foreigners were living in

Exchange Buildings, were soon on the scene. At about 11.30 p.m., Bentley, Tucker, Bryant, Choate and Woodhams effected an entry into 11 Exchange Buildings, to be met with gunfire from a man standing on a staircase and another who had just appeared in the hallway. Bentley was seriously wounded, his spine severed; Bryant was shot in the arm and chest and Woodhams was shot in the leg.

The occupants of the house, apparently a sizeable gang of men, attempted to escape, but as they ran up Exchange Buildings they were intercepted by more officers, and shooting resumed. Sergeant Tucker was shot twice, one bullet hitting him in the heart, causing instant death, and PC Choate, while attempting to apprehend one of the gang, was shot in the leg. As he went down, other gang members began firing their weapons, shooting Choate twelve times; in the chaos, Choate's quarry was also injured by a stray bullet. The gang began to beat a retreat from Exchange Buildings carrying their injured colleague with them, leaving one police officer – Tucker – dead, and four others – Choate, Bentley, Bryant and Woodhams – seriously injured. Although the latter two would survive, they would never fully recover from their injuries; Choate and Bentley died in hospital the following day.

The background to the incident was an organised gang having taken possession of 11 Exchange Buildings with the aim of breaking into Harris's Houndsditch jeweller's shop at the rear. The leader of the group was the wounded man, George Gardstein; with him were also believed to be Jacob Peters, Yourka Dubof, Fritz Svaars, William Sokoloff, Peter Piatkoff, Karl Hoffmann, John Rosen and Max Smoller, all of whom were Latvian political activists. Some were known to be fugitives from justice, having been convicted of terrorist offences, robberies or agitation in Poland, Russia and Latvia. They were also believed to be allied to the Jubilee Street Club in Stepney, the successor of the notorious International Working Men's Educational Club in Berner Street.[15] Radicalised by their experiences in Russia, all had extreme socialist and anarchist views, believing that the expropriation of private property was acceptable to further their political cause.[16]

Gardstein was taken by the group to the lodgings of Piatkoff and Svaars in Grove Street, Commercial Road, and a doctor was called. With a bullet lodged in his chest, it was suggested Gardstein be taken to the London Hospital, but to no avail; soon the injured man would succumb to his injury. The recalled doctor saw the corpse and reported it to the coroner, unaware that the dead man or his fatal injury had anything to do with the dramatic events of the previous evening. When the coroner informed the police, a team of officers, headed by Frederick Wensley, by now a detective inspector, descended on the house in Grove Street. Papers found there linked the crime to anarchist groups active in the East End, and by the next day, Dubof and Peters, along with several other co-conspirators, were located and arrested. The others remained at large.

But the Houndsditch tragedy did not happen in isolation. In January 1909, two Russian anarchists, Paul Helfield and Jacob Lepidus, had attempted an armed robbery on a van that was bringing the weekly wages into the Schnurmann rubber factory in Chesnut Road, Tottenham, where Helfield worked. The two men, who were both armed, failed in their attempt to grab a bag of cash, and to fend off factory workers who were attempting to bring them down began firing their guns at anybody who dared to intervene. Two people were injured in the gunfire and the two robbers made good their escape, pursued by two police officers who had heard the gunshots from nearby Tottenham police station. A colossal cat-and-mouse chase ensued through the then respectable suburbs of Tottenham and Walthamstow, involving a growing number of police officers, passers-by (including a group of game shooters who were ordered to fire on the running men), and on one occasion, a hijacked tram. One policeman and, tragically, a young boy caught in the crossfire perished, and a total of fourteen innocent bystanders were injured in the long-running battle; Helfield was seriously injured and was apprehended, but Lepidus put a gun to his head and shot himself dead. The 'Tottenham Outrage', as it was immediately named, was called 'the most dramatic and daring crime of recent years',[17] and sparked a renewed upsurge in anti-immigrant rhetoric from the press:

We have at last reaped the reward of our insane toleration of the anarchist outcasts of other countries . . . these are the sort of people we receive with open arms as political refugees . . . With people who are animated with genuine political ideals, however fantastic they may be, we can afford to be tolerant, but anarchists have no ideals . . . The Governments of Europe should hunt them down for the homicidal maniacs they are.[18]

The East End, with its high density of Eastern European immigrants, was naturally a fertile breeding ground for radical ideas. A club in Thomas Street, Whitechapel, hosted the Fifth Congress of the Russian Social Democratic Labour Party in May 1907, famously attended by such future luminaries of post-revolutionary Russia as Vladimir Lenin, Joseph Stalin, Leon Trotsky and Maxim Litvinoff, and, in June of that year, the Second Congress of the Latvian Social Democrats was held at King's Hall, Commercial Road. Lenin had also given lectures at Liberty Hall, Whitechapel, as well as at the Jubilee Street Club earlier in the decade.[19] The anarchist clubs of the East End were suggested to have links to a plot by Catalan anarchist Mateu Morral to assassinate King Alfonso XIII of Spain during his wedding to Princess Victoria Eugenie of Battenberg in May 1906. Prior to the nuptials, fifteen anarchists left London for Madrid, believed to be armed with either small bombs or revolvers, and once in Spain they met others from France, Belgium and Italy, a total of sixty conspirators. Five men were to be placed on the steps of the church, ready to throw the bombs at the wedding party when they emerged;

however, only one device was thrown, but this alone caused the deaths of fifteen people and injuries to many others, although not to the intended royal targets. Following the inquiry into the incident, it was noted that the bombs had come from London, and police intelligence at the time revealed that the execution of the plot and its aftermath had been discussed in various clubs around the East End. A meeting at the Jubilee Street Club spoke of proclaiming a commune in Spain, along the lines of the one that governed Paris in 1871, following a successful assassination of the king, and other possibilities were discussed at a club in Spelman Street, Spitalfields. Further meetings at a house in Wilkes Street spread the news of the anarchists' arrival in Madrid.[20]

The association with political anarchism and violent crime became a strong one, causing significant concern amongst the public, all bolstered by the regular anti-immigrant invective published in the press. In the cases of the Tottenham Outrage and the Houndsditch murders, attention was given to the fact that the protagonists in both incidents were armed with high-quality automatic weapons, which rendered utterly ineffective the modest truncheons possessed by the police: 'The unarmed alien is the exception', claimed one police authority; 'the automatic pistol, known as the Browning pistol on the Continent and as the Colt automatic in this country and America, is the most common arm carried . . . They are imported into this country by their owners.'[21] This concern over the presence of highly organised, seriously armed agitators and criminals would reach its climax in the new year of 1911.

The Siege of Sidney Street

The high-profile publicity surrounding the investigation into the Houndsditch affair bore fruit on the evening of 1 January when a member of the public came forward to give information regarding a house at 100 Sidney Street, where it was believed that Fritz Svaars and

William Sokoloff were lodging with Sokoloff's mistress, Betty Gershon. Just after midnight on 3 January, 200 police officers, many armed as a precaution, established themselves in Sidney Street and began evacuating the block of tenements in which no. 100 stood. Carefully, all the tenants left the building, and when Betty Gershon was lured out on the pretence that her husband was ill, she was seized. Svaars and Sokoloff were the only two people left in the house, seemingly unaware of the events unfolding around them. Storming the house was deemed too risky due to its cramped internal layout and so further action was delayed until dawn, when at 7.30 a.m. a police officer knocked at the door. In the absence of any response, stones were thrown at the window, eliciting a reaction from the besieged men who appeared at the window and, seeing the assembled crowd of officers, opened fire with automatic weapons. In the opening salvo of gunfire, Detective Sergeant Ben Leeson was seriously wounded; as the gunshots rang out, the armed officers were permitted by protocol to return fire.

The short-range weapons used by the police were no real match for the anarchists' more sophisticated firepower, and it soon became apparent that further assistance was required. In what was the first occasion of the London police calling upon the military, twenty-one volunteer marksmen from the Scot's Guard were called in, and after setting up their positions at around 10 a.m., the shooting continued, but without either side gaining any advantage. The arrival of Home Secretary Winston Churchill later that morning prompted a derisory response from the crowds, who were kept at a safe distance from the drama by innumerable police officers. As the shooting continued and intensified, smoke was suddenly noticed coming out of one of the windows of no. 100; Sokoloff stuck his head out and immediately fell back in, presumably shot. The fire within intensified, prompting the arrival of the fire brigade, which, according to Churchill years later, created a dilemma:

Suddenly with a stir and a clatter, up came the fire brigade, scattering the crowds . . . The inspector of police forbade further progress, and the fire-brigade officer declared it his duty to advance. A fire was raging and he was bound to extinguish it. When the police officer pointed out that his men would be shot down, he replied simply that orders were orders . . . I now intervened to settle this dispute, at one moment quite heated. I told the fire-brigade officer on my authority as Home Secretary that the house was to be allowed to burn down and that he was to stand by in readiness to prevent the conflagration from spreading.[22]

One apocryphal version of events claims that Churchill mumbled to himself, 'Let the bastards burn'.[23] At about 2.30 p.m. shooting from the house ceased, and the now blazing fire caused the roof to collapse, all of which suggested that in all likelihood the two men inside were dead. When the fire brigade finally extinguished the blaze and effected an entry, the body of Sokoloff was found; Svaars's body was discovered several hours later. The siege had lasted seven hours and, as well as the deaths of the two protagonists, saw the injury of Detective Sergeant Leeson and the death of one fireman who was crushed by a collapsing interior wall.

The events of 1910 and 1911 continued to bring the 'Anarchist Problem' to the fore. Whilst there was a guarded admittance that not all anarchists were hell-bent on mayhem, the characters involved at Houndsditch and Sidney Street continued to reveal activism of a most dangerous nature, one which was deemed almost unique to the immigrant:

They are ordinary housebreakers, familiar possibly with Anarchist literature, and using political anarchism as a cloak for their crimes, but devoid of any real political aim. Doubtless there are other gangs

183

in London of the same type. They differ from the British house-breaker in the use of the pistol, and their advertisement of the power of the pistol may have deplorable effects.

From this it will be seen that the Home Secretary's task is one of immense difficulty. Does the Houndsditch affair really indicate that official anarchism contemplates an active and militant campaign of terrorism in the only European land of political asylum?[24]

CHAPTER 12

Mob Town

Lawless gangs of youths belonging to rival factions came into collision ... in some cases with serious consequences ... and the police had the greatest difficulty in obtaining satisfactory evidence, as respectable people were afraid to speak.

Illustrated Police News (1912)[1]

The violence of the pre-war East End was not just the preserve of immigrant gangs, for home-grown mobs were also proving to be no small challenge for H-Division's officers, in their turn producing notable characters in local villainy. Perhaps the best-known personality of this period was Arthur Harding (real name Arthur Tressadern), who would become a major thorn in the side of the ubiquitous Detective Inspector Wensley. Harding was a true product of the harsh East End, born illegitimately into the slums of the Nichol during its last days[2] and brought up in Dr Barnardo's children's home in Stepney. As a child he ran errands for a local villain named 'One-Eyed Charlie' Woodgar, his introduction to crime, before moving into petty theft and armed robbery, and from the

185

age of fourteen he acquired a string of early convictions, many for pick-pocketing.[3] By 1911, Harding was a career criminal, and the de facto leader of a Bethnal Green gang known as the Vendetta Mob, a thirty-strong team of roughs who made their living from thieving and holding up illegal gambling clubs (the latter activity proving lucrative until the victims clubbed together to make a forcible stand). 'We were a collection of small-time thieves ripe for any mischief', recalled Harding; 'we were ready to stake anything. Sometimes we went in couples, sometimes alone – it was only when there was a big fight on that we went as a gang.'[4]

The vendetta

The cohesive efforts of this gang would become evident in September 1911 in what became known as the 'East End Vendetta',[5] demonstrating the violence that could result when rival groups came face to face over their spoils. The Vendetta Mob, effectively based at the Bethnal Green end of Brick Lane, came into conflict with another gang led by Isaac Bogard which controlled protection and prostitution in and around Whitechapel High Street. Bogard was Jewish, but his dark skin had earned him the nickname 'Darky the Coon', and his gang were known as the Coons.[6] Problems had developed between the two groups over a clash of interests surrounding the protection of a market stall in Walthamstow. Bogard had assaulted Vendetta Mob member Thomas Taylor in August; a revenge attack ensued on 10 September 1911 when Harding, joined by sundry members of his gang, attacked Bogard in the Blue Coat Boy public house on Bishopsgate, inflicting serious injuries upon his perceived rival. Several men smashed glasses and struck Bogard around the face with them, one of the gang announcing, 'That's for Taylor, you fucking bastard.'[7] 'As it was we did a lot of damage', Harding would later recall. 'The Coon had a face like the map of England. He was knocked about terrible. I hit him with a broken glass, made a terrible mess of his face.'[8]

The following week, the Vendetta Mob attacked Bogard and another man, George King, on the corner of Gibraltar Gardens, on Hackney Road; shots were fired, injuring a newspaper boy. King and Bogard were arrested for fighting and disorderly conduct, but as they were being conveyed to the station they were again set upon by the mob. When Bogard and King had been bailed, the police had to escort them home, and when they appeared at Old Street Magistrates' Court the following Monday, the Vendetta Mob returned in force, having come to the conclusion that the prisoners were about to break the criminal code and commit the heinous act of asking for police protection. After the hearing, despite police warnings to disperse, the gang attacked the two prisoners as they were escorted from the court, rushing at Bogard and King, ignoring the police guards who had great difficulty driving them away. Some of the mob had their hands in their coat pockets, suggesting they had revolvers in their possession. A little later, in Shoreditch High Street, King was pulled away from the escort and kicked in the eye. Bogard was also assaulted; a revolver was seen to be passed amongst the crowd, and was later recovered by a police officer.[9]

Numerous arrests were made during the two-hour incident, and eight men, including Arthur Harding, appeared at Old Street on numerous charges, mainly of breaking the peace and rioting. Mr Sefton Cohen addressed the court, explaining that 'an organised gang of armed men existed in the East End, who terrorised men and women who happened to incur their displeasure. Some of that gang were before the court, and it was hoped that the East End would be relieved of the terror they had practised for so long.'[10]

In connection with the attack in Gibraltar Gardens and the riot in Old Street, all were found guilty at the subsequent Old Bailey trial and given various concurrent sentences for rioting, assault, wounding and, in the case of one man, Stephen Cooper, shooting. Mr Justice Avory, who presided over the case, expressed his concern:

I wish to say before I leave this case that for any portion of London to be infested by a number of criminal ruffians armed with loaded revolvers is a state of things which ought not to be further tolerated, and, if the existing law is not strong enough to put a stop to it, some remedial legislation must be effected.[11]

As the leader of the mob, Arthur Harding warranted special mention by Wensley, who described him as 'the captain of a band of young desperadoes. He had developed into a cunning and plausible criminal of a dangerous type.'[12] Harding's lawless career continued, but without the drama of the 'East End Vendetta' case, resulting in imprisonment for offences ranging from assault on a police officer to receiving forged banknotes. In the end, it was because of his wife that he left behind the life of crime: she laid down the law after he was involved in a street brawl in 1926, and from that moment on, Harding kept on the straight and narrow.[13]

Death of the Milsteins

The end of a dramatic 1911 for east London provided the district with one final flourish of tragedy, namely a shocking double murder in Hanbury Street, Spitalfields, a thoroughfare that was still associated in many people's minds with the terrible events of 1888. Early in the morning of 27 December 1911, the dead bodies of Solomon Milstein and his wife Annie, described as 'pleasant, quiet, soberly conducted people,'[14] were found in the small back bedroom of their restaurant and tea shop at 62 Hanbury Street. Paraffin had been poured over some bedding, and hot pokers had been left on the bed, causing a small fire. The smoke alerted the attention of a lodger, Marks Verkbloot, who had summoned a nearby police officer to investigate. Both victims had been bludgeoned with a sturdy instrument, probably a fire-iron, and stabbed multiple times, and it appears that the paraffin was used in an unsuccessful attempt to burn the bodies, or the property, after the deed. Two bloodstained knives, one belonging to the premises, were found in the room along with a small bottle of paraffin. Although it appeared that robbery was a possible motive, as a cash box was found to be missing, it was curious that, although several drawers had been opened, certain items of jewellery had not been taken.

Detective Inspector Wensley and his team went to work, and it was not long before the crime's intriguing back story emerged. For so long, the fortunes of the restaurant had relied chiefly on the patronage of numerous workers at a nearby warehouse; however, in the autumn of 1911, the workers had gone on strike, and so by November, with the prolonged absence of so many regular customers, the Milsteins found that they were beginning to struggle financially. Solomon Milstein, much to his wife's chagrin, decided to let out the restaurant's cellar as a 'spieler', or small gambling club, going into partnership with Jack Slovotinsky; the card game faro would be played for threepence a round, and a levy of 5 shillings a week would be imposed for the use of the room, all of which, it was hoped, would alleviate the Milsteins' precarious financial situation. Before long, Solomon began to find himself working not just with Slovotinsky but also with a local boxer, Joseph Goldstein, who was brought in by Slovotinsky to act as a kind of bouncer to monitor and regulate the behaviour of the players. Goldstein, who boxed under the name Joe Goodwin, would also receive a payment for his services.[15]

Despite the popularity of his new venture, Solomon Milstein began to realise that he was not quite on top of the situation as much as he would have liked, and his wife's growing agitation over the illegality of the enterprise, and her distaste for the rough individuals who patronised the basement spieler, put considerable pressure on a man who now found himself out of his depth. On 23 December, Milstein announced to his two partners that the club was to be wound down; it continued until Boxing Day when, at the close of play in the early hours of the 27th, the remaining gamblers were told that it was all over. Less than four hours later, Solomon and Annie Milstein would be found brutally murdered in the smouldering back room.

Inspector Wensley's investigation unearthed the identities of many of the regular players at the Hanbury Street spieler, and several gave themselves up willingly to exonerate themselves from any complicity in the murder. In the early hours of 28 December, one of the club regulars, Harry Sojcher, was on his way to Leman Street police station to give an account of himself when he saw Myer Abramovitch, another regular, at a coffee stall by Gardiner's Corner.

Abramovitch was unkempt and his hand was bandaged, and though he appeared troubled, Sojcher persuaded him to accompany him to the station where the police were keen to see him. In fact, before even reaching Leman Street, an officer, Inspector John Freeman, spotted Abramovitch and told him he was wanted; the police had been looking for him all the previous day. On arriving at the station, Abramovitch began to open up: 'What is the matter with your hand?' asked Freeman. Abramovitch replied, 'I got it cut in Hanbury Street this morning.' The wanted man was taken aside by Wensley, who had been informed of his arrival:

He accompanied me to my office. When he got to the door he said, 'I know what you want' ... Then taking this leather purse from his right-hand trousers pocket, he handed it to me and said, 'This is his. You will find all the money there.' It contained £2 10s. in gold. In various pockets I found 3s. 3d. silver and 2s. 8¼ d. bronze. I told him he would be detained for the present on the suspicion of the murder of Mr. and Mrs. Milstein yesterday morning.[16]

The dishevelled Abramovitch replied pathetically, 'I done it . . . I done it because I lost all my money at gambling.' As he removed his layers of clothing, it was also discovered that some of his garments belonged to

190

Solomon Milstein, and there were traces of blood on them. He was also presented with a silk handkerchief which was found at the scene of crime, which he confirmed was his.

It transpired that not long before the closure of the Hanbury Street gambling den, Abramovitch had found that he needed to vacate his lodgings in Underwood Street after his landlady, Rose Beckdanoff, announced that her family were moving to South Africa. At this time, Abramovitch owed the Beckdanoffs 30 shillings in rent arrears, but the regular gambler had frittered away any money he had acquired to pay the debt. Myer Abramovitch was a desperate man, and had gone to desperate lengths to alleviate his predicament.

The trial at the Old Bailey lasted two days. A witness who had known Abramovitch for years said that he was known as 'Myer the Fool' and 'Myer the Insane',[17] but any argument that Abramovitch was thus unaccountable for his actions was roundly rejected. On 8 February he was sentenced to death: he would be hanged on 6 March at Pentonville prison.

As Abramovitch awaited his fate there occurred another serious case, this time not resulting in murder, but also reflective of the potentially dangerous nature of East End gambling dens. When a coffee house in Sclater Street, Bethnal Green, which had also been used as a spieler, was raided, it was found to be frequented by 'low class foreigners, some of whom carried revolvers in their pockets'.[18] Twenty-one young Chinese seamen were also arrested during a raid in a club on Limehouse Causeway, where fan-tan was played for money. The bankers netted 90 per cent of the stakes and the sheer scale of such operations was revealed when a safe on the premises was opened and found to contain over £156 in cash and gold.

The tragedy of the Milstein murders, born of the desperation that was often the result of illegal betting, was a most notable case of its time, and naturally brought further undesirable attention to the East End, in much the same way that the Wainwright and Lipski cases, the Whitechapel murders, and the dramatic events in Houndsditch and Sidney Street had done. In the spring of 1912, crime statistics for the East End over the previous twelve months were released, and showed a massive increase in charges heard at Thames Police Court: from the thousands of summonses issued, over 9,300 cases were heard, an increase of 1,300 over the previous year.[19] Perhaps as a result of what was seen as yet another resurgence of lawless behaviour in east London, the Shoreditch Public Welfare Association announced its intention to stage a great 'moral crusade' through the East End, to denounce 'drink, gambling, and impurity as enemies of the home, the state and the race'.[20]

Anti-German unrest

The years of the First World War once again saw the East End struggle with its role as a first point of entry into London for successive waves of European immigrants. The number of Eastern European Jews had continued to rise after the end of the nineteenth century, joined now by those from Austria, the Netherlands and Germany. There had been a significant German presence in the East End for some time, originally in the form of merchants who were later joined by artisans, booksellers and bookbinders, and then by sugar refiners. Other businesses, such as confectioners and butchers, had also become trades dominated by German settlers, and the presence of several German churches in the East End was testament to the growth of this community.[21] The war years, not unexpectedly, saw resentment directed at Germans in the United Kingdom, particularly during the early stages of the war, before internment was introduced: great uprisings of violence against German citizens became par for the course. Some of the worst incidents took place in several major cities across Britain during the second week of May 1915, with the East End of London seen as the epicentre of many of the most explosive confrontations.

On the evening of 11 May, a number of riots broke out in Poplar and Bromley, overwhelming a local police force which was stretched to breaking point; so many officers were injured that when further disturbances resumed the following morning in Poplar, there were not enough fit officers available to deal effectively with the chaos.[22] During these renewed attacks, the crowd's anger initially focused on a butcher's shop; windows were smashed, and the occupants took refuge in the police station as the shop and living quarters were ransacked and their furniture was thrown out into the street. A considerable amount of looting took place and violence soon spread:

> During the attack on a bakers shop a few of the assailants, led by a woman, swarmed up a ladder to a lift. Bags of flour were seized and thrown on to the people below. The Poplar rioters also looted a lodging house in Hole Street, believed to be tenanted by a German. Everything movable was thrown out of the windows and taken possession by the crowd in the street.[23]

A tobacconist's, owned by A. Schoenfeld, was similarly ransacked, and furniture removed through the broken windows was passed over the heads of the mob. In Duckett Street, a crowd that included 'scores of little boys and girls' attacked the shop of a German baker:

> They seized him and his assistant, and unceremoniously bundled him out onto the street. The baker and his assistant were in a frenzy of fear, and soon fled. Left in possession of the premises, the crowd enjoyed themselves immensely, and soon Duckett Street was covered with the contents of the shop. This done, the shop was set on fire.[24]

On the Minories in Aldgate, Germans were 'attacked and subjected to a good deal of rough handling by the frenzied crowd'.[25] In Aldgate High Street, a German barber was pulled from his shop and given 'a terrible beating' in the street; an Austrian barber was thrown out into the road and narrowly avoided being run over as a mob ransacked his shop, stealing razors, shaving pots, cigarettes and cigars, as well as hurling chairs into the roadway and slashing the upholstery. After these two incidents, a group of around thirty Germans were chased down the road under a hail of stones and other missiles, causing several injuries.[26]

Major incidents took place in Canning Town, where over 200 police officers were brought in to control a riotous attack on the premises of a furnishing company alleged to have German owners. It was also said that the military were to be drafted in to deal with the seriousness of the problem as it began to escalate out of control. It was of these incidents that one newspaper commented that 'the most disgraceful feature of the whole business was that in the majority of cases, women appeared to be ringleaders and encouraged children to carry off spoils from the pillaged shops. The women had brought especially wide aprons in order to carry away the loot.'[27]

Racism, then, does not seem to have been the sole cause of the riots in the East End, where a form of 'rent-a-mob' were hell-bent on profiting from the spoils of the wrecked shops and houses. Again in Poplar, half a dozen houses were attacked simultaneously in the course of one afternoon, and everything from horse-drawn carts, handcarts and perambulators were used by the crowds to ferret away stolen items from the wrecked properties. There were pianos, dressers, chests of drawers and other heavy household furniture making their way down the streets; one man, who had possession of several mattresses, was heard to cry, 'Here is wealth for the taking!' as he drove his overloaded donkey-cart along Chrisp Street.[28]

Upper North Street, the location of a number of German bakeries, was besieged by upward of 3,000 people, with only one lone police constable present to deal with the dangerous situation. Needless to say, he could not, and as heavy bags of flour were tossed out of the upper windows of wrecked shops, the officer received a direct hit on the head. Three young women went up to the first floor of one shop and, giving a warning for

194

the crowds below to move out of the way, proceeded to hurl a piano out of an upper-storey window which crashed spectacularly onto the pavement. The officer present described it as 'the most nerve-trying experience he had ever had'.[29] The *Daily Mirror*, in an editorial asserting that the only action needed to win the war was military action where it mattered, namely on the front line, stated strongly that it knew exactly what the solution was to the unfortunate state of affairs on the streets:

> The people who break shop windows ought to join the Army at once. That should be their way of 'getting it off the chest'. If you can smash a German pork butcher's head you can hold a rifle. Go and do it, then, instead of exposing our policemen here in London to injury and giving them more work than they need.[30]

The Germans, like any other immigrant settlers in east London, had, by the First World War, become absorbed into the culture of the East End, and possessed significant roles within the wider community. The original Russian and Polish Jewish refugees, once vilified by many in their struggle for acceptance and survival in the only country that appeared to give them a chance, were also now an established part of that great melting pot, and were already introducing a second generation of indigenous-born children into east London's continuing evolution. The eruption of violence during the anti-German riots strongly hints at a volatile district, whose people, for so long seemingly poor and down-at-heel, would – if a significant excuse could be found – erupt into mindless lawlessness at the drop of a hat; often, despite the improvements that had been made since the dark days of the late nineteenth century, for personal gain. Such behaviour would do little to shake off the area's unpredictable and ungovernable reputation.

195

CHAPTER 13

Anti-Heroes

The social reformer desiring in days gone by to see poverty and squalor in their acutest forms naturally turned to the East End, knowing that there he would find both in full measure. Today the East End has been transformed.

Dundee Evening Telegraph (1915)[1]

Anti-German riots aside, the years of the Great War saw a change in the fortunes of the East End. With so many men away in the trenches, work became more readily available, especially for women; the war effort meant that many were employed in the munitions factories or by companies who had begun to change their output to contribute necessary equipment for military and civilian purposes. Arthur Harding would later call this period 'The Gold Rush':

The First World War had made a great change in Bethnal Green. Before then it was practically impossible to find work. But with the war every firm was getting busy and the people they said was 'unem-

196

ployable' became the people to fill the jobs . . . and the widows and mothers were getting large sums of money as allowances for their boys and husbands.[2]

People with more disposable income spent freely, borrowed more willingly; money-lenders and buyers and sellers of clothing and gold (known as wardrobe dealers) reaped the benefits. Poverty was not eradicated altogether – it never could be – but the fortunes of the East End had noticeably changed. 'Probably no part of Great Britain has been more radically affected by the war than East London', proclaimed one newspaper. 'If poverty has not been entirely eliminated through causes due to the war it has largely disappeared, and the toiling people are enjoying a degree of prosperity such as they have never known before.'[3]

One contributing factor to such industry was the change in licensing laws, put into effect by the Defence of the Realm Act of August 1914, which limited pub opening hours to three hours around lunchtime (midday until 3 p.m.) and another three hours in the evening (6.30 until 9.30 p.m.).[4] Alongside other measures, this was intended to limit distraction from the war effort, and for an area such as the East End, with its past history of perceived drink-related degeneracy, it helped propel its residents' upturn in fortunes: the press reported that, 'Thanks to the restrictive measures passed to curtail the drink traffic, there has been no noticeable increase in drinking. Instead families have been buying new clothes and furniture, and generally raising the standard of living.'[5]

That said, a rise in crime rates amongst the young was noted during the war years, 'brought about largely from the fact that fathers in many cases are at the front and mothers engaged on some kind of war work. In consequence the boys are more at liberty and without restraint.'[6] Desertion from the army, whether on moral grounds or for other reasons, was now increasingly an issue, and was a punishable act. The case of Abraham Libovitch, aged eighteen, of Brady Street Buildings,

Whitechapel, was typical: ignoring the call-up, he resigned his position as a tobacconist's manager and went into hiding for seven months before he was caught and charged with absenteeism. He carried a 'No-Conscription Fellowship' card and described himself as a conscientious objector, none of which cut any ice with the authorities, who fined him £10 and handed him straight to the military. Libovitch was described as 'one of hundreds of young men in Whitechapel who had successfully evaded service for a long time'.[7] Davis Levinsky, a tailor, was fined £100 or, in default, two months' imprisonment for employing two army deserters: Corporal F. Robins, who was investigating Levinsky and his premises, had found one of the young men hiding on the roof.[8] The same month, Michael Goldberg was fined £20 at Thames Police Court for attempting to bribe a police officer not to charge him with employing an absentee.[9]

As indicated by the names in the cases above, absenteeism amongst naturalised Jewish men was common. Lieutenant Gorham D'Arcy, recruiting officer for Stepney, claimed that

there are some 4000 men in that area hiding from military service . . . The absentees are mostly Jews and men of foreign extraction who have lived here all their lives and become naturalised. Great numbers have gone to Ireland, which would be well worth scouring . . . There are still many hundreds hiding in Stepney [where] . . . Army dodgers hide and earn big wages.

They are making bigger wages every week, because the district is practically denuded of British men of military age. The fine on an absentee, usually £2, has no terror to them.[10]

Other more serious incidents in the East End during the First World War included the attempted murder of Jane Woods, a married 48-year-old woman, who was attacked in Leman Street one Saturday night in May 1915 by a man who cut her throat with a sharp instrument before dashing off down an alleyway in the direction of Stepney.[11] The presence of mob violence was still evident when a dispute between a group of soldiers and some Russian Jews in September 1917 developed into a free-for-all in Blythe Street, Bethnal Green, which involved between 2,000 and 3,000 participants, a riot which the police found almost impossible to quell.[12] The end of the war, however, saw an increase in crime, as men returned from the trenches to rebuild their lives. By the end of 1919, the level of unemployment had spiked to 6.6 per cent,[13] and between 1915 and 1930, crime rose by 5 per cent a year.[14] It was during this period of post-war rebuilding that the concept of organised crime truly came into its own; the East End of London would provide history with some of its most notable exponents over the decades to come.

Heroes and villains

Brilliant Chang (real name Chan Nan) was born around 1886 in Canton to a wealthy mercantile family; their business interests in Hong Kong and Shanghai had made them successful and wealthy and the young Chang was well educated, studying chemistry and learning several languages. He came to Britain in 1913 as a student, and later ran a restaurant in Birmingham, although hospitality may not have been all he was involved in. A police drug raid in 1917 uncovered paperwork which mentioned Chang by name,[15] and soon after he moved down to London to help his uncle in his various business interests which included a restaurant in Regent Street. It is possible that Chang began dealing in drugs as early as his time in Birmingham, as the evidence suggests, but certainly once in London he had begun dealing in opium, cocaine and heroin; the Regent Street premises became a centre for trafficking and Chang often attended secret cocaine parties across London.[16] He was usually surrounded by young women attracted by his charm, charisma and the promise of a fine night out; in time he gathered around him a coterie of female admirers who would become his lovers and, ultimately, his customers.[17]

Several drug-related fatalities of young women, most notably that of actress Billie Carleton in 1918, placed the illicit use of recreational drugs in the sights of moral crusaders and Scotland Yard. Freda Kempton, a 'dance instructress' who worked in a bar and earned extra money by charging partners to dance with her, died of a cocaine overdose in March 1922; Kempton was a regular user, and the cocaine allowed her to work long hours. At the inquest it transpired that Chang had been with her the night before her death and was seen to have given her a small bottle of white powder, but Chang unsurprisingly denied any involvement with drug dealing. It was known that Kempton had been depressed and comments she had made prior to taking the drug suggested she was contemplating death; she had also written a note to her mother which apparently read, 'Forgive me. The whole world was against me. I really meant no harm.'[18] As a result, the inquest jury delivered the verdict of suicide while temporarily insane; there was insufficient evidence to convict Chang of manslaughter, and he was set free.

The inquiry brought to light the possibility of a white slave network linked with interracial sex and drug trafficking; outrage against 'dope clubs' ensued in the media, and in some quarters, immigrants were held responsible for the moral corruption of young girls. The author Rebecca West described how 'One only has to go to any night club and see the Chinese and South Americans, and aliens of all degrees of colour, to see that the best brains of every country's roguery are attending to these things.'[19]

Chang's association with the whole seedy affair was disastrous for his reputation and his business and so, under a cloud, he moved to Limehouse in 1923, setting up another restaurant, the Shanghai. Chang based himself in one room of a three-storey house on Limehouse

Causeway, but this modest home was lavishly furnished, undoubtedly financed by his now heavy involvement in drug dealing. Couriers would buy the drugs in Limehouse (where smuggled narcotics would often first enter London via the docks) and transport them to the West End where demand was great; and it was not long before the comings and goings at the property were attracting police attention. It was the apprehension of one of Chang's regulars, a chorus girl named Violet Payne, in the Commercial Tavern in Pennyfields that led to his downfall; Payne was found to have cocaine hidden in the lining of her coat and marks on her arm suggested use of a hypodermic needle, the sign of a true addict. Her statement to the police implicated Chang and his premises were raided, revealing a bag of cocaine hidden behind a cupboard. Arrested and charged with possessing and supplying cocaine, Chang was sent to trial at the Old Bailey in April 1924, where revelations claiming that Payne often stayed with Chang opened up further allegations of inter-racial sexual activity. One officer stated, 'This man would sell drugs to a white girl only if she gave herself to him as well as paying him. He has carried on the traffic with real Oriental craft and cunning.'[20]

Chang, despite using his wit, intelligence and excellent command of English to put up a spirited defence, was sentenced to fourteen months' imprisonment, to be followed by deportation. The case drew considerable attention, and for many reinforced the opinion that the close Chinese community of the East End was calculating, sinister and inseparable from the seedy world of drugs, a world which, manifesting itself in the flamboyant bohemia of the West End, was claiming young lives. Sax Rohmer's stories of Fu Manchu continued to excite the notion of the 'Yellow Peril', and the reputation of Limehouse as the nexus of London's squalid opium dens was a not too distant memory. Chang, as the charming, opulent and almost romantic face of London drug culture, was publicly demonised in the subsequent moral backlash:

Brilliant Chang, dope fiend and uncrowned king of the underworld from the dark alleys of Limehouse to the brightly-lit night clubs of London, has at last been run to earth. Impassive, cunning, and bland, he has lived a lurid life in London for several years, decoying hundreds of innocent girls to a life that is worse than death.[21]

The judge at Chang's trial made his own opinions abundantly clear: 'It is you and men like you who are corrupting the womanhood of this country. Girls must be protected from this drug, and society must be purged.'[22]

The attention aimed at the issue of drug trafficking after Chang's imprisonment led to a downturn in dealing, as those who profited from the business prudently looked for other ways of earning a living. Armed robbery and protection racketeering were, however, on the increase, in line with growing post-war crime rates. Gambling at the horse and greyhound racetracks – the only places where it could be legally undertaken by the working classes – boomed in the years following the First World War. The racecourses had always drawn large crowds, targets for roaming pickpockets, but they also provided tremendous opportunities for making money from protection and even extortion. The Sabini brothers, Charles and Ullano (better known as 'Darby'), from Clerkenwell, were major players at the racetracks in the early twentieth century; their gang, sometimes known as 'the Italian Mob', was arguably the most famous of the early organised crime groups in London, and a force to be reckoned with when it came to blackmail, extortion and protection. On the racecourses of Epsom, Brighton and Hove, the Sabinis' boys would threaten violence to bully bookmakers into vacating their pitches before selling them off or letting them out to their associates. Other scams included putting a group of roughs in front of a bookmaker's stall to prevent punters from reaching it to place bets, or indiscriminately wiping odds off blackboards, all of which could be avoided by the handing over of cash. The Sabinis were well connected with the police, and as well as avoiding unwanted attention by offering bribes to complaisant officers, they were also willing to use the threat of informing the police on any villains who refused to see things their way as a means of gaining cooperation. Despite coming from Clerkenwell, the Sabinis had strong connections with east London, working in tandem with gangs from Hoxton, Hackney and Aldgate, the latter known as the East End Jews.[23]

The East End certainly provided its own notable home-grown criminal characters during this period. One, Bethnal Green's Jack 'Dodger' Mullins, was a veritable terror in the area, having racked up his first conviction (for wounding) at the age of sixteen; he would become a significant addition to the fearsome Bethnal Green Gang. He was described as 'scruffy, often with food hanging from his mouth, and always scrounging something from someone, whether he had a need for it or not'.[24] His attempts to establish himself on the racecourses were unsuccessful, so he built up a formidable reputation on the streets of east London through a wide-ranging network of protection rackets on bookmakers, clubs, pubs and billiard halls, administered with a reputation for ready violence, often with an extremely vicious razor-wielding friend, Timmy Hayes, in tow. Mullins worked alongside Arthur Harding as a bodyguard during the General Strike of 1926, protecting strike-breakers at the docks and ensuring the unhindered movement of goods, but he would later turn against his old associate and by 1930 was regularly demanding money from him. Ultimately, Harding, on the way out as a major force in East End gangland, could take no more. One day, Mullins and another man, Jackie Berman, broke down the door of Harding's home to be confronted by the old trooper pointing a pistol at them. Mullins and Berman fled, unaware that the gun did not work, and Harding went to the police; he refused a bribe to twist the evidence and Mullins got a six-year sentence for demanding money with menaces. Mullins would later find further infamy as a major player in a serious mutiny at Dartmoor prison in July 1932, and would go on to be known as 'the old guvnor of the East End'.[25]

Jimmy Spinks was a titan of a man who was leader of the Hoxton Boys and a prominent bare-knuckle fighter of the day. His face was said to be patterned with razor scars and his great nephew, the boxer Lenny McLean,[26] described him as 'a "ten-man job", because to bring him down you would have to go ten-handed or turn up with a shooter'.[27] Spinks was much respected and feared by the local community, as the following remarkable story makes perfectly clear:

> During a row with his girlfriend he had grabbed a heavy mirror off the wall and smashed her over the head with it and killed her, and her blood had splashed all over him. In a drunken panic, his first thought was to get away from the scene, so he ran out of the house and tried to get on a bus. When the bus conductor saw this wild-looking man, obviously drunk and covered with blood, stumbling to get his feet up on the platform, he refused to let him on, and pushed him away, and the bus pulled off without him. Several passengers saw this scene, which would not have been easily forgettable, so putting a case against Jimmy was essentially a matter of establishing the identification: was the blood-covered man that all these people saw Jimmy Spinks? None of the witnesses could say. Confronted with Jimmy, not a single one of them could remember.[28]

One of the period's great personalities was the little-mentioned Tommy 'Wassel' Newman from Old Ford, a character if ever there was one, who combined old-school villainy with a fearsome reputation. On one occasion, Newman, having been swindled by a market trader, surreptitiously attached the man's barrow to a nearby stationary omnibus, and watched in delight as the vehicle began to pull away down Cambridge Heath Road, dragging the unfortunate trader's wares with it.[29] Another time, disgruntled with the slow service in his local butcher's shop, he suggested that he should have his meat for free and that all the other customers present be given the same offer. The butcher was in no position to deny them all the luxury; as a boxer of some reputation, Newman was prone to demonstrating his strength on any given occasion, and one of his favourite diversions in a pub was to stand stock-still and challenge people to throw darts at his head.[30] Wassel Newman, like Dodger Mullins and Jimmy Spinks, would be spoken of by later generations of rogues as role models, 'fearsome tough fighting men who didn't give a toss for anyone', in the words of the Krays. 'Even the coppers were scared stiff of them. They ruled the streets of the East End when we were kids, but they always played by rules which we admired.'[31]

Jack Spot, who would become a major figure in London's organised crime for decades, was on the rise during this period and is still often considered one of the East End's most famous underworld overlords. Born Jacob Comer[32] in April 1912 to Polish Jewish parents, and raised in the slums of Fieldgate Mansions in Myrdle Street, Whitechapel, he first became part of a gang at the age of seven. The area around the dwellings had two distinct Jewish and Irish Catholic communities and there were frequent battles for supremacy on the street: with his willingness to fight tooth and nail, Spot soon became leader. It was said that around this time he earned his famous alias on account of a prominent mole on his cheek. At fifteen he made early forays into organised crime, becoming an apprentice to a Petticoat Lane protection racketeer before joining forces with a prominent bookmaker as a runner and then working as a lookout for a local housebreaker.

Bookmaking led him to the racecourses where for a while he set up a scam called 'Take a Pick' which saw punters pay sixpence for the privilege of pulling a straw from a container in the hope that it indicated the winning of a cheap prize. The reward for the customer may have been small, but Spot would net up to £40 a day, and by taking the same operation to the bustling Petticoat Lane market on a Sunday morning, his profit would effectively double.[33] It was in the East End that Spot would become a face, particularly to the Jewish community he protected (for money, of course):

> I didn't have to buy nothing. Every Jewish businessman in London made me clothes, gave me money, food, drink, everything. Because I was a legend. I was what they call a legend to the Jews. Anywhere they had trouble – anti-Semitic trouble – I was sent for . . . and I'd go up and chin a few bastards. The Robin Hood of the East End, a couple of taxi drivers told me once. 'You helped everyone,' they said.[34]

'Mosley shall not pass'

One of Spot's more dubious claims was that he was a participant in the famous Battle of Cable Street in October 1936, which history has remembered as one of the defining moments of the East End's chequered history. It was also a moment that reinforced the area's reputation for recurring turbulence.

The severe economic depression of the 1930s, known as the 'Great Depression' or 'Great Slump', had caused industrial output in Britain to halve and unemployment to more than double, with many in work only possessing part-time jobs. The privations faced by those affected created a polarising of political views, with a significant rise in the popularity of both communist and fascist ideologies. Extreme right-wing principles spoke loudly to those in the UK who were dissatisfied with a hung Labour Parliament which appeared to be providing weak leadership in response to the economic hardship. As was seen in Italy and Germany, a political force that appeared to a frustrated electorate to have strong direction gathered momentum. As G.D.H. and Margaret Cole observed in 1937, 'Men turn to Fascism when they have lost faith in the continuance of the conditions under which they have managed to find a tolerable accommodation with life. They turn Fascist out of a desire to do something where inaction seems to threaten them with disaster . . .'[35]

The East End, despite its strong links to the left and unionism, also became a breeding ground for fascism, and the area was severely tested by its opposing loyalties. The question of race in this developing situation cannot be ignored. Hitler's brand of fascism was characterised by an obsession with racial issues, in particular relating to the Jews. Following the ravages of the First World War, the number of Jewish immigrants settling in the East End had significantly dwindled, but the major influx of the previous decades had made an indelible mark on the area. As much as these poor newcomers were effectively now part of the East End demographic, they had always been on the receiving end of antagonism in times of crisis: they made a convenient scapegoat when one was needed, whether it was being condemned for causing strain on the labour market, at fault for filling up dwellings, or, as was seen in 1888, being blamed for the Whitechapel murders. In the 1930s, a time of hardship, fascism therefore found its advocates in east London. The *Jewish Chronicle* put forth an appraisal of such support:

> There has always been a combination of several types of working class element influenced by Fascism. They included some unemployed and many wives of unemployed workers ... a number of municipal workers who held a Trade Union card and were dissatisfied with conditions under a Labour Borough Council, some Catholics, many unorganised workers in small workshops and factories ... costermongers and smallholders who felt that the Jews were depriving them of their livelihood and a large number of shopkeepers ...[36]

Founded in 1932, Oswald Mosley's British Union of Fascists (BUF) garnered interest in areas such as Whitechapel, Bethnal Green and Limehouse, where support campaigns had concentrated on issues of exclusion, bolstered by growing resentment towards the performance of socialist councils. In West Ham and Poplar, strong Labour traditions remained dominant and prevented the right wing from gaining any significant foothold, but in Shoreditch, where the Jewish population was less significant, the pre-eminence of an indigenous people with a strong tradition of suspicion of outsiders led to more notable action against the minority Jewish community. The BUF in Shoreditch and Hackney was aggressive, often launching direct action against Jewish businesses, and thugs were occasionally hired to do a little dirty work.[37]

One element of Mosley's homespun fascism was protectionism, with no room for the multiculturalism that the BUF felt was a cause of a breakdown of social cohesion. Little was made of the Jewish question officially; indeed, Mosley could count a number of Jews as supporters. Yet some elements, like the Shoreditch wing of the organisation and other rogue groups, did feel it necessary to make clear that for them the Jewish presence was not welcome; Jewish people found themselves attacked by groups of men with iron bars wrapped in cloth, or followed into quiet thoroughfares and beaten.

In August 1936, a procession of Jewish ex-servicemen in Victoria Park, congregating as a show of strength against fascist aggression, attracted an ugly element of the BUF who shouted fascist slogans at the crowd. James Brown, a hawker from Stepney, was said to have shouted, 'Down with the Jew', and while he was being apprehended for using insulting language, he hit and bit a police officer. Brown received a fine for the insulting behaviour and two months' hard labour for the assault on the officer. Four other men received fines for the more minor offence of throwing apples at the procession.[38] Amidst such rising turbulence, the decision, made in September 1936, to stage a number of fascist meetings at different points in the East End was deemed provocative and generated significant opposition. Deputations from the Jewish People's Council presented their views to the mayor of Bethnal Green, Councillor Harry E. Tate, regarding the first march, due to take place on Sunday, 4 October; they prepared a petition calling for the event to be banned, which they were confident would receive upward of 100,000 signatures. 'The East End is in a state of ferment over the proposed march', claimed the protesters.[39] The day before the march, there was a real concern that conflict might result: 'Feeling is said to be running very high in the East End. Communists and the I.L.P. [Independent Labour Party] have appealed to workers to rally to a counter demonstration against the Fascists half an hour before the march begins.'[40]

When the day came, the different organisations, bolstered by thousands of supporters, rallied to the cause. Just over thirty minutes before Mosley's parade was due to start from Royal Mint Street, communists poured into the Minories; a yellow car bearing the legend 'Mosley shall not pass' drove through the crowds, adding to the confusion. Police set up barriers to keep the opposing sides apart, but the numbers of those against the march began to swell. Accordingly, police reinforcements were bused in, eliciting cries of derision from the crowds, and batons were used in Royal Mint Street as tempers flared and scuffles broke out. Stones were thrown at the police and further reinforcements were brought in to deal with similar disruption in Leman Street. Other disturbances looked ready to flare up at Gardiner's Corner, the busy junction of Leman Street, Whitechapel High Street and Commercial Street, and police drew their truncheons in readiness.

> So tense became the situation . . . that Mr. Fenner Brockway, secretary
> of the I.L.P., telephoned to the Home Office urging them to stop or

divert the procession as at least 100,000 were determined that it should not pass . . . It was not until an hour after the parade was about to start that Sir Oswald Mosley, the Blackshirts' leader, appeared. He made his way to a side street where he was told by Sir Philip Game, Commissioner of Police, that the meetings and parades were to be abandoned.[41]

The march continued, now wisely moving westwards, away from the East End, but by the time the BUF was on its way towards the Embankment, events in Cable Street had taken a more dramatic turn. Protesters had already erected barricades, festooned with placards bearing the words 'They shall not pass'. Some of these barriers were made from builder's materials and wrenched-up paving stones, and when a lorry was wheeled out of a yard and overturned in the street to add to the obstructions, the police moved in. Showers of stones and other debris flew from open windows, incurring the arrival of further reinforcements, who took decisive action:

> Mounted police with drawn truncheons galloped along the street, while women and children cowered in doorways. From behind the lorry came a shower of paving stones and pieces of glass, and several policemen were injured.
>
> As the police reached the overturned lorry, three missiles were thrown over the top . . . They exploded with a loud noise and everyone for a hundred yards ran for their lives. These missiles were afterwards found to be small boxes of gunpowder, used as home-made bombs. The police stormed the lorry and the defenders behind it ran down adjoining streets . . .[42]

Mosley never made it into the heart of east London on that occasion; so it could indeed be claimed that the violence in Cable Street was wholly unnecessary. The BUF opined that the authorities were clamping down on free speech and cowering under the influence of the 'Red Terror'; their opponents described it as a successful fight against the far right, one of the most significant ever seen. But the fascists still managed to hold marches in the East End after that fateful Sunday; the passing of the 1936 Public Order Act, a direct result of the events in Cable Street, meant that permission from the Metropolitan Police had to be sought before organising any political demonstrations in London,[43] and although there was none of the large-scale disruption that accompanied the events of 4 October, incidents of violence were not uncommon. Less than a fortnight after Cable Street, an arson attempt was made on the headquarters of the Bethnal Green branch of the BUF in Green Street.[44] In November 1936, a fascist meeting in Bethnal Green attracted a number of isolated protesters who set upon the marchers. Dealing with the various incidents at Old Street, magistrate Herbert Metcalfe expressed his annoyance at the repetitive instances of violence presented to him:

> The trouble is that people come down to this part of London – which for years has been quiet and peaceful – and kick up a row with their escapades. Whether they are Mosley's crowd or not doesn't matter. It is a disgraceful business, and it means a lot of extra work for the police. The whole performance bores me stiff on a Monday morning.[45]

That great leveller, the Battle of Cable Street, resulted in many injuries, arrests and complaints of police brutality, but it did not quash the rise of fascist support in east London, which grew steadily in the last few years of interwar peace. But it was the highly charged events in that particular long, narrow thoroughfare that became symbolic of the tension, the friction and the passionate fight stirring at the very heart of the East End itself.

The ravages of war

Jack Spot's claim to have been at Cable Street, where he apparently knocked a few Blackshirts' heads, is dubious by merit of the fact that the battle was between the people and the police, and that there were no BUF members present. That is not to say this rough defender of the Jews failed to make a stand against the fascists; in 1937 he received six months' imprisonment for causing grievous bodily harm to a Blackshirt, which, miraculously for this career gangster, was the only prison sentence he would ever serve. Unusually for a criminal, Spot served in the Second World War and was stationed in Cornwall with the Royal Artillery. In his absence, crime flourished in the East End – not because the great protector was away, but because the war created its own climate for lawlessness which affected even those for whom breaking the law was once something others did.

Crime during the period 1939–45 rose by 57 per cent: harsh conditions, rationing, bomb damage and blackouts may well have imbued the people of the most affected cities with a spirit of unity and defiance, but this also benefited the common criminal, as well as the once law-abiding citizen who realised that a better quality of life could be attained by bending or breaking the rules. Many of the standard offences remained a constant – theft from homes, business premises and the docks, gambling and prostitution – but these were accompanied by a burgeoning black market economy, desertion and, noticeably on the increase, looting.

Of all crimes associated with the war, looting was considered the most morally reprehensible, and officially, under the terms of the Defence of the Realm Act, was punishable by execution, although prison sentences were the norm. There was a difference between picking up things that were found in the street, which somebody else would probably purloin if you didn't, and going into a property with the express purpose of stealing for one's own benefit. Unfortunately, some of these thefts were carried out by men in positions of responsibility, such as air-raid wardens, who had the task of guarding bombed buildings to deter looters, and who would sometimes take advantage of their position. The wrecked factories and workshops of the East End provided ample targets for looters and stealing from business premises saw a marked increase. One gas company inspector told the East London Juvenile Court in February 1941 that his company had lost more than £800 from stolen meters in 3,000 incidents in the space of three months, invariably from bombed houses.[46] Raids on properties left vacant by evacuees became so commonplace that it was observed that people were becoming too frightened to use the air-raid shelters, choosing to take considerable risks by staying at home in order to protect their property.[47]

Popular items for theft were alcohol and cigarettes, clothing and other little luxuries, which would find their way onto the streets via the colourful character known as the spiv, born of the depression years and profiting again in wartime. The spiv has become another cliché associated with the cockney heartlands east of Aldgate, and although such individuals flourished everywhere, the sharp-dressed, pencil-moustached, wily entrepreneur, dispensing his cheeky patter to the market-going masses on Petticoat Lane and Brick Lane, remains an archetype of the East End's past. Different from the gangster, who was usually prepared to use violence, the spiv became a tolerated and endearing element of the black market economy who did little more than dupe unsuspecting customers out of a little money, under cover of verbally dextrous banter and charm. Many of these men were deserters, earning their living from selling on stolen goods at inflated prices, safe in the knowledge that such items were in high demand and that those who bought them were unlikely to speak to the police and scupper their enjoyment of a little wartime luxury. At one stage, people were prepared to pay a shilling for a single egg without any complaint.[48]

As early as the opening bombardments of the London Blitz in September 1940, furniture removers began fleecing the thousands of vulnerable residents of the East End who were attempting to flee the bombing, often charging double rates. The local council provided facilities for moving property within the borough free of charge, but when families wished to move outside its borders – not an unlikely desire given the East End was one of the most heavily bombarded districts of London during the period 1940–41 – unscrupulous operators would descend like vultures. 'It's heartrending to see these poor people cheated. The removers know they want to get out quickly, and put the price on', said one councillor.[49]

Crime amongst women was seen to increase, as well as that involving children. In one case, a group of four girls aged between fourteen and sixteen formed themselves into a gang and simultaneously absconded from their jobs to embark on a thieving spree, targeting bedrooms, offices, workshops and shops, before pooling the spoils and returning home, pretending to have done a normal day's work. When their case was heard at the East London Juvenile Court, fourteen incidents were recorded, and Chairman Basil Henriques described it as 'one of the worst series of thefts and housebreakings which had come before the Court'.[50] Another case saw three women charged with stealing more than 100 men's ties from a goods depot in East Ham, for which two were fined and another sentenced to hard labour.[51]

In December 1940, three boys aged between ten and thirteen went before the East London Juvenile Court on a charge of looting toys worth 5 shillings from a damaged warehouse. The eldest boy had not attended school since the start of the war, apparently due to his father keeping him at home because the boy's mother was ill, an excuse that was deemed by the chairman, Basil Henriques, to be 'absolutely scandalous. You would dare not make this excuse during peacetime.'[52] One story that received wide syndication across Britain was that of a petulant youth who was sentenced to approved school, only to tell the magistrate, 'I think you are a fool. I will not stay there.' The magistrate promptly sent him to borstal. The newspaper reports and court records from hearings at the East London Juvenile Court amply display the growing presence of youth crime during this period, much of it involving theft, which was believed to have increased by between 40 and 50 per cent during the period 1940–41.[53] In a letter to *The Times*, John A.F. Watson, chairman of Southwark Juvenile Court, felt he was in an excellent position to divulge the causes:

> Young people in war-time are intrinsically no more wicked than in time of peace. The recent increase in juvenile crime is due rather to a combination of extraneous circumstances ... These include the absence of fathers on active service, the disruption of family life caused by bombing and evacuation, and the closing of schools and clubs.[54]

The East End, which was devastated by air raids, has often been looked upon as epitomising the 'Blitz spirit', as the chirpy cockney waves a metaphorical fist in defiance at Hitler's Luftwaffe – 'for though a bomb can shatter an East End home, it cannot affect an East End heart'.[55] But of course there were many who benefited from the unique circumstances; in the words of the famous London gangster 'Mad' Frankie Fraser,[56] 'I'll never forgive Hitler for surrendering.'[57]

CHAPTER 14

Gangland Legend

It was on that night, with me and Ron done up like dogs' dinners in our bow ties and dinner jackets, and surrounded by the rich and famous, that I realised that we were well on the way to making it to the very top . . . I felt nothing was going to stop us . . .

Reggie Kray (1988)[1]

Following the Second World War, the shattered East End was still under the cosh of the organised mobs that had found their footing there in the early twentieth century, as men like Jack Spot established themselves as kingpins of protection rackets, drinking clubs and illegal gambling dens, and plotted robberies and heists. Spot's public image was reminiscent of the Chicago-style gangsters of the 1920s, and he was now well known, feared and respected throughout the East End, backed by a loyal gang of hand-picked local Jewish toughs. Morris Goldstein, a talented card-sharp and ex-boxer from Stepney, was also known as 'Moishe Blueboy', or 'Blueball', as it was said he had a discoloured testicle.[2] Another former pugilist, Hymie Rosen, was known as 'Little Hymie' or

216

'Hymie the Yid'; Bernard Schack was known as 'Sonny the Yank'; and Solly Kankus, on account of his dark complexion, was usually referred to as 'Solly the Turk'.[3] These and others formed part of the gang that would accompany Spot in his dealings on the racecourses of the southeast and his protection rackets in the East End. The lucrative West End of London was conquered owing to a successful coalition with another notable London villain, Billy Hill.[4] He and Spot defeated all rivals in often bloody battles for control of the West End, becoming the self-styled 'Kings of the Underworld'.

Prostitution and protest

It would be easy to say much more about the further rise of the established gangsters of the East End during this immediate postwar period, to the exclusion of anything else, and we shall return to the subject later; however, the remainder of the 1940s and 1950s were also notable for the resurgence of a much older profession. In the years immediately following the war, Commercial Road between Alie Street and Watney Street, and the districts around Cable Street further south, were coming under scrutiny for what was deemed to be a significant increase in vice. Foreign men, many of them described as 'coloured', were said to be cohabiting with white women who were little more than prostitutes. Many of these women had come to the area 'with the deliberate intention of trading on the coloured men',[5] and many of those involved in such relationships were believed to carry sexually transmitted diseases which, out of either ignorance or nervousness of the authorities, they failed to have treated.

> Almost all these women are below normal intelligence and, according to officials who have dealt with them, over-sexed. With the exception of those who have married, these women have very little moral sense.

They will leave one man to go with another if the second will give them more. While accepting a monthly allowance from one man while he is at sea, they will live with others until he returns, and will encourage men in any activity, such as black marketing, that will help provide more clothes and food.[6]

Much of this business, which as far as the local authorities and clergy were concerned signified a moral black hole, was conducted in cafés in which black and Asian men were believed to meet white women and above which they often rented rooms. Although interracial relationships are nothing unusual today, it must be borne in mind how scandalous such liaisons would have been in those less tolerant days, exacerbated in this case by the perception that prostitution was at the heart of it all, and that the girls were intentionally targeting what was seen as a vulnerable clientele of unattached, often isolated men. The issue would escalate, prompting the presentation of a petition bearing 30,000 signatures to Stepney Council in autumn 1947, protesting the conditions in and around Cable Street: 'Grave moral and physical danger exists for both young and old people in this area ... We express the opinion that the contributory causes are the excessive number of cafés in the street open at a late hour and the disgusting conditions in some public houses.'[7]

By the 1950s, little had changed. Prostitution and brothel-keeping in the area were now being linked to West Indian immigrants and Maltese gangs, the latter having become synonymous with vice racketeering; in 1956, twenty-seven of the thirty-five convicted for living off immoral earnings in Stepney were Maltese.[8] Such connections with immigrant minorities therefore made vice in the area a racial as well as a moral issue; the arrival of a significant number of West Indian immigrants in the late 1940s and early 1950s had made a small impact on the area around the docks, and even though these communities were not large, the media obsession with people of colour being at the heart of the local vice problem merely added to the moral outrage. The publication and recommendations of the *Report of the Committee on Homosexual Offences and Prostitution* (known as the Wolfenden Report) in September 1957, which threatened to take the profit out of prostitution, scared pimps and their girls away from the area following a concerted anti-vice campaign by local residents backed by the *East London Advertiser*. But it was a short-lived respite; by the summer of 1958 the situation had become as bad as before: 'From Alie Street to Watney Street, and along the Commercial Road, one could see groups of two or three street-walkers waiting for custom. "They take their clients into old dilapidated dwellings or bombed sites and ruined houses – which should have been demolished years ago." '9

The problem for local residents was further exacerbated by being disturbed at all hours of the day and night by the frequenters of the pubs and cafés; the noise of revving cars and motorcycles and the shouting of the roughs in the street, cries invariably filled with obscenities, were a nightly occurrence. Some residents who spoke to the local press chose to remain anonymous for fear of reprisals; one young mother exclaimed, 'It is really terrible. One night my family and I were awakened by screams and shouts coming from Cavell Street. There was a coloured man thrown out of a window.'10 The area had earned such a bad reputation that one woman, Ethel Pollard, was discovered carrying a razor in the street simply to defend herself against the 'dangerous men in the area.'11 The lengthy drag of the Commercial Road had become a black spot once again, and Councillor Barney Borman, chairman of the Dorian Estate Tenants' Anti-vice Committee, was ready for action: 'We local residents have declared war on the prostitutes and their pimps', he was quoted as saying. '[Vice] is on every street corner. It is disgusting.'12

The following week, the police swooped on the area, arresting twenty-four prostitutes aged between eighteen and thirty-eight in a single evening. It was not unusual to have around four prostitutes per morning up before the magistrates, but on this occasion many of the women were unfamiliar, and the magistrate Cecil Campion noted, 'It seems we have a record number of prostitutes this morning, and it's quite apparent – because I don't know some of the faces – that they seem to be moving in from other districts.'[13]

The frustration felt by the local residents boiled over into anger at a stormy meeting at the Bernhard Baron Settlement in Berner Street[14] on 15 July. Feelings ran high, with the local press describing the situation as like 'a powder keg about to explode';[15] cries of 'Enough said, nothing done' punctuated proceedings, and at one point the possibility was brought up of using vigilante patrols to clean up the streets, a suggestion that was roundly rejected to avoid interfering with the work of the police. Tempers flared further at subsequent meetings, particularly when one Bethnal Green councillor, C.F.F. Fleet, declared that there was no prostitution in his particular borough, which met with derisory shouts of 'Fool!'[16] Mr Fleet was obviously deluding himself, for prostitution was burgeoning amongst the battered slums of post-war east London.

The findings of the Wolfenden Report and the significant media profile given to the anti-vice campaign in the East End informed the passing of the Street Offences Act of 1959, intended to deal with the rising tide of prostitution at that time. Local residents might have made a good go of their campaign, and legislation might have resulted, but prostitution was never going to fade away that easily, and it would be the removal of the dilapidated and damaged buildings following a compulsory purchase order in 1963 that caused the slow exodus of vice from the Commercial Road and Cable Street areas, which for so long had seemed to be the natural successors to 'Tiger Bay'.[17] Many of the pimps and girls found pastures new around Brick Lane, particularly in Old Montague Street in Whitechapel. Appearance-wise, it was remarkably similar to Cable Street, a narrow thoroughfare with decrepit shops and houses, and innumerable narrow passageways such as Green Dragon Yard and King's Arms Court adding to the sense of claustrophobic clutter. Many of the Jewish citizens who once dominated this street had begun to move on to London's northwest suburbs; properties now deemed unfit for habitation were being left empty, and were soon being used as vice dens. The Davenant Foundation School on Whitechapel Road backed on to Old Montague Street, the ungodly sight of which was shielded from the pupils by frosted glass. Jewish children at the school had to take kosher lunches at Canon Barnett School in Gunthorpe Street, and the route there was arduous, as one former pupil of this time vividly remembered: 'We were told to walk quickly and not stop and talk to anyone because it was populated by meths drinkers and prostitutes. It was very, very run down – it wasn't a place you'd want to live in. It looked as though a bomb had landed on it the previous day!'[18]

The twins

The shelf-life of Jack Spot and Billy Hill, after an eventful, successful and often bloody rule, followed by a falling out that generated more violence, was coming to an end by the mid-1950s; they were about to be replaced by an arguably more enduring criminal legend. It was not a takeover as such, but rather a slow rising through the ranks, helped along by the two retiring gangland personalities, but the new faces in east London's gangland would eclipse them both in terms of celebrity and notoriety, if not necessarily success.

As leaders of a London gang with family ties, Ronald and Reginald Kray would not be unique: north London most notably had the Nash brothers, the Webbs and the Adams family; south London was home to the Heywards and, most famously, the Richardsons. East London could also boast the Dixon brothers and the Tibbs family, among others, but it is fair to say that the Krays held the lion's share of notoriety and media attention during the violent period of the 1950s and 1960s. Much of this was to do with their being identical twins, giving them a clear-cut image that made them stand out from their contemporaries; their love of the limelight, which manifested itself in innumerable posed photographs with family, associates and celebrities, kept them in the public eye when others who followed the same criminal path kept their heads down. Because of this, the Kray twins became household names at the height of their career, inspiring respect and admiration as well as fear and hatred in many quarters, even from those who had little or nothing to do with them.

Born into the gritty world of interwar Hoxton in 1933, the twins were the product of two notable East End families, the Krays of Hoxton and the Lees of Bethnal Green. Their father Charles was frequently absent from the home, bringing in a reasonably comfortable income as a 'wardrobe dealer' or 'pesterer', travelling London and often farther afield to buy up unwanted clothes and jewellery which he would sell on at a profit in Brick Lane market. Their mother Violet thus took on much of the upbringing of her children and famously doted on her twin sons, much more than their elder brother Charlie, creating a life at their famous home in Vallance Road[19] that the boys found safe and loving, but which at the same time imbued them with a sense of entitlement that would become a driving force in the way they treated others their entire lives. Occasional run-ins with the law in their youth galvanised their antipathy towards the police,[20] and their education in crime came from the many entertaining stories of local villains told to them by their colourful grandfathers, Jimmy Kray and Jimmy Lee, as well as from their time spent on the run from the army in the early 1950s, during which they associated with established criminals and learned their methods.[21] Their very brief but successful careers as professional boxers, following in their elder brother's footsteps, gave them the physical fitness and pugilistic skills which would come in useful on countless occasions when they were required to assert their authority.

Their real breakthrough came in the mid-1950s when, as regulars at the Vienna Rooms on the Edgware Road, they acquainted themselves with Billy Hill and Jack Spot, who by this time were in their twilight as the real force in London crime. Hill was admired and appeared to actively encourage the brothers' evolution in villainy, but Spot was essentially used by the twins – who had become muscle for Spot-controlled betting pitches at the races – to obtain a vital foothold in the London underworld. 'It wasn't that we liked him', claimed Ronnie later. 'We despised him really. We just turned out with Spotty to show everyone that we was the up-and-coming firm and didn't give a fuck for anyone.'[22]

When the takeover began, it proved not to be an easy ride. Established East End gangsters such as the Watney Streeters and the Maltese mobs of Shadwell, resentful of these confident upstarts from Bethnal Green, were only too willing to put the young men in their place, resulting in some spectacular battles which the twins, as a formidable combined fighting force, invariably won. Ronnie's attack on a gang of Maltese protection racketeers at the Regal billiard hall, during which he used a sword to disperse the gang, was one such incident, even being re-created (with tremendous artistic licence and enhanced violence) in film.[23]

Ronnie was imprisoned in 1956 for grievous bodily harm and carrying a loaded revolver following an attack on Terry Martin outside the Britannia public house in Shadwell. The whole incident stemmed from a tit-for-tat feud between Martin's brother Charlie and Billy Jones, a business partner of Kray associate Bobby Ramsey, over work allocation at the London Docks. The dispute spiralled out of control and on the night of 28 August 1956, Ronnie got himself involved, inflicting tremendous violence on Terry Martin, a scapegoat in his brother's absence.

While Ronnie was detained at Her Majesty's pleasure, Reggie and Charlie set up their first proper business venture, the Double R Club on Bow Road, the beginning of their love affair with the high life and early encounters with celebrities outside the boxing world. In prison, Ronnie's mental health issues manifested themselves, and after being moved to Long Grove Asylum in Surrey he was diagnosed with paranoid schizophrenia, a condition which went some way to explaining his spontaneous violence and unpredictability. When he was sprung from Long Grove by Reggie and some friends on Whit Monday in 1958, the press were already describing him as 'a violent criminal' who posed a danger to the public;[24] one report stated that he suffered from 'a persecution mania' and that 'he may use violence if he thinks he is near recapture'.[25] After being caught and returned to Long Grove and later Wandsworth prison to see out the remainder of his sentence, Ronnie Kray would spend the rest of his life dependent on medication to control his illness, not always effectively. This only added to the twins' legendary status: the suggestion was that – with Reggie the more calculating, more patient brother, Ronnie the overtly violent one – the twins balanced each other out in a skewed representation of Ying and Yang, as if they were two sides of the same person.

By 1960 the Krays were established, with a formidable portfolio of protection rackets to bring in the cash, as ever from local spielers as well as cab firms, cafés and pubs. They had also become involved in 'long firm' business fraud, masterminded by Leslie Payne and his partner Freddie Gore, which swelled the coffers and allowed them to pay their coterie of hangers-on, known as 'the Firm', in cash, clothes, food and drink, inspiring tremendous loyalty. One utterly dependable individual was not actually part of their world as such, but could be trusted to help out in some of the most awkward circumstances. Dr Morris Blasker was certainly a character. Born in Stepney in 1904, he was a compulsive gambler and a lover of music who at one time had been the resident medico at Repton Boxing Club in Cheshire Street, one of many clubs used by their twins during their days as amateur and professional boxers. He operated from his modest surgery at 2 Manchester Grove on the Isle of Dogs, and was a first port of call for the Krays (and probably other ruffians) when injured in gangland altercations and in need of some late-night stitches or bullet removal. Blasker had come up before the General Medical Council on at least one occasion for supplying false documents and certificates for the illegal procurement of passports, and in 1961 was nearly struck off the Medical Register, but was acquitted.[26]

In the small hours of 6 February, Selwyn Cooney (also known as 'Leeds Jimmy Neill'), a West End nightclub owner, went to the Pen Club in Duval Street,[27] Spitalfields, for a late drink with one of his barmaids, Joan Bending. The club, undoubtedly the haunt of many a felon, had apparently been named in honour of a robbery at the Parker Pen factory: the proceeds had been used to set it up.[28] At the club was Jimmy Nash, a member of the north London crime family, and several friends; Nash's brother Ronnie had apparently been beaten up by Cooney in Notting Hill some time previously, and when Cooney was pointed out, Nash and his companions John Read and Joey Pyle attacked him. Witnesses claimed that, after breaking Cooney's nose with the first blow, Nash had pulled a gun and begun shooting, hitting Cooney almost at point-blank range in the head, and then fleeing with his friends. One individual, Billy Ambrose, an associate of the Krays, was shot in the stomach, but survived; Cooney was not so lucky – his limp body was dragged out into the street where it became apparent to all that he was dead.[29]

The resulting murder trial at the Old Bailey garnered considerable public and press attention. The police could not help noticing that the Kray twins were in attendance on every day of the proceedings; they had a fragile relationship with the Nash brothers which teetered on the edge of tolerance provided they did not tread on each other's toes. An anonymous letter had also been received from what appeared to be a disgruntled member of the local community, earnestly advising the police of how big a concern organised crime was becoming in the East End:

they have been operating all sorts of gambling clubs in the east end of London in the Bow district, it is pretty evident that these men are not doing these things without some assistance from the police why is this being allowed to continue they are getting money from all sorts of operations they have been known to have machine guns and shot guns in hordes what exactly is going on when it is common knowledge and the police are powerless to do anything about it it will not stop at this one murder and I think that you should make some effort to stop it . . .[30]

The verdict of the jury in the Pen Club murder trial saw Nash sent down for three years for the initial assault on Cooney, but due to lack of evidence (one witness had failed to turn up and two had withdrawn their evidence, suggesting intimidation) he was acquitted of murder.

A campaign to stamp out London's gangland, spearheaded by the *Daily Mirror*, gained fresh impetus from incidents like the Pen Club shooting. As major players, the Krays were an urgent case, as an internal report by Detective Superintendent Tommy Butler made clear:

During the last three years the Kray twins and their older brother Charles James KRAY . . . assisted by the notorious NASH family, have welded themselves into a formidable criminal association. They have organised the 'Protection' technique, and the keystones of their confederacy are VIOLENCE and INTIMIDATION. At present this is mainly directed towards club owners, café proprietors, billiard hall owners, publicans, and motor car dealers, operating in the East End of London. That they will spread their operations to other districts in due course may be taken for granted. Their reputation is already such that persons threatened almost frantically deny visitations by anyone connected with the Kray twins. Not one victim can be persuaded to give evidence against anyone connected with their organisation. The fact that Ronald Kray is certainly mentally unstable (to put it at the very least) is of immense importance to the others, and adds considerably to the victim's undeniable urge to comply with demands made upon him, and to his atrocious memory when questioned by Police at a later stage.[31]

The upshot of all this was the closure of the Double R Club and the Regal (the scene of Ronnie's sword attack), as well as the Wellington Way Club, a spieler off the Bow Road that was part-owned by the Krays. Although the Regal's closure was due to the impending demolition of the hall, the demise of the other two concerns was in part due to Reggie's concealment of Ronnie Marwood, a man wanted for killing a police officer in 1958 (and who eventually gave himself up on 27 January 1959: he was hanged at Pentonville prison on 8 May 1959). The police knew that Reggie had hidden this fugitive, even bringing him in for questioning at Bow police station, but they had insufficient proof: 'I was told by the governor of the station that they knew I had looked after Marwood, so in future the spotlight would be on me wherever I went and in whatever premises I opened as clubs.'[32]

The Krays did have the ability to bounce back from any allegation the police could make against them, and their continued professional relationship with Leslie Payne maintained the steady income from long firm frauds, along with several protection deals that had slipped under the police radar. Esmeralda's Barn, a Knightsbridge club of which the twins became co-directors in time to enjoy the proceeds of the recently liberalised gambling laws,[33] gave them an established presence in the West End and a foothold in higher-grossing protection rackets from clubs frequented by the wealthy and privileged. When the American Mafia began fronting London casinos in the early 1960s, they sought out the Kray organisation for muscle, leading to highly lucrative scams such as the selling of stolen Canadian bearer bonds across Europe. Some of this money was put into the establishment of another East End club, the Kentucky on Mile End Road, where many of the twins' highly publicised charity functions were held and recorded for posterity by the press; the quality of celebrities who floated within the Krays' orbit increased significantly and included such prominent personalities as Judy Garland, George Raft, Liza Minelli and even an alleged association with Princess Margaret and Lord Snowdon.[34]

The Krays' love of big money and big names threatened to blow up in their faces in 1964 following a scandal involving the eminent Conservative peer Baron Robert Boothby, a regular at Esmeralda's Barn: under a front-page headline 'Peer and a gangster: Yard inquiry', the *Sunday Mirror*'s crime reporter, Norman Lucas, presented the world with the scenario of a homosexual relationship between that best-known of peers and Ronnie Kray, something that also implicated other pillars of the establishment. The sexual relationship between Boothby and Kray was non-existent, but they were certainly friends and had socialised on numerous occasions after Boothby had been approached as an investor in a profit-making construction project in Nigeria that Leslie Payne was masterminding with the twins' involvement. Non-relationships aside, it was an incendiary acquaintance, and with a general election looming it was deemed necessary to bury the story before damage was done to all involved, including the former chairman of the Labour Party, Boothby's friend Tom Driberg, who was having a dangerous affair with Kray associate 'Mad' Teddy Smith. The establishment won out, and the journalists of Fleet Street were warned off from negative reporting about the Krays, which in turn boosted the twins' power and notoriety. The Krays were lucky in other ways too. Detective Inspector Leonard 'Nipper' Read, newly appointed to Commercial Street police station, was engaged in a concerted effort to bring the Krays down at the time of the scandal; the evidence that had been patiently collected was rendered almost unusable, riddled as it was by surveillance reports containing compromising material on establishment figures.[35]

In a way, the Boothby affair gave the Krays a short reprieve. A few days into 1965, the twins and Teddy Smith were arrested by Detective Inspector Read for demanding money with menaces from Hew McCowan, a nightclub owner who also happened to be heir to a baronetcy.[36] McCowan was one of several people who, like Boothby, had been approached over the Nigerian development project; he too was unable to oblige, but showed the Krays his new club, the Hideaway, in Soho's Gerrard Street. The opportunistic twins spotted another lucrative partnership in the West End, but their attempts to put their men on the door of the club were rejected again and again by McCowan. Eventually Smith snapped, going into the Hideaway drunk one night and causing a fair amount of damage. In a meeting with McCowan afterwards, Reggie made the Krays' position crystal clear:

> You see the sort of trouble we can save you. If you had our man on the door, Smith would run a mile. We know everyone in town and they know us. If four of them had come in and smashed the place up you wouldn't have liked it. Anyway, now you're open we would like you to sign an agreement for us to protect you and we would do that for 20% of the takings.[37]

McCowan was now well aware that this had become a case of 'demanding money with menaces' and went to Marylebone police station to file a complaint. On 6 January 1965 the arrest was made at the Glenrae Hotel in Finsbury Park, one of the many clubs which had come under the Krays' control.

The resulting trial in February was a sizeable media affair but came to nothing when the jury, some of whom had been influenced by members of the Firm, failed to reach a unanimous verdict. A retrial was

229

ordered, but the ever-resourceful twins ensured that McCowan's supporting witnesses had been persuaded to 'forget' evidence or be absent from court, leaving him an isolated figure in the prosecution's case; they had also employed George Devlin, a private detective, to dig up anything that would wreck McCowan's standing as a witness. The results were effective: McCowan was exposed as a police informer and practising homosexual with a criminal record to that effect, and the case was thrown out.[38] The three acquitted men pulled up outside Vallance Road that day in a Jaguar to shake hands with well-wishers, family and friends, all in the gaze of the national media; that night, Ronnie and Reggie would appear on BBC television being interviewed about the case.

The twins continued to revel in the media spotlight. With a projected article about them in the works for *The Sunday Times Magazine*, they attended a photo session (along with brother Charlie) at the studios of *Vogue*, where David Bailey, the most prominent fashion photographer of 1960s London, recorded the pair for posterity in what has become a truly iconic image of the decade. The essay that accompanied the photograph when it was published in late 1965 in Bailey's *Box of Pin-Ups* described the twins as 'an East End legend – their exploits have inspired almost as many stories (both false and true) as those of Frank and Jesse James'.[39] The Boothby and McCowan cases, although not tied to the East End per se, also reinforced the Kray twins' almost untouchable status; they had powerful friends in the establishment, and the sensationalist press and now even the law found them out of reach. Reggie's high-profile marriage to Frances Shea in April 1965 further cemented the Kray name in the public eye.

But the night of 9 March 1966 brought it all back home to the East End. Much has been written and said about the shooting of George Cornell by Ronnie Kray in the Blind Beggar pub on Whitechapel Road that night, and the event has seared itself into criminal, and London, history.[40] The result of a combination of long-standing feuds and personality clashes, as well as the victim's unfortunate choice of drinking hole on that particular night (although accounts vary as to the exact cause), the death of Cornell, an east Londoner who had once had connections with the Watney Street gangs in the 1950s, saw the East End rocked by an audacious gangland assassination. It also demonstrated just how feared the Krays had become: although the killing was highly public in its execution, a 'wall of silence' shot up almost immediately, and H-Division's Detective Superintendent James Axon found himself coordinating a murder inquiry with which nobody was willing to cooperate. Not even an identity parade held at Commercial Street police station the following August, which included Ronnie and his comrade in arms that night, Ian Barrie, managed to jog any memories. A key witness, the barmaid of the Blind Beggar, failed to materialise. It is revealing that although two witnesses, the barmaid and Johnny Dale, one of Cornell's drinking companions, did disclose the identity of the gunman to the police a few days after the event, neither was prepared to set it down in a vital statement:

John Dale was ashen white and obviously frightened but after what seemed some minutes' hesitation he said, 'All right, it was Ronnie Kray'.

Superintendent Axon returned to the room and I said to John Dale, 'Tell Superintendent Axon the name of the man who killed George Cornell' and he said, 'It was Ron Kray'.

Mr. Axon asked him if he would put that down in writing and he said, 'No and I shall not identify him. It is more than my life is worth. I shall be scared to leave here tonight'.[41]

Despite the metaphorical 'wall of fear', the word on the streets had it that Ronnie Kray did the deed; an anonymous postcard received by

231

police on 9 August made this all too evident: 'Keep plugging at it. Ronnie Kray did the shooting.'[42] It was one of several such missives. Be that as it may, what the authorities needed was not unsolicited opinion but eyewitnesses who would cooperate fully. But there was no way they would be given such a luxury – not for a while at least.

The events of March 1966 again put London's gangland on the front page. Connections were made with the death of Cornell and the disappearance of 'Ginger' Marks the previous year, as well as the shooting dead of Dickie Hart in a Catford nightclub during a fracas between members of south London's Richardson gang and a rival group led by the Heyward brothers.[43] The press spoke of a feud that was now coming to a head between rival gangs 'who are both trying to lead the profitable protection racket at betting shops, gaming casinos and clubs in the east End and south London'.[44] Police were convinced that this was now 'part of an underworld war which has been going on for months'.[45] Such opinions were given further impetus by the discovery of the body of Ernest Isaacs in the basement of his house in Penn Street, Hoxton, in May 1966. Isaacs, known to all as 'Jovial Ernie', had been shot to death, and the fact that his wife and two children slept soundly in the rooms above suggested the considered use of a silencer. He worked as a street trader, but was known to the south London gangs and was also apparently on first-name terms with George Cornell. His friend Cyril Brown said that 'he was inclined to be rather a loudmouth', adding, 'I fear I may be the next person on the list to be murdered. I am very scared and feel quite sick. I am frightened to say more about it.'[46]

When the Richardson gang were finally rounded up for good later in the year, the trial exposed tales of 'mock trials' and 'punishments ranging from death – the sentences being carried out by an imported executioner – to beatings and torture',[47] in which George Cornell was posthumously found to be a main player. Ronnie Kray would later write that the methods used by the Richardsons 'made the Kray twins look like

232

Methodist lay preachers', and that Cornell, as 'chief hatchet man and torturer ... was extremely well qualified for the job'.[48]

The murder in the Blind Beggar drove divisions within the Kray Firm, as those who had benefited from the comfortable yet aggression-ridden lifestyle became disenchanted: what was seen as unnecessary violence threatened to bring them all down. At the end of 1966, the twins exacerbated these problems by masterminding the breakout from Dartmoor prison of Frank Mitchell, 'the Mad Axeman', an East End criminal legend and scourge of the prison system. Born in Canning Town in 1929, Mitchell's life of crime, which began in 1939, was a continual cycle of law-breaking and crushing punishment which only served to brutalise the simple-minded giant. By 1955 he had been declared 'mentally defective', and subsequently spent terms at Rampton Secure Hospital in Nottinghamshire and Broadmoor in Berkshire, escaping from both. While at Wandsworth in the late 1950s he had met Ronnie Kray and a friendship developed, with a large measure of hero-worship on the part of Mitchell. When he was transferred to Dartmoor in 1962, he was not given a release date and the twins came to his assistance. The idea was ultimately a stupid one: spring Mitchell from the outdoor working party on Dartmoor and bring him back to London where he could communicate with the authorities to bolster public sympathy and demand a release date, which, if given, would guarantee him handing himself in to the authorities. 'Yes, ludicrous as it sounds, that was the deal the twins had persuaded Mitchell to believe. He didn't think it was ludicrous because to him, Ronnie was a God.'[49]

It was a desperate act and despite the original escape going to plan, the aftermath became a nightmare as the unstable Mitchell began to bristle at being held under house arrest by a small coterie of Kray gang members, which included Jack Dickson, Albert Donoghue and Billy Exley, in a commandeered flat in East Ham. Even the services of an escort girl, Lisa Prescott, could only temporarily soothe the big man's frustration:

> I had more fucking freedom in Dartmoor. At least I wasn't cooped up – I could get out and see a bit of sunshine. How long do they think they can keep me here? I want to see Ronnie. He's fucking letting me down – if he doesn't get here fast I will be looking for him. He was supposed to have me out of London days ago.[50]

When Mitchell began making such threats towards the Krays, the decision was made to get rid of him. On Christmas Eve 1966, on the pretence of taking him to spend the festive season in the country, he was driven away from the flat in a van; within seconds of the van doors being closed, the contents of two pistols were emptied into Mitchell's torso and head by a ready Freddie Foreman, the prominent south London bank robber and close friend of the Krays, and his sidekick Alfie Gerrard. Mitchell's body has never been found.[51]

As actual murder was added to the Krays' criminal curriculum vitae, the goodwill quickly began to drain from the Firm. Reggie's murder of lone villain-for-hire Jack 'The Hat' McVitie at a basement party on Evering Road, Stoke Newington, in October 1967 came just as Nipper Read, now detective superintendent, returned to have one more crack at the Kray empire. He found a gang beginning to lose its cohesion and operating through fear; as Albert Donoghue, one of several once trusted members of the Firm, later recalled:

> Around the murders the twins were getting even more paranoid. Reggie was drinking more and more. Instead of getting drunk once or twice a week, he was drunk practically every night. Ronnie would hole up with crates of brown ale and whether he was drunk or not, to him everybody was a spy, everybody was trying to fuck the twins up.[52]

The sheer weight of evidence given to the police by Leslie Payne and other deserting Kray luminaries such as Billy Exley, Alan Cooper and Paul Elvey triggered the highly planned wholesale arrest of the Kray Firm on 8 May 1968. With the entire operation effectively behind bars at Bow Street Magistrates' Court, and with no chance of bail, more witnesses opened up. Others turned Queen's evidence in return for leniency and immunity. Although the original arrests had been on charges of grievous bodily harm, assault, financial fraud, conspiracy to murder and other misdemeanours, new evidence emerged regarding the deaths of George Cornell, Frank Mitchell and Jack McVitie, now set in stone with written statements taken from once reluctant witnesses, making a High Court trial for murder inevitable.

The life sentences for the murders of George Cornell and Jack McVitie handed down to the Kray twins by Justice Aubrey Melford Stevenson at the Old Bailey in March 1969, along with the variable punishments given to most of the Firm, including brother Charlie, were seen by some as a message to the underworld, a warning to anybody who wished to fill the yawning chasm of villainy now left by the incarcerated brothers Kray. The East End of London had again become the centre of attention for its criminality; the *Daily Mirror* spoke of 'The Kray Manor', printing a small gazetteer of locations relevant to the twins' crime story, such as Green Dragon Yard (home to a prominent gambling club under Kray protection) and favoured public houses like the Lion in Bethnal Green, and the Grave Maurice and Blind Beggar on Whitechapel Road.[53] The revelations that came to light during the Kray case, wrote the *Guardian*, cast 'a sordid shadow over the eastern half of this city', a domain populated by 'This-brothers and That-brothers, a world of nicknames straight out of a sick Damon Runyan'.[54]

The Krays ensured their legendary status through their strong public image and media profile, the latter being kept up throughout their prison years. Despite the attention lavished on the twins by their supporters as

235

firm-but-fair protectors of the innocent who only hurt their own, they were dangerously flawed. In many ways, they ruined everything they touched, including many lives, not least their own. As this author once observed,

They had the ability to be very successful criminals, and for a brief period they were. Had they gone about things differently, they could well have retired to the country or the south of Spain, as so many have. They would be a small chapter in British criminal history, as opposed to the iconic, David Bailey-immortalised gangsters who are now a big part of London's iconography.[55]

CHAPTER 15

A Low Ebb

You and your men require the full commendations of the public for bringing this gang to justice. It was a difficult task, thoroughly, honestly, efficiently and fairly discharged.

Mr Justice O'Connor, addressing Superintendent Albert Wickstead at the Dixon brothers' trial (1972)[1]

Whilst the Kray brothers attracted attention in abundance, even after their incarceration, the East End underworld provided the media with a number of other notable characters. On 2 January 1965, as drinkers in the Carpenter's Arms in Bethnal Green made the most of their Saturday night, gunfire echoed around nearby dingy Cheshire Street. A hail of bullets had rammed into the body of Tommy 'Ginger' Marks, a local haulage operator[2] and villain, as his companion, Jimmy Evans, hid behind him. Firing the shots from a car was Freddie Foreman, accompanied by his driver, Alfie Gerrard. Evans fled in fear as Marks's lifeless body hit the ground – it was picked up by the two assailants, bundled into the car, and never seen again. All that remained were the dead man's spectacles, hat, some bloodstains, and a bullet hole in the wall behind where he fell. The mystery of 'What happened to Ginger Marks?' was born.

The reason for the shooting, like the Pen Club incident, was an act of personal revenge rather than justice meted out for 'business' reasons or as a means of establishing gangland supremacy. Freddie Foreman's brother George, who had been having an affair with Jimmy Evans's wife, had been shot in the groin at point-blank range by Evans with a sawn-off shotgun at the door of his home in Lambeth in December 1964.[3] George Foreman survived, and obeyed the criminal code of staying silent about the culprit when questioned by police, but his incensed brother waited for the right moment to exact justice. So the gunfire that had opened up in Cheshire Street that January night was meant for Evans – and he had used Marks as a human shield. Evans broke his silence about the incident, and Foreman was charged with the murder in 1975, but was acquitted. He later admitted that the body had been disposed of in the English Channel – one of Foreman's nicknames was believed to be 'The Undertaker'.[4]

The disappearance of Marks was certainly symptomatic of the gangland problem in the East End, and although the truth regarding his death would come to light with Foreman's confession in the 1990s, Ronnie Kray for one had his own ideas about what had really happened, blaming George Cornell for the incident. Kray made the claim that he had broken up a heated disagreement between Marks and Cornell some time before, and that Cornell had said that he wanted to blow Marks's head off – an act he later admitted to Kray some time before he himself would become the victim of the dangerously unstable twin.[5] Such claims by Ronnie Kray were obviously aimed at vindicating his old friend Freddie Foreman, while in the process implicating his arch-enemy for murder: such was the skewed morality of villainy.

238

Pretenders to the empire

Despite the punitive effects of the pummelling fist of the law in 1969, the vacuum left by the Krays did not remain unfilled for long. It was another notable family, the Dixons of Canning Town, specifically brothers George and Alan, who seemed prepared to take on the mantle of East End overlords as the optimistic 1960s gave way to the troubled 1970s. The Dixon brothers had been around for a long time, and had frequently crossed paths with their infamous predecessors. Famously, George Dixon, barred by Ronnie Kray from the Regency Club in Stoke Newington for his heavy drinking and careless remarks about Ronnie's sexuality, nearly met his end when the mentally ill twin attempted to shoot him in the head, only to be saved by the failure of the gun to go off.[6] The Dixons made a name for themselves as hard men and bouncers for various clubs and pubs, as well as efficient strong-arm debt collectors. After they helped publican Phil Jacobs fend off the unwanted attentions of the Krays, a professional relationship developed, which would ultimately branch out into protection and fraud. Jacobs, known as 'Little Caesar' on account of his height of 5 feet 2 inches, was the mastermind behind the growing Dixon operation.

Dixon enforcer Mickey Flynn, described by Detective Chief Superintendent Albert Wickstead as 'huge, one of the most formidable men I have ever seen',[7] fell out spectacularly with his employees when Brian Dixon apparently gave him some rough treatment after he had beaten his wife. Flynn made a complaint to West Ham police station and as the investigation proceeded, more witnesses to the deeds of the Jacobs–Dixon alliance came forward. Albert Wickstead, apparently under orders from the Home Office to 'stop another possible recurrence of the Kray regime',[8] drew together a team with the aim of bringing down the new threat in pretty much the same way that Nipper Read had done three years before.

239

The arrests were made on 25 August 1971 and the trial commenced on 12 April 1972. Much of the time was spent challenging the evidence of the police, for a considerable amount of it was in the form of verbal admissions, with no written statements to be drawn upon.[9] Several defence witnesses gave evidence against their former colleagues, having already secured deals from the police. Seven men in all were up for sentencing on the last day of the trial, 4 July. Brian Dixon, originally charged with conspiracy to cause grievous bodily harm, conspiracy to blackmail and conspiracy to assault, was acquitted along with Lambert Jacobs. George Dixon, whom Phil Jacobs was believed 'to have sponsored as successor to the Krays',[10] was jailed for twelve years for demanding money with menaces from two motor dealers and conspiracy to demand money with menaces from a publican. He was also convicted of conspiring to assault Raymond Washbourne, road manager for the Bee Gees; Alan Dixon received nine years' imprisonment for the same offences. The other convicted men were Leon Carlton (six years), Brian Taylor and Michael Bailey (both five years) for crimes ranging from blackmail and affray to conspiracy to do grievous bodily harm.

The downfall of the Dixons did not see the end of old-school crime families in the East End; others, like the Tibbs and Nicholls clans, continued with their own brand of mayhem, although none of them would ever reach the lofty heights that the Krays had occupied during their heyday.

George Davis is innocent, OK

The last luminary to shoot to nefarious fame during this sensational period of 'classic' East End villainy was George Davis. He was born and raised in Poplar in 1941 to a good working-class family. His early life gave no hint of any future life of crime; he passed his eleven-plus exam and went to grammar school, after which he secured a job as messenger boy for the Port of London Authority and became a father at the age of sixteen, marrying his girlfriend, Rose Dean. Davis did, however, associate with local gangland characters and even ran his own illegal drinking den for a time. Having lost his job as a lorry driver for drink driving in 1972, he supplemented his income with minicab driving and petty theft,[11] and that year was convicted of receiving stolen goods; but it was the events surrounding an armed robbery on the London Electricity Board offices in Ilford in April 1974 that earned him a place in the annals of crime.

The dramatic incident involved commandeered vehicles, a lengthy chase and a shootout with police that resulted in injury to the robbers and one officer. Davis was not arrested at the time, but was taken into custody later following the testimony of an eyewitness who claimed to have seen him climbing out of a getaway car, and others who put him at the scene. Davis claimed that he was driving a minicab on the fateful morning and was apparently seen doing so by friend Peter Chappell, Davis claiming that he was the only driver on duty that day. Significantly, tests on blood found at the crime scene revealed no match with any of the accused, but the results were apparently not ready in time for the committal hearings, and thus the decision to go to trial in the High Court relied solely on eyewitness testimony. At the ensuing trial of the four men charged with the robbery, all were acquitted except Davis, who received a twenty-year prison sentence in March 1975. Rose Davis was convinced that something was amiss with the evidence and, aided by Peter Chappell, began a tireless campaign against what she saw as an obvious miscarriage of justice.

It was Chappell's enthusiasm for highlighting the plight of his friend and his talent for generating publicity that catapulted the case into the public domain. Graffiti reading 'George Davis is innocent' and variants thereof began to spring up around the East End, on walls, buildings and railway bridges. In May 1975, Jim and Colin Dean staged a seven-hour rooftop protest at St Paul's Cathedral; Chappell daringly drove a lorry into the glass doors of the *Daily Mirror* offices in Fleet Street and a car through the gates of Buckingham Palace. With the graffiti campaign spreading beyond the East End, several protesters, including Chappell, broke into Headingley Cricket Ground on 19 August 1975 and vandalised the wicket on the eve of a crucial test match between England and Australia; the match was cancelled, robbing the hosts of an Ashes victory.[12] Despite gaining national attention for the campaign, it also resulted in an outcry; one commentator said, 'Can we hang these people for this?' and Davis was threatened by cricket-loving inmates at Albany prison on the Isle of Wight, where he was serving his sentence.[13] Chappell, along with several other co-activists, received an eighteen-month prison sentence, by which time the campaign had gained enough traction to instigate a police review of the evidence. It was discovered that the blood analysis results had actually been in the possession of the police during the committal proceedings, and it was noted that had they been released when they should have been, the negative results would probably have seen Davis released there and then.[14] Doubts over the police evidence which had convicted Davis led Home Secretary Roy Jenkins to exercise the Royal Prerogative of Mercy: 'My conclusions about the shift of evidence in the case are such that it would not be right for Mr. Davis to remain in prison', said Mr Jenkins, and the prisoner was released on 11 May 1976. Davis arrived back home in Bow to considerable crowds and waiting journalists, filled with praise for his supporters: 'I can never find words to express how I feel about all these people . . . the knowledge that they were fighting for me is what kept me going. And as for my wife Rosie, well, what can you say?'[15]

George Davis was also a celebrity. His name now adorned innumerable architectural features across the UK and he was being celebrated in the mass media. The Who's Roger Daltrey famously wore a jumper bearing the ubiquitous slogan during the group's 1975 UK tour, and even three years later the same words were being sung by Jimmy Pursey's band, Sham 69.[16] But it came at a price. Davis's sudden profile saw him go off the rails; his son Rick later observed that 'He was full of himself when he came out. He went on a bender for about eighteen months. All he was doing was getting drunk, coming home, and they [George and Rose] were having rows. He wasn't the same man as when he went in. He was the famous George Davis.'[17]

Davis was arrested on 23 September 1977 as he sat in a waiting car during a raid on the Bank of Cyprus in Holloway Road, north London. There were guns on the seat next to him and he was also apparently wearing a balaclava when a police officer tapped on the window. Asked what he was doing, Davis replied, 'Shopping.' For his role in the raid he received a fifteen-year prison sentence, and on this occasion there was little doubt of his guilt. There would be no campaign from his now disappointed wife and divorce soon followed. In March 1986, two years after his release, he received another prison stretch, this time for two years for attempting to rob a London-to-Brighton mail train. His reputation as a salt-of-the-earth cockney who had been the victim of police corruption, riding high in the mid-1970s, was now in tatters and Davis willingly dropped out of the public eye.

But the events of 1975–76 demonstrated what James Morton would describe as 'the greatest instance of the East End rallying to one of their own'.[18] It's a rare sight, but occasionally around east London one can still see the faded daubs on railway bridges and isolated walls declaring Davis's innocence.[19] Despite the reminders, some have come to the conclusion that Davis was anything but innocent, even casting doubt on his original release in 1976, as one article written shortly after his wife's death attested:

The truth is that George Davis is not an innocent man. Despite what his gullible Left-wing supporters thought at the time, his original conviction may have been correct and it has never been officially overturned. His other convictions are beyond question.[20]

243

The East End in crisis

If the East End of the 1960s was portrayed in a quasi-glamorous light, albeit one immersed in the seedier side of life, the 1970s would see a decline that was impossible to ignore. This most troubled period in British history – beset by industrial action, power cuts, terrorism and a crippling oil crisis – saw the East End at one of its lowest ebbs since the dark days of the nineteenth century. The area was full of slum dwellings and many cleared bombsites still awaiting development. In Spitalfields, detritus from the market was a regular feature on the streets, picked at by groups of homeless men and women, and the once fine Huguenot houses were in a sad state of repair with cracked windows, crumbling brickwork and peeling paint; many of them had by now become sweatshops. In the riverside areas, dock closures, brought about by the dominance of container shipping based farther up the Thames Estuary, left empty warehouses decaying over streets that had once teemed with life and industry. Selective slum clearance programmes during the 1960s had vacated large areas of land, and what was left was often in poor condition as Tower Hamlets lurched into a major housing crisis. As had been seen many times before, neglect now exposed the underbelly of the East End once again.

It is ironic that a social housing project that was created in the philanthropic fervour of the late nineteenth century to replace the slums should have become a slum itself. The streets are familiar to us – Flower and Dean and Thrawl Streets – and the model dwellings that had replaced the disreputable doss-houses had themselves become obsolete. On visiting the area in 1971, historian Jerry White wrote that 'Spitalfields was something else. Its tenement blocks were worse than anything I had seen in the Clerkenwell or Farringdon Roads. Rothschild Buildings, as I stood awestruck in their virtually abandoned courtyard, were bleak, barren, smoke-blacked, sadistically ugly. They looked as though they had been designed by a medieval torturer.'[21]

By that point many of the flats were empty as the authorities attempted to vacate them as a prelude to demolition. It was a long process, however, for despite the squalor and the unsatisfactory sanitary arrangements which made the flats unsuitable to modern life, five stalwart residents, all of them long-standing tenants with strong links to the community, would not leave. In April 1972 the body of a 17-year-old girl was found in a flat in Winifred House; she had been dead for several hours and had apparently been 'savagely beaten about the head'.[22] The following year, Elizabeth O'Connor, a mother of three, was found strangled to death in her flat in Strafford House. In Rothschild Buildings, an elderly woman was raped and another committed suicide.[23] Excrement and rubbish littered the stairwells and tramps often broke into empty flats for shelter, occasionally bringing prostitutes with them for immoral purposes. The surviving tenants felt it necessary to plaster placards on their front doors announcing that their flats were occupied in an attempt to avoid the ever-present threat of a break-in: one man said, 'I stay in my flat guarding it against the dossers . . . I've got an iron bar and piece of wood ready'.[24] Playwright Arnold Wesker visited Rothschild Buildings in the autumn of 1973 as they were finally being demolished and, taking a photographer into the half of the building that still stood, ascended its staircase to get a bird's eye view of the scene, only to be confronted by an angry woman who made it clear that she was still living there.

The fate of Rothschild Buildings and its surrounding barrack-like tenements echoed that of Blackwall Buildings only a few years previously. Like their Spitalfields counterparts, when they were first built in the late 1880s the buildings, situated off Vallance Road, appeared an oasis of decency in an otherwise seedy area. By the late 1960s they had deteriorated sufficiently for them to be condemned, and many of the flats were already empty; some were commandeered by prostitutes who would also use the passageways with their clients, resulting in discarded condoms lying in the general refuse alongside used hypodermic needles.

The Kray twins once possessed flat 2, a grim hovel which John Pearson claimed was so awful that the last time he had witnessed anything so squalid was in a slum in Calcutta. When Pearson spent some time there in 1967 at the behest of the Krays, he was visited by two prostitutes, who were obviously familiar with the place – one remarked how dreadful the bed was. The flat was known by the Kray Firm as 'the Dungeon' and was later ransacked by police in their search for the body of Jack 'The Hat' McVitie.[25]

Other slums which would attract local media attention for their seediness were the model dwellings on Wentworth Street and Goulston Street, close to Petticoat Lane market. Wentworth Dwellings, Brunswick Buildings and Davis Mansions[26] may have been erected following the great drive of rebuilding instigated by the 1875 Artisans' and Labourers' Dwellings Improvement Act, but, like the other tenements mentioned, they too were in an awful state of repair by the 1970s. Conditions in Wentworth Dwellings were so bad that by April 1978 flats were infested with mice, bugs dropped from the walls, there was no hot water and residents were claiming to be killing sixty to seventy rats a week.[27] Flats were frequently broken into and meths drinkers congregated on the litter-strewn, unlit staircases, and a case of typhoid was even reported in October the same year.[28]

The East End was in terrible shape; the devastation of wartime air raids may have been three decades past, but the district was still littered with barren bombsites and decrepit houses which, owing to their unsafe condition, were officially empty. As we have seen, such dwellings became a target for illicit behaviour, particularly prostitution and drug dealing – and there was plenty of them.

CHAPTER 16

Culture and Conflict

... the stereotype of what a good patriotic British citizen should look like: it was White, short hair, and large boots. And if you didn't fit that stereotype, then you will be abused, whoever you are.

Reverend Kenneth Leech (2006)[1]

Whole streets lined with boarded- or bricked-up houses were a common sight in east London during the difficult 1970s, and Tower Hamlets was now going through a major housing crisis. Competition was fierce: waiting lists for council property were long, with many people in limbo, seemingly indefinitely, waiting to be relocated from homes that were about to be condemned or which should have been years before. Needy residents found themselves crammed into squalid rooms while properties around them lay empty. It was believed that in the mid-1970s over 3,200 council-owned properties were vacant, enough to clear the waiting lists at a stroke, but nothing was being done by a council that appeared to be at best inefficient, and at worst corrupt.[2]

Squatting was one reaction to the dearth of officially recognised available housing. One Bangladeshi resident of Tower Hamlets, Nooruddin Ahmed, recalled that 'People thought with some political mind, what a waste of resources, you let the people suffer in a polluting condition, yet you are leaving properties empty, this cannot be done. So people started squatting in to those houses, putting pressure on . . .'³ At this time, squatters were isolated in individual properties. Roads around the London Hospital such as Varden Street and Nelson Street were owned by the hospital; empty properties on them were commandeered on a random basis, eliciting complaints from the hospital that electricity was being used illegally. Pelham Buildings, a block of flats in Woodseer Street, was targeted in 1976; out of sixty available and usable flats, only six or seven were occupied, and so on Easter Sunday Terry Fitzpatrick and five or so other men broke in and commandeered the building. By the end of the year, it was unofficially home to 300 people, nearly all of them Bangladeshis.

The East End had always had links with ethnic Bengali and Sylheti peoples, as from the 1870s onwards a number had settled there after coming over as lascar sailors and cooks working for the East India Company. During the 1950s and 1960s, Bengali men came to Britain looking for work on the promise of a more secure future, and with its busy and predominantly Jewish clothing trade, where workers were always needed, the East End became a popular destination: 'They came expecting to work for a short time and to return home with the bulk of their earnings to be able to offer their families a better future in Bangladesh . . . It became clear to the Bengalee [sic] workers that the streets of East London were not paved with gold. Lonely men in an alien world yearned for their families . . .'⁴

At that time the Asian population was almost entirely male, working in the rag trade and sharing living space in cramped micro-communities, but as the Jewish population increasingly moved out of the area in the mid-1960s, Bangladeshis began to take over their clothing shops and factories. The Bangladesh Liberation War of 1971 led to a dramatic influx of refugees, predominantly from Sylhet, who now found themselves in the rundown district of the East End, where others from their original communities were already settled. Changes in the UK immigration laws tightened up the acceptance criteria, and from 1972 only those with already established families could settle in Britain, which resulted in the arrival of women and children joining husbands and fathers.

The Pelham Buildings intervention was a result of a growing need for housing for these new arrivals in the face of what was perceived as open racial discrimination in local government. Leading housing activist Terry Fitzpatrick explained:

[I] pointed out to the GLC housing department down in Aldgate, that there was a flat in Kingwood House which has been empty for a year or something. I was told it was reserved for White people. Kingwood House, the new Chicksand Estate, was at the time virtually all White apart from a few West Indians . . . We had no difficulty whatsoever in getting Bangladeshi people to squat. There was always a massive queue. There was always a huge list of people who wanted to break into places.[5]

In reality, many, regardless of ethnic background, were desperate to find proper homes; however, groups such as the Bengali Housing Action Group (BHAG) – *bhag* means 'tiger' in Bengali – cofounded by Fitzpatrick, helped politicise the Bangladeshi community, and squatting became a popular means by which to solve their desperate housing problem, as well as forcing the hand of local government to address the needs of its newest community. Although those finally rehoused had been found homes owing to an immediate need, immigrant families were accused of queue-jumping by those who claimed to have been waiting for longer. This became part of the catalyst for growing resentment. The immigration debate was a fierce one, and letters pages in the local press were filled with comment from an impassioned public keen to address the sudden changes. Some of the opinions demonstrated a nationalistic fervour verging on outright racism, the like of which would be unimaginable in a local publication today: one writer, from Robin Hood Gardens in Poplar, wrote that 'England is being invaded by races not of her own kind . . . it is not right that they should over-run this small country'.[6]

Blood on the streets

In 1975, a local community newspaper reported the case of Gerald Byrne, the publican of the Railway Tavern on Grove Road in Bow, who refused to serve foreigners, particularly black people. As far as he was concerned, 'they are all queers pimps and prostitutes'.[7] His barring of people merely for the colour of their skin evoked a protest; draymen were encouraged to cease deliveries, but, to the disappointment of the protesters, they sided with Byrne, even going so far as to say they wouldn't have blacks employed as draymen. It would become indicative of the growing hostility faced by non-white East Enders.

Early problems came from isolated racist thugs or small gangs. Attacks on Bangladeshi and other non-British people increased, as the term 'Paki-bashing' entered the vocabulary. And 1976 proved to be a bad year. The sheer number of assaults became difficult to ignore: a scouring of the local press of that time reveals attack after attack, all racially motivated. The East End was heading towards crisis. Three Asian families fled in fear from the Canada Estate in Poplar after being subjected to regular assaults and arson. A white woman was targeted by thugs because she was married to a West Indian; as well as obscene letters, she and her family had to put up with smashed windows, the vandalism of their car, and threats against the children. On one occasion, the woman's two sons were burnt when a car, dumped on the estate deliberately, exploded in front of them; their mother received a chilling letter afterwards, stating 'It is a pity it didn't kill them.'[8]

Rawal Singh, a 41-year-old building worker, was attacked twice in the space of a week near his home in Bow. On the first occasion, in Eric Street, he was beaten so badly that one of his eyes was damaged; the second time, as he walked along Bow Common Lane with the express purpose of avoiding the scene of the first assault, he was ambushed by a gang who beat him and hit him with bottles before one of them attempted to slit his throat. As his wife stood there screaming, nobody from the neighbouring flats was prepared to open their doors and assist, probably in fear of retaliation.[9] Another young family in Bethnal Green returned to their squatted mobile home one evening to find it in flames, the culmination of several weeks of continual threats; 'A man told us they are not having "Pakis" on the estate and they are going to burn us out.'[10]

Incidents such as these were sadly becoming routine, and the apparent indifference of the police to the growing violence drew a strong reaction from the Asian community. A meeting in Brick Lane's Naz Cinema was called to announce the setting-up of defence groups:

We can no longer stand by and see Asians stabbed and beaten up in the streets. We have documentary evidence of almost 100 assaults that have taken place in the East End this year. The majority of these attacks have been reported to the police, but many go unreported because Asians in the area know that nothing official will be done.[11]

The *East London Advertiser* reported that the Asian patrols were needed almost immediately. On the first night, a group of white men were spotted following two Asians up Commercial Street:

251

We drove our car ahead of the men, and as the two Asian men turned into Toynbee Street the six white youths suddenly ran at them. We drove up, jumped from the car, and they ran off through the grounds of the Holland Estate.

The patrols consist of four cars touring the most vulnerable areas. In each car there are about six men. We were stopped by police and searched for weapons on the first night out. There is a heavy police presence in the area.[12]

The extreme-right National Front (NF), founded in 1967 and invariably described as fascist and neo-Nazi, was also making a provocative show of strength on the streets of the East End at this time. It had found growing support during the 1970s and its all-white membership, reinforced by the popular skinhead youth movement, added significantly to the anti-immigrant violence. The Reverend Kenneth Leech, a lifelong anti-fascist activist and campaigner for social equality, remarked:

there exists in Inner London a highly vulnerable population of disillusioned, alienated and frustrated youth who are a prime target for exploitation by racist groups. As far as the East End is concerned, and I include Hoxton, they live in an area where mainstream politics seems to have betrayed them. For many, vandalism is the last available form of social action. The coming of the National Front into this situation of mass despair represents at one level, the expansion of vandalism into a political movement. It has given these kids an identity for the first time.[13]

The aggression manifested itself in schools: in July 1976, a run of attacks on Asian children took place inside and outside Daneford Street school, and in some cases, as in Vallance Road, Asian teachers were also assaulted.

There were even examples of white teachers verbally abusing non-white students.[14]

Interestingly, many of the most provocative gatherings took place at the Bethnal Green end of Brick Lane, where Mosley's Blackshirts had gathered forty years before; the demarcation line was the railway bridge across the street, north of which was a no-go area for anybody, not just Asians, who fell into the category of outsider:

On Sundays, particularly the Sundays was the worst day for racist violence; because that was when the National Front used to turn out in force and take a whole park or pavement, and they would abuse verbally and sometimes physically, not just black people, not just Bengali people but anybody who looked different, who didn't look as if they were National Front supporters . . . So people who looked like students would be abused, white people with long hair would be abused, people who looked as if they might be gay, how the people looked gay I don't know, but they thought might be gay, people wearing Anti-Nazi League badges, or almost any badges apart of the Union Jack badges – all were abused.[15]

Further attacks continued throughout 1977: NF supporters waged a vendetta against Bangladeshi squatters in Limehouse in May, patrolling the streets in minicabs and using their car radios to coordinate an organised search for likely victims. On three successive nights Asian men were threatened, racially abused and beaten in Aston Street and York Square, and in the latter case, a lone Bangladeshi man was set upon by a dozen white men who beat him with sticks and broken bottles, splitting his head open, an attack which required hospital treatment. Further attacks were deterred by a heavy presence of local residents and the police were informed; but as seems to have often been the case during this period, little was done, resulting in a complaint against the police for their apparent apathy towards investigating racist violence.[16] One family from Aylward Street in Stepney had suffered repeated attacks on themselves and their home throughout 1976 and 1977 which sometimes involved attempted arson. The police seemed reluctant to act, to the point where the head of the household began reporting the incidents directly to an inspector at Scotland Yard in the hope that something would be done. Sadly, the family were then visited by officers from Arbour Square police station who stated that 'if complaints were made over their heads again, nothing would be done to help them'. The family were even told to catch the culprits themselves and turn them in to the police. In another incident, following an attack on a boy by forty youths in Bishopsgate, the victim, who was left bruised and bleeding at a bus stop, claimed that police from Bethnal Green police station merely laughed and mocked him.[17] Life for many immigrants in the East End was becoming impossible and the threat of intimidation was everywhere, as John Newbigin, who worked with Bangladeshi youth groups in the 1970s, would later recall:

There was a good deal of open intimidation on the street, women and children being shouted out, people having bricks put through their windows, shit put through their letter boxes, clothes drying on the line would be cut with razors, cars would be damaged, incredible level of violence and the response of the police was absolutely pathetic. Very often the police did virtually nothing.[18]

The key year was 1978, when the increasing frequency of threats and violent assaults on Asian residents, despite the attempts to fight back with organised self-defence groups, came to a head. The turning point was local election night, 4 May. That evening, a 25-year-old mechanic, Altab Ali, who had recently arrived in London from Sylhet, was walking home after working late in a sweat shop on Brick Lane, when he was chased down the street by three youths. They caught up with him at St Mary's Gardens on Whitechapel High Street where he was attacked and stabbed by one of them. Ali managed to stagger to Adler Street as the three attackers ran off, but died in a pool of blood. The three youths involved in the murder were Roy Arnold of Limehouse and Carl Ludlow of Bow, both aged seventeen, and an unnamed 16-year-old mixed-race boy from Bow. It was the latter who stabbed Ali; when he was asked why he did it, his reply was chilling: 'For no reason at all', he said, adding, 'If we saw a Paki we used to have a go at them. We would ask for money and beat them up. I've beaten up Pakis on at least five occasions.'[19]

The murder of Altab Ali was seen as the final straw. Shams Uddin, a friend and the last person to speak to Ali before his death, said that 'The blood of Altab Ali made us realise we couldn't ignore it, or who would be next? We knew there would be no place for us unless we fought back.'[20] On 14 May, Ali's funeral procession took an unconventional route, from Adler Street to Downing Street via Trafalgar Square and Hyde Park, followed by upward of 7,000 Bangladeshi protesters demanding police protection from the increasing racist attacks. Ali's murder had inspired one of the largest demonstrations by Asians ever seen in Britain, and mobilised a downtrodden community who simply wanted to settle peacefully in Britain, free from ignorance and hate.

Tower Hamlets' proposed plan to house Bangladeshi families in specific tenements led to accusations that the council was trying to create 'ghettos', while anti-immigration sympathisers felt that the policy was favouring the Bangladeshis over whites in the struggle for homes. The politicised immigrant community vowed to fight these unhelpful policies and to combat violence with violence if necessary, leading to an upsurge in incidents involving NF supporters and Bangladeshi activists. On 11 June, numerous shops, including Taj Stores, the East End's oldest Asian grocery, and the Clifton restaurant[21] were vandalised as a mob of NF supporters, most of them from outside the borough, rampaged down

255

Brick Lane, smashing windows, hurling missiles and yelling abuse. The thankfully short burst of violence ended after groups of Asians and whites intercepted the mob at the junction with Hanbury Street, but out of the twenty rioters who were arrested, only three were charged. The damage, however, was extensive; one man had to have stitches and two teeth removed after a piece of rubble that had been hurled through his shop window hit him in the face. Confectioner Harry Fishman looked on helplessly as one rioter jumped onto the roof of his Mini, denting the roof and causing a window to fall out, and customers in the Clifton restaurant had to be locked in by the owners as stones crashed through the windows.[22]

That five minutes of chaos on Brick Lane, the most violent incident of many – invariably taking place on Sundays, when representatives of both far-right and far-left groups vied for dominance of the streets during the busy market period – became known in the local press as the 'Battle of Brick Lane'. Even the police, accused for so long of complacency when it came to racial issues in the area, felt compelled to act; 'We'll be bringing in more men,' said Chief Inspector John Wallis, the Metropolitan Police's community liaison officer; 'we're not prepared to let this sort of thing go on'.[23] The result was the setting up of Brick Lane's own police station in November 1978, a small property perched in the heart of the business community on the corner with Heneage Street, 'aimed at improving the police's local image and reassuring the local community of the force's willingness to help'.[24] It was staffed by a uniformed officer with the assistance of a police interpreter, as it was felt that language issues often prevented Bangladeshis with little or no English from reporting hate crime.

The turning point of the summer of 1978 was important, but it could never eradicate the violence overnight. One month after the murder of Altab Ali, Ishaq Ali, a 50-year-old restaurateur, was killed in Hackney, followed by the murder of a young Guyanese motor mechanic, Michael

Ferreira, in Stoke Newington in December. Occasional outbursts of racially motivated mob violence continued in the Brick Lane area, such as one notable incident in 1979 when a group of 200 of the British Movement, another far-right extremist political group, stormed down the street, smashing shop windows and overturning market stalls. But it became harder for the extremist groups to operate against the will of the increasingly cohesive local community and the larger police presence, and when a march of anti-racist demonstrators came face to face with NF supporters in the latter's stronghold at the top of Brick Lane in March 1979 – a confrontation that only a year before would have ended in bloodshed – sloganeering on both sides was the only thing that prevailed, and the incident passed without issue.[25]

CHAPTER 17

Fighting the Good Fight

Step into the wrong patch of land, wander into the wrong street, and violence can be swift and brutal. Often it is their own . . . that pay the price.

Nick Ryan, 'Children of the Abyss' (2005)[1]

The 1980s were a time of considerable change in the East End. The previous decade had seen the area at one of its lowest ebbs since the notorious late Victorian period, and its infrastructure was still under great strain as housing problems continued to bedevil the local authorities; streets were still encumbered with battered housing, and swathes of corrugated iron shielded undeveloped demolition sites. By the waterside, the East End's Docklands were now a skeleton, as over the previous decades containerisation at locations farther east had rendered these once tremendous feats of engineering and architecture obsolete. Between 1960 and 1980, all of London's premier docks were closed, resulting in an 8-square-mile slab of unused land, a once busy world of claustrophobic cobbled streets, lofty derelict warehouses, abandoned machinery and demolition sites. The impact on the local community was significant and negative, resulting in considerable unemployment levels, increased poverty and the social problems that went with it. The Conservative government's establishment of the London Docklands Development Corporation in 1981 was an attempt to reinvigorate the now obsolete district, offering potential businesses competitive financial packages to establish themselves in what was intended to become a serious rival to the City, a financial hub on a world scale. The policies of Margaret Thatcher's government were not popular with the local population, who could see nothing for them in the location of high-end financial institutions in their neighbourhood, bringing with them middle-class home comforts such as warehouse conversion apartments, leisure amenities and wine bars. The promise of new housing, looked upon suspiciously as beneficial only to the corporate-sector 'yuppies' pending their imminent takeover, cut little ice with the long-suffering working classes of Wapping, Limehouse and the Isle of Dogs: 'We keep hearing they're gonna build so many homes and so many flats and there's gonna be squash courts and swimming pools and all wonderful things ... all very well but it's meaningless to the average working class person round here.'[2]

The Battle of Wapping

Initially, local protests against such moves were noisy and militant but wholly non-violent affairs, but the arrival of News International, Australian tycoon Rupert Murdoch's dominant media empire, to Wapping in 1985 brought dispute and, ultimately, violence to the streets of the East End again. Admittedly, the trouble surrounding what has become known as the 'Wapping dispute' and the 'Battle of Wapping' had little to do with the homespun issues experienced by the East End citizenry as a whole, but it was certainly a product of the changing face of the area at the time and, ironically, along with the failure of the miners' strike of 1984–85, contributed significantly to the dismantling of the powerful union system that the workers of east London had been so instrumental in forging a century before.

At the new plant in Wapping, where Murdoch-owned newspapers such as *The Times*, *The Sunday Times*, the *Sun* and the *News of the World* were to be printed, new technology was to be introduced which would effectively put 90 per cent of the former Fleet Street type-setters out of work. A range of redundancy packages were offered but were rejected by closed-shop unions; on 24 January 1986 a strike was called, resulting in the dismissal of 6,000 employees, and News International forged ahead using workers predominantly from the non-closed-shop Electrical, Electronic, Telecommunications and Plumbing Union (EETPU). Union pickets assembled on The Highway in Wapping in support of the sacked workers, attempting to block shipments to and from the plant. Journalists defying the decisions of their own union, the National Union of Journalists, were bused into the plant in reinforced coaches. Police were on hand to clear the way for staff vehicles, shipment lorries and 'scabs' (workers who were defying the industrial action), and on some occasions, Wapping was 'locked down' as roads were closed off to prioritise the arrival of employees and material in the face of growing obstruction from the demonstrators. The protests grew more heated and began to attract outside activists who appeared to disregard the unions' call for a peaceful demonstration. The protest became polit-icised almost immediately, as the behaviour of Rupert Murdoch was seen as yet another attempt to crush unionism at the behest of the Tory government; Brenda Dean, leader of SOGAT '82, one of the leading unions in the dispute, nailed her membership's colours to the mast, declaring, 'We owe it to ourselves, to our families and to Britain as a nation to return a Labour government. That above all must be our priority. We must not allow anything to come in the way of that.'[3]

On 15 February, serious clashes between police and 5,000 demonstrators broke out: for the first time during the dispute, police bore riot shields, and mounted police were on hand to break up sections of the angry crowd. On that day of violence, eight police officers were injured; one, a 27-year-old sergeant, was taken to hospital with serious head injuries. Fifty-eight people were arrested. Police blamed the 'rent-a-mob' element of outsiders for sparking off unnecessary violence: 'We saw the classic example of honest well-intentioned union members supporting their cause being joined by diverse elements whose only interest was in causing as much trouble as possible. They were intent on disrupting business and assaulting officers.'[4]

Further disturbances continued as the standoff dragged on throughout the year. The effects of the dispute did not just manifest themselves in the highly visible clashes on the streets of Wapping, for the post-dismissal hardship took its toll on families who now struggled with poverty and depression; there were even cases of suicide. Andrew Neil, then editor of *The Sunday Times*, recalled that 'for 13 months my life was blighted by physical attacks, death threats, bodyguards everywhere I went and 5,000 screaming, violent pickets at the doorstep of my office every Saturday night.'[5] Tragedy struck on the night of 10 January 1987, when 19-year-old Michael Delaney was killed by a TNT lorry at the junction of Butcher Row and Commercial Road. The vehicle had just dropped off a delivery at 'Fortress Wapping', as the News International plant was now being called, and was spotted idling at traffic lights by Delaney and his friends, who were walking home after a night out drinking. They yelled at the driver, calling him a 'scab', and as Delaney slapped the cab door, the lorry began moving off, dragging him underneath its wheels and crushing him to death.[6] The driver did not report the incident until he had reached Heston services on the M4 in Hounslow. The inquest in April delivered a verdict of unlawful killing, which was overturned later through lack of evidence.[7] The 'Battle of Wapping' ended soon after, a depressing defeat for the unions and a triumph for what many on the left saw as the systematic destruction of the powerful union system in Britain. The East End was witness to one of the many nails hammered into its coffin.

Jack's back

'This is the year of the Ripper.' These words were penned by Deborah Cameron in the *Guardian* in March 1988 in reaction to the book *The Age of Sex Crime* by Jane Caputi, published the previous year.[8] Caputi's book ventured 'a feminist analysis of sexualised murder of women by men in modern Western society, a subject that is at once frightening and enraging', bringing up the case studies of a number of male serial killers, and including the East End's most famous monster, the centenary of whose first murders was fast approaching. In her piece, Cameron made it perfectly clear how she felt about the constant interest in the Ripper:

> The hopeless obsessive quest to unmask Jack the Ripper deflects our attention from what should be obvious: the extreme desires and fantasies which animate sexual killers are shared to some extent by a great many men, growing up as they do in a culture which promotes them, not least by its portrayal of murderers as heroes. If we want to do something about sexual serial murder, it's the culture and its attitudes that need to change.[9]

The latter part of 1987 and the early months of 1988 had revealed that Caputi and Cameron were not alone in their perceptions of and attitudes towards the Ripper story, and those who could foresee the resurgence of interest created by the imminent centenary took their grievances to the streets. But to appreciate the motivation behind the debate, a little context is required.

Undoubtedly, at the time of the Whitechapel murders they provoked a media sensation without equal, and yet, even before the killings had run their course, the mysterious predator – 'Leather Apron', 'Saucy Jack', whatever name was given to him – was already becoming the stuff of myth and legend. The absence of a confirmed identity automatically stripped what was effectively a depraved sexual murderer of any hard reality and thus, from the moment the papers hit the newsstands during that autumn of 1888, the Whitechapel fiend had become part ghoul, part maniac, and a malign, undying presence. This amply explains how the Ripper could metamorphose into literally anybody, whether factual or fictional, depending on the claims of any given amateur sleuth or scriptwriter. A mad doctor, a surgeon, a butcher, an escaped lunatic, a foreigner, a toff, a member of the upper classes or even the royal family – the Ripper has been them all and many more. The movie industry set in stone the classic and now ubiquitous super-villain costume of top hat, cape and little black bag, all immersed in the heaving melodrama of gaslight and fog, and turned the victims into attractive cockney dolly birds whose deaths invited little sympathy. April 1980 had seen the Ripper immortalised in a grisly waxwork tableau in Madame Tussauds' Chamber of Horrors, complete with a mutilated Catherine Eddowes and a despondent Mary Kelly leaning against the door of the Ten Bells pub, which proved to be highly popular.[10]

The Ten Bells in Commercial Street, Spitalfields, had earned the largely unfounded reputation of being the pub the victims drank in, or the one the murderer frequented when on the hunt, and so in 1975, at the behest of two East End businessmen, Bobby Wayman and Mickey Taheney,[11] the pub was given a Victorian makeover and rechristened the Jack the Ripper, with one eye firmly on the tourists. The walls were plastered with newspaper cuttings and Ripper-themed imagery, and the frontage sported two (admittedly attractive) hand-painted signs

263

listing the victims. The opening night in April was announced to great fanfare in the local press,[12] and nobody seemed to mind the change, probably because by now, for many, the Ripper was no more real that Sweeney Todd, Mr Hyde or Count Dracula. Naming a pub after such a notorious mass murderer is obviously unthinkable today, but the rebranding caused no ripples of dissent from any quarter, and the pub thrived. As the Ripper's centenary loomed in 1987, the then owners, Ernie and Yvonne Ostrowski, began selling Ripper-themed souvenirs and memorabilia, and even an over-priced blood-red cocktail called the 'Ripper tippler'.[13] This was the kind of culture that still predominantly surrounded the Ripper as his hundredth anniversary approached, and as well-timed books on the subject hit the shelves and guided tours of the area began to swell in numbers, it was apparent that there were some who most definitely felt that the subject had been exploited to such an extent, and for so long, that it had reached the point where nobody cared about what it really entailed: the horrific murder of vulnerable women on the streets of the capital, echoes of which persisted into the modern day.

Women's protest groups mobilised in earnest. A small collective became an almost constant presence outside the Jack the Ripper pub, collecting signatures for a petition to have the name changed back to the original Ten Bells. Kelly Ellenbourne of Women Against Violence Against Women (WAVAW) said it was 'outrageous that anyone should be using the historical and horrific murder of women as a tourist attraction to make money'.[14] Spokesperson Anne McMurdie of the recently created Action Against the Ripper Centenary group (AARC) reiterated that the trivialisation of the Ripper crimes ignored the fact that 'women are still being murdered and there are still men like Jack the Ripper',[15] making comparisons with the recent discovery of a woman's torso found dumped outside a women's refuge.[16] Some members of the public added their voices of support to the correspondence pages of local newspapers, making the point that the streets of the East End were not safe for women, and even the local Spitalfields prostitutes were interviewed, revealing the dangers of streetwalking a century after the 'autumn of terror'. Many still served their clients in the street:

> You get knives pulled on you and everything. If the market people hear you scream, they will come running out to help you . . . but the rest of the people around here they just don't give a damn. I've had a knife at me throat and I talked my way out of it. I know a lot of prostitutes has been murdered – a few of my good friends have been murdered. That is the chance we take.[17]

A number of prostitutes were, however, willing to take risks to benefit from the renewed interest in the Ripper case. The then derelict and deserted Durward Street, formerly Buck's Row, and the narrow alleyway of Wood's Buildings leading from it into Whitechapel Road (now closed), were known prostitute haunts and some were happy to pose for tourist photographs on the streets of Whitechapel to earn extra cash. More disturbingly, some clients wanted sex at actual Ripper murder sites:

> The punters actually ask for the sites of the Ripper murders by name. They seem to get some extra turn-on from having sex in the streets that they have heard about. The people are all ages, but most of them are City types . . . It's a way of earning an extra few bob. I usually charge £15 but it's double when I get these requests.[18]

In spite of this apparent sanctioning of the Ripper 'industry' by a minority of streetwalkers, the message was still very much against profiting from the commercialisation of the crimes. Unsurprisingly, the sentiments were also strongly feminist and at times became antagonistic towards men in general:

In the reporting of sexual murder, the media focuses on the women's age, appearance, dress, sexual history, marital status, class and race where these are usually irrelevant, yet gives no analysis of male sexual violence. We believe the media should not present these murders in isolation, but place them in a context of masculinity, male power and male sexual violence.[19]

A peaceful 'March against male violence' took place on 24 September 1988, organised by the WAVAW and AARC. Attended by 300 women, it set off from Bethnal Green Gardens and ended at 'Itchy Park', the local name for the churchyard of Christ Church Spitalfields. A minute's silence was held to remember the Ripper's victims, and the Ten Bells, which by then had reverted to its original name (but still displayed its Ripper paraphernalia inside), again became the focal point of yet another lively demonstration.[20]

The Ripper, at once a significant part of London's history, a universally recognised horror icon, and a mystery crying out to be solved, ensured that any campaign to stymie public interest and media exploitation was doomed to fail. Demonstrations again appeared outside an exhibition, 'The Jack the Ripper Experience', at the London Dungeon in the summer of 1993, where grisly depictions of murdered women upset campaigners from the Campaign Against Pornography (CAP). Picketing the exhibition, the women protesters encouraged customers to boycott the event, hoping that 'our presence will help eat into the profits they are making out of the murder of women'.[21] The name of the exhibition's restaurant, 'Ripper's Rapid Snacks', which served a 'Ripper steak sandwich', and its gift shop, 'Ripper Mania', which sold Ripper-branded paraphernalia such as T-shirts, mugs and bookmarks, only helped to reinforce the accusations made by groups like the CAP that this was little more than 'the glorification of a serial killer', which blatantly used 'the brutal murder of five women as entertainment'.[22]

266

The same year, publican Steve Kane of the Alma in Spitalfields found himself accused of using local funding to finance a Jack the Ripper 'museum'. Kane, who was already running Ripper and East End history tours from his pub,[23] was furious at the suggestion that he was going to use £12,500 from the City Challenge neighbourhood fund to set up a museum to the Whitechapel murders in the upstairs rooms. 'I think that would be a little bit gruesome', he said. 'No-one can deny he was part of Spitalfields, but not a very nice one.'[24] However, despite his denial that the pub was going to house a Ripper museum and the management's outrage that such a claim had been made, that is precisely what transpired.

Further attempts by local residents to curb the growing number of Ripper walking tours a few years later caused considerable debate in the local press. In the wake of the Docklands' redevelopment, which was by then fully realised, parts of the East End were in the midst of changes of their own: Shoreditch was opening up to new-media professionals, with trendy bars and shops materialising to cater for the young newcomers who felt at home in the gritty urban milieu. Spitalfields in particular had seen a transformation following the closure of the Truman Brewery on Brick Lane in 1989 and Spitalfields market two years later, and these available locations became the venue of choice for artists looking for studio space, or independent market traders dealing in antiques and arty ephemera. Brick Lane itself was now predominantly comprised of Asian restaurants and had benefited from local funding to improve the outlook and profile of the area, renamed 'Banglatown' in 1998, which made this once tatty street a popular leisure destination. The dilapidated Queen Anne townhouses in Fournier Street and neighbouring thoroughfares were now being bought by property developers and wealthy middle-class professionals with the aim of restoring them to their former glory, and it was these new residents who were up in arms about the tours in their neighbourhood:

The idea that the area will be regenerated by Jack the Ripper walking tours is rubbish. The people who go on these tours spend an hour walking the street being told in grisly detail about the murder of prostitutes, buy a pint in the sponsoring pub, then leave with the image of the East End as a seedy, dangerous red-light district firmly reinforced in their minds.[25]

Again, all attempts to curb such activities failed, partly due to the fact that such tours were not actually breaking any laws, and local councillors could find no legislation that would help them hammer out a regulatory licensing system or outright ban.[26] The problem was insoluble, and thus the walking tours prevailed and ultimately thrived.

Further troubles for the Bangladeshis

The Bangladeshi community of the East End had cohered by the 1980s and 1990s in the wake of the racist onslaught of the 1970s. Community groups set up for businesses, families and young people demonstrated that the newcomers were here to stay and had officially become part of the local demographic. The opening of the East London Mosque on Whitechapel Road in 1985 offered facilities not just for prayer but also for health and financial advice and local government and police liaison.[27] This was one of the first mosques in Britain permitted to broadcast the *adhan* (the call to prayer) from loudspeakers in its minaret, and almost immediately this caused a local controversy. Complaints were levied against the mosque on the grounds of noise pollution, and some of the correspondence received by the local press suggested that despite the successful immigrant integration, now into its second generation, there were still elements of intolerance. When one complainant was reminded that the twice-daily call to prayer constituted no more of a nuisance than the ringing of church bells, they replied, 'What bells? You hardly ever hear them these days. I'm sure I would sooner listen to the tolling of church bells than someone screaming out words I cannot understand and don't want to.'[28]

In July 1989, hundreds of Bangladeshis, in a show of unity not seen since the dark days of 1978, assembled in protest in St Mary's Gardens, scene of the Altab Ali murder, to demand police action to protect the Asian community from violence once more.[29] In May, Sao Miah had been kidnapped from his East End home, and was found a few days later tied up and burned to death.[30] The following month, a middle-aged Bangladeshi woman was seriously injured after she fell 53 feet, having either jumped or been pushed from a second-storey window as her flat in Sunbury House on the Boundary Estate in Bethnal Green was raided by masked robbers. Soon after, a most shocking murder triggered the outrage of a community and instigated the protest. On 9 July, a group of three men, two black and one white, broke into a flat on Flower and Dean Walk, Whitechapel, armed with a handgun and a knife. They made demands of a woman occupant, Asiaun Ali, who was four months pregnant, but grew frustrated when she could not understand what they were saying; one of the intruders beat her to the ground with the butt of his gun. Two children hid terrified under a bed in an upstairs room. Asiaun's husband Waris was also attacked by the men, receiving five stab wounds inflicted with a terrifying 10-inch blade. His brother Esmoth attempted to save him, but the men set about him, stabbing him in the chest, before running from the flat with a total of £1,000 in cash; Esmoth died on the doorstep in a pool of blood. Waris, severely injured, was taken to the London Hospital where a kidney was removed in an attempt to save his life, but after falling into a coma he failed to regain consciousness and died almost a year later. At the protest on the Saturday following the attacks, feelings ran high. Aodul Gaffur, vice-chairman of the Bengali Welfare Association, told the crowd, 'We have paid for the police with our money, we have as much right to aid as anyone else.'[31] Angry scenes developed as youths engaged in confrontation with police and riot teams were drafted in to contain the deteriorating situation; twenty-five arrests were made. Local businesses contributed a £5,000 reward for the capture of the attackers, but regrettably, no charges were brought against anybody for the deaths of Esmoth and Waris Ali.

In the aftermath of the killings, police believed they had uncovered a probable motive for the robbery. The Alis were constantly referred to as respected pillars of the local community and were involved in a *hawala*, 'acting as a kind of bank to local friends, collecting money from families in this country and sending it back to loved ones abroad'.[32] In fact, a *hawala* was often employed as a sophisticated banking and money-laundering system, sometimes used to finance drug smuggling, which could net the banker rich rewards: it was believed that Esmoth and Waris Ali could have been earning the considerable sum of £100,000 a year in commission.[33] The suggestion has been made that the Alis were involved in banking for some of the area's shadier characters, making their operation known to local Bangladeshi gangsters, and although the attackers were known to be black and white, as confirmed by a driver who had nearly run them over as they fled the scene, Asian miscreants may have been behind the robbery. Sao Miah, kidnapped and burnt the previous May, also ran a *hawala*. His death, too, remained unsolved.

Return of the right

Continuing incidents of far-right violence during the 1990s reflected the East End's inseparable relationship with politics and race.

The first was an attack in 1993 by the now defunct neo-Nazi group Combat 18[34] on the Freedom Bookshop in Whitechapel. The Freedom Press remains Britain's oldest anarchist publishing house, founded in 1886 by a core group of anarchists which originally centred on the radical Charlotte Wilson. The monthly *Freedom* newspaper was launched in October of that year, and was produced from a number of offices during its formative days; pamphlets, books and translated political material became the press's main output, and in 1898, under the guidance of Alfred Marsh, it found a permanent base in Ossulston Street, London, close by the British Library. The First World War resulted in the oppression of anarchist clubs and literature and anarchist principles became less popular; *Freedom* foundered, in part also due to internal conflict between its staff over their principles regarding the war, and it became an irregularly produced newsletter until interest grew in anarchism once more with the onset of the Spanish Civil War. The Freedom Press then bought Express Printers at 84a Whitechapel High Street in 1942, and the relaunched newspaper continued publication throughout the Second World War and beyond, with the headquarters shifting to 84b in 1968 after the former site was purchased by the Whitechapel Gallery.

The Freedom Press and its associated bookshop have continued on this site ever since, and it is these premises, hidden down the diminutive Angel Alley, which have become the target for far-right attacks. Several took place in the 1990s, when neo-fascists were again in conflict with anti-fascists in the East End; fledgling extremist group Combat 18, an ultra-violent successor to the National Front, were instigating renewed attacks on Asian shops in the area and the Freedom Press was also seen as an obvious target. The bookshop was attacked by representatives of the group on 27 March 1993, and the incident, which caused £5,000 worth of damage,[35] was described in considerable detail in the subsequent edition of *Freedom*:

Shortly after the Freedom Press Bookshop opened last Saturday, 27th March, the building was invaded by five young men wearing balaclava helmets and carrying long wooden truncheons, one with a spike . . . They smashed up everything smashable . . . They knocked

271

over the bookshelves . . . Before they left, the attackers sprayed 'C18' in large letters on the wall above the office door. Combat 18 is the name of a group describing itself as a 'fascist paramilitary organisation'. They left behind a bottle of petrol, which fortunately they made no attempt to explode. It was clear the attackers knew what they were doing. The operation was carried out with military precision.[36]

The shop suffered another break-in in May, when the laser printer and photocopier were stolen, and an arson attack on 4 June, which caused considerable damage.[37] In the latter incident, it was only the quick response by the fire brigade which prevented the flames spreading to adjacent premises, all of which, fortunately, were unoccupied at the time.

These incidents were part of a spate of attacks during 1993, indicating a worrying rising tide of extreme right-wing violence, which also saw a strike on the offices of the socialist newspaper the *Morning Star*, the burning of the 121 Centre in Brixton (also an anarchist bookshop), and a mass assault on the participants of a march in London commemorating the Bloody Sunday massacre in Northern Ireland in the 1970s, which resulted in the arrests of over 300 fascists.[38] Thankfully nobody was killed in the course of these incidents. The same could not be said for a series of nail-bomb attacks in April 1999, committed by neo-Nazi militant David Copeland; and one of these occurred in the East End.

The Brick Lane bombing was the second of three aimed at London's gay and immigrant communities: the first, in Brixton, targeted the area's sizeable black community and resulted in forty-eight serious injuries; the last bomb was detonated in the Admiral Duncan pub in Soho, a popular gay venue, injuring forty-eight people and killing three, including a pregnant woman. In Brick Lane, Copeland, targeting the area's Muslim population, had left a holdall containing the nail-bomb in Hanbury Street. A passer-by found it and took it to Brick Lane police station, which he found to be closed and thus left the bag in the boot of his car, which was parked outside 42 Brick Lane. The man was calling the police when the bomb went off, injuring thirteen people.[39] Scotland Yard's anti-terrorist branch declared, 'This is another vicious atrocity with terrorist impact. Early indications are that this is a similar device to that in Brixton. We are treating this as a racist offence.'[40]

Rumours of a possible racist attack had been circulating around the area for weeks, and after the incident, four far-right groups claimed responsibility. Oona King, MP for Bethnal Green, called it 'the ugliest face of racism I have ever seen'.[41] David Copeland, diagnosed with paranoid schizophrenia, was found guilty on three counts of murder and was sentenced to six concurrent life sentences, with the High Court ruling that he serve a minimum of fifty years. After the trial in June 2000, he was described as 'a disaffected loner, sexually confused and driven by homophobia, Nazism and deep-seated racism', who intended his campaign of bombings to start 'a race war across Britain'.[42]

Years later, old ghosts returned when the Freedom Bookshop was hit by an arson attack which caused irreparable damage to much of its stock. An appeal for financial help was made – the bookshop, unable to afford the fees, had allowed its insurance to expire – but there was a willing stream of volunteers who turned out in numbers to help clean up and salvage books and other paraphernalia.

East London massives

A sense of the existence of a sizeable Bangladeshi gang culture in the East End began to surface at this time, as the former minority, united against common problems such as poor housing, poverty and racial prejudice, became established and ultimately the majority. The proliferation of support groups, successful businesses and the sheer dominance of Bangladeshis in the East End had seen many of those problems reduced, though not eradicated entirely; however, the next generation, born and bred in Britain, did not necessarily feel such a strong connection with the traditions of their parents or the struggles of two decades before:

> the issues of elders were very much distanced from the youth. In that sense there . . . existed a paradigm between youth and adult issues. The large families and limited space of housing meant that youths would socialise more outside the house. As a second-generation Bengali, you are often brandished with family deeds making it harder to individualise oneself.[43]

For East End Bangladeshi youths, unemployment and boredom were a prospect for those unwilling to embrace the culture of their parents, or the prospect of working in the family business. Joining youth groups – aimed at giving young Bangladeshis a voice and purpose within the community – was a safe option, but in time Asian youths began to find their own identities by forming gangs.

One of the earliest was the Brick Lane Massive, formed in 1979 to combat the racist attacks of the NF, but they would later evolve to become one of the most notorious gangs in Tower Hamlets, and they survive to this day. Rana Mia was only twelve years old when he joined them 'for the fun of it', but he soon found himself involved in robberies, violence and drug dealing: 'The drug dealing and the money we got was to entertain ourselves and go places because we were from poor backgrounds.'[44] It was a common enough experience for many youths, who joined gangs seeking a sense of belonging and a solution to the challenges posed by bigotry and poor prospects. The Brick Lane Massive were quickly joined on the East End's streets by the Cannon Street Posse and others; conflict between these groups, when it came, could be the result of any number of circumstances, from feuds over drugs or a girlfriend to a question of honour or integrity, but often it was territorial. Journalist Nick Ryan, on patrol with Tower Hamlets' Robbery Squad, wrote:

Usually composed of young men between 14 and 25, the gangs 'claim' patches of territory, estates ... Each estate has its own 'firm', a local probation worker tells me. 'The firms start selling drugs and a lot of them are into fighting; it's all about their territory. That's where getting your "rep" comes from.' A survey has revealed that nearly three-quarters of all Bangladeshi primary-school children rated fighting as a friend's most important attribute.[45]

Fights that had once been carried out with fists and sticks were now involving 'machetes, knives, meat-cleavers and baseball bats',[46] and it was only a matter of time before the escalating violence of the 1990s gangs spiralled out of control. A turning point came in early 1998 when fifteen members of the Cannon Street Posse were ambushed in a park by a collective of fifty representatives from three other groups, the formidable Brick Lane Massive and the smaller Stepney Terror Posse and East Boys from Bethnal Green. Cannon Street Posse members were seriously injured in the assault; one lost the use of his arm after it was slashed open, another was left with his ear hanging off. A local community group, the Brick Lane Youth Development Association (BLYDA) was tipped off about possible reprisals from the Cannon Street Posse and, spurred on by the rumour that guns were being acquired for the task, a BLYDA representative and former member of the Brick Lane Massive, Abul Khayar Ali, persuaded the heads of all the gangs to get together and broker a truce. Nobody would agree on whose 'turf' to hold the meeting, and so they met on the neutral territory of the East London Mosque. The forum was a success: peace between the major Bangladeshi youth gangs was achieved and maintained through the use of mediation to resolve differences before disagreements became violent. One mentor said, 'We want to stop the cycle of violence with our generation and develop friendships rather than being rivals. We don't want the younger kids to have to live like we had to.'[47]

Nevertheless, gangs of youths of all creeds continued to flourish, their numbers increasing as different allegiances were forged and splinter groups made their mark: thirty-seven such collectives were recorded in 2012.[48] Whereas many gangs go undocumented, those with names set out to be noticed and acknowledged as a significant force, and many, as has always been the tradition, use their locale in their titles to stake their claim to their own unique part of the East End. Some defined themselves by region, such as the E3 Bloods, Globe Town Massive, Cubitt Town Massive, IOD (Isle of Dogs) and the Wapping Mandem. Streets were popular signifiers of territory (hence Devons Road, Tiller Road Boys, Brady Street Massive, Trellis Square Boys) and housing estates (Aberfeldy Massive, White Flatz, Brune House Boys, Ennerdale, Lincoln State Massive). It is such territorial claims that have always given rise to many of the disputes between gangs, whereby the infiltration of any group from one 'turf' into another's, for whatever reason, becomes a catalyst for violence. Sometimes, such insurgence can be put down to the settling of a score, sometimes just an act of provocation, but it can be serious business, and has been known to end in tragedy.

In one incident, Ischan Nicholls, a member of the IOD (Isle of Dogs) gang, was murdered in January 2010 when he and several friends drove into the territory of the E3 Bloods in what was considered to be an act of wilful provocation. His car was surrounded by members of the Bow-based gang in Parnell Road, forcing it to stop, and in front of horrified onlookers, the mob proceeded to smash the windows, chanting 'Bow E3 E3!' Nicholls was hauled from the car and dragged a short distance up the road before being beaten and stabbed; he died two days later from injuries to his abdomen and thigh. Forensics linked three men to the killing – Simeon Hunter and Joel Ofori, both from Bow, and Mully Tambwe from

Romford – and they were charged with the murder four years after the attack.[49] The jury at the Old Bailey trial cleared Ofori and Tambwe, but Hunter was found guilty on a separate charge of manslaughter, apparently showing no emotion as the verdicts were read out.[50]

The anxiety generated by the territorialisation of parts of the East End has also been felt by those who have no links with gangs. In 2016, teenagers from Stepney Green's Harpley Youth Centre staged a protest at the planned relocation of the facility from Globe Road to the Columbia Centre, a mere 500 yards away. The problem had little to do with the relocation itself, but more to do with the move to a different area; the original youth club, based in an E1 postcode, would be moving the short distance into the E2 district, and the young people feared for their safety. One teenager told the local press,

It's only 10 minutes away, but there's been a postcode war for 10 years. I feel unsafe going into E2. My mum won't let me. You don't even have to be part of a gang – it's just that you're from another neighbourhood. We don't like postcode war, but we can't ignore it.[51]

CHAPTER 18

A Battle of Wills

We have won unprecedented talks that show . . . our determination, energy and persistence . . . We can stop them.

Ian Bone, founder of Class War (2014)[1]

Drugs go hand in hand with gangs, in east London as much as anywhere. But the East End seems to act as a crucible, magnifying drug taking and drug dealing to significant levels. In 1993, drug raids in Limehouse and the Isle of Dogs revealed the shocking fact that children as young as eleven years were dealing in crack, heroin, cocaine, amphetamines and cannabis.[2] In 2005, Chief Superintendent Mark Simmons, police area commander, stated bluntly that 'Unemployment is high. Canary Wharf is an anomaly. This is one of the worst half-dozen boroughs in the country in deprivation terms, and it therefore has all the problems that you'd expect. The area has been called the heroin capital of the UK. We have significant issues with class-A drugs.'[3]

In 2009–10, 12 per cent of all 'notable' offences in Tower Hamlets were drug-related, at that time the second-highest rate in London, and a

Communities and Local Government Survey of the same period claimed that 61 per cent of residents were concerned that drug-related crime was a serious issue in the borough (across London generally the figure was 37 per cent).[4] Five years on, Tower Hamlets' drug crime rate had declined sufficiently to see it rank fifth in London, and although the number of people in the borough who felt that drugs were a serious problem had also declined, it was noticeable that almost the same proportion believed that alcohol-related crime and disorder were becoming a major cause for concern.[5]

This is not surprising considering the changes that have taken place in key areas of the borough, particularly Shoreditch and Spitalfields, which for many years have been absorbing much of the nightlife from the City after office hours and at weekends. Brick Lane, continuing to assert itself as a microcosm of everything that is the East End, is a key 'area of note' for the Metropolitan Police, and its 'night time economy' is directly linked to high levels of alcohol-related violent crime, making it a 'long term hotspot for violence in Tower Hamlets despite dedicated police efforts'.[6] The high density of visitors to the Sunday markets brings with it a multitude of problems and generates a significant proportion of drug use, stealing, sale of stolen property and theft, which account for a high proportion of the borough's crime figures. In 2013, the borough was recorded as having the second-highest rate of antisocial behaviour in London, after the City of Westminster, which earns that top spot as home to the clubs, bars and theatres of the West End.[7]

Prostitution in the East End remains high. In 2005, a police estimate stated that approximately 250 prostitutes, the majority being white British, were working the streets of Tower Hamlets.[8] A large proportion of those have substance misuse issues; of 100 new women seen by one particular drug treatment centre during 2008–9, 70 per cent were regularly involved in prostitution. In an echo of the past, in 2007, half of all arrests for kerb-crawling were made on Commercial Road, with most of the others being in Wentworth Street;[9] other prostitution hotspots were Commercial Street and Old Montague Street.[10] Violence against women and girls is also a significant problem in the borough, and it has the sixth-highest number of recorded sexual offences in England and the third-highest in London.[11]

In 2011, two residents of the Flower and Dean Estate in Spitalfields, Lily Islam and Shabana Begum, spoke out about the rising levels of anti-social crime and prostitution taking place in its midst. The estate had been seen as a successful development at its opening in 1984, and its self-contained community feel was instrumental in making it a safe place for families. But its insular layout would become its undoing as the neighbouring area around Brick Lane rose in popularity in the following decades. The estate's position between this now busy location and the main road of Commercial Street made it a shortcut for many revellers, as well as prostitutes and vagrants:

> Each morning, the mothers taking their children to school say they have to plough their way through the debris of condoms left after yet another night of prostitution.
>
> They also feel overwhelmed by having three major charities for the homeless on their doorstep drawing in more strangers.
>
> 'There are not gates or CCTV on our estate, just alleys, arches and dark corners,' Lily points out, finally losing patience after 15 years of it. 'We have young children and there's the youth centre – that's the danger with strangers loitering, urinating. We also get excrement. They're disrespectful to the families living here.'[12]

Consultations and meetings with other concerned residents set out prostitution as the first matter to be dealt with, and, with the involvement of local police, bail conditions which prevented prostitutes from using the estate were put into effect. These conditions had been used successfully to reduce kerb-crawling in Bethnal Green several years previously, and had the same effect on the Flower and Dean Estate; however, there was some criticism that the new rules merely moved the problem elsewhere.[13] To tackle this, activists from the estate allied themselves with Toynbee Hall's Safe Exit programme, which was set up to provide intervention outside the legal system to break the cycle of offending and arrest amongst prostitutes, as well as providing strategies for women to escape the sex trade and stay out of it.

Class war

As the City encroaches confidently into the western fringes of the East End, the traditional heated battles between political ideologies have manifested themselves yet again. One Commercial Street, a twenty-one-storey residential development above Aldgate East underground station, finally graced the east London skyline in 2014 after being abandoned by its previous constructors, John Sisk and Son, during its construction in 2008 owing to the property market crash. Five years later, Redrow completed the task and the 207 apartments (and substantial office space) were ready for occupation. In line with planning legislation, affordable housing was integrated into the scheme, this residence being given the name Houblon Apartments and its own entrance in adjacent Tyne Street, a narrow alleyway used occasionally by prostitutes and drug dealers. These effectively segregated entrances quickly became known as 'poor doors', and an investigation by the *Guardian* revealed that this was becoming common practice in new developments. One Commercial Street made it into the exposé:

> The brochure for the upmarket apartments ... on the edge of the City, boasts of a bespoke entrance lobby ... [with] a concierge, on hand 24/7 to service the every need of residents paying a minimum

of £500,000 – which only buys a studio flat – to live in this booming part of the city.

But the lobby is out of bounds to some of those who live in the building. What the brochure doesn't mention is a second door, with a considerably less glamorous lobby, tucked away in an alley to the side of the building . . . This is the entrance for One Commercial Street's affordable housing tenants.[14]

The resulting controversy sparked a lengthy protest in front of the main entrance: anti-capitalist group Class War, joined by other demonstrators from the area, staged weekly protests for nineteen weeks in 2014 and 2015. Although the demonstrations were boisterous and sometimes threatened to spill over into violence, they were predominantly without incident, although a few arrests were made. According to Class War, one woman was arrested on 2 April 2015 for allegedly putting a sticker on a window of the lobby and holding up a poster of a graveyard bearing the slogan 'We have found homes for the rich'. Another was arrested for standing by a banner emblazoned with the faces of all the major UK political party leaders over the words 'All Fucking Wankers'.[15] On one evening, an effigy of Boris Johnson, then London's mayor, was burnt. After eighteen weeks, the developers, Redrow, sold their stake in the property, and the new owners, Hondo Enterprises, agreed to meet the protesters. For a while at least, a truce prevailed.

Class War were back in the East End again the following year after the opening of a Jack the Ripper museum in Cable Street, which appeared to glorify the Whitechapel murders with grisly interpretations of a murder scene, a mortuary and a host of inaccurate exhibits. This was bad enough, but much of the furore over its opening stemmed from the fact that the project had been proposed to Tower Hamlets as a museum of East End women's history. What Cable Street got instead was a tacky exhibit which made things worse by selling Jack the Ripper souvenirs featuring the silhouette of the top-hatted gentleman, complemented by a splash of blood. In August 2015 an angry protest saw Class War joined by other anarchist groups, Fuck Parade and the Women's Death Brigade; demonstrators blocked the road, entered into heated standoffs with the police, damaged the frontage of the museum and left after breaking a window. Other less rowdy demonstrations ensued, but the founder of the museum, Mark Palmer-Edgecumbe, refused to bow down to what he believed was bullying. 'We are absolutely staying open. I've been a victim of bullying at school and the one thing I learned is that you should never give in to the bullies', he said. 'There's no way I'm going to give in to them.'[16]

These protests were as much about the perceived capitalism of the project, namely the idea of profiting from sexual murder, as they were the tastelessness of the subject matter, which had provoked the anti-Ripper protests in the 1980s; but the demonstrators on this occasion were far more vocal and aggressive. Martin Wright, veteran activist, declared passionately, 'It's not just the Ripper museum. That's just a symptom of the disease – it's the disease of Manhattanisation. We're competing with millionaires for everything – space, accommodation . . .'[17] At the time of writing, the Jack the Ripper museum has defied closure, proving again that no matter who tries, no matter how hard, nobody has managed to successfully suppress what Wright called, along with those other notorious east London characters, the Kray twins, 'a lurid footnote in the history of the East End'.

Afterword

An air of stagnation hangs over the whole district. Somehow one feels that Spitalfields is cursed, that this is unhallowed ground ... Even the bricks seem to give off an odour of poverty and vice.

Tom Cullen, *Autumn of Terror* (1965)[1]

The words of American journalist Tom Cullen, written in the mid-1960s, could just as well apply to many other parts of the East End of the time. Cullen was making direct reference to the Jack the Ripper murders and the locations that they made famous, in an era when many were still as they had been in 1888. Today, those places have either been redeveloped beyond recognition or wiped off the map of London altogether, and yet one is made constantly aware of their former presence as hundreds, even thousands, of people visit them every week on guided walking tours.

In 1956, the proposed demolition of the row of red-brick houses where the great Siege of Sidney Street took place attracted the opposition of those who wished to preserve no. 100 as a historical monument. Stepney Borough Council, as was, were having none of it, claiming that

284

as far as they were concerned there was no merit in retaining it at all. 'We do not consider the house historic or famous', said one councillor.[2] Yet the cluster of flats subsequently built farther down the street was named Siege House, joined later by Peter House and Painter House in honour of Peter Piatkoff, or 'Peter the Painter', one of the gang who organised the Houndsditch robbery of 1910, and who, after his disappearance following the siege, became a local folk hero. Down on Cable Street, a prominent mural, completed in 1983, commemorates the street's own infamous disturbance, and a Freedom Bookshop placard standing outside Angel Alley in Whitechapel reminds us that anarchist activism, such a part of the East End milieu before the First World War, still has a place here.

The Blind Beggar pub is a popular haunt for those curious to see the location of George Cornell's murder, and a few pictures on its walls remind customers of its gangland associations; curiously, the Kray twins rarely patronised 'the Beggars', preferring the intimate surroundings of the Grave Maurice further along the road, but this does not stop Kray tours from starting there, or regular Kray-themed parties and book launches from being held in its beer garden. The Carpenter's Arms in Bethnal Green, once a Kray stronghold, may not cater to the interested tourist in the same way, but it still displays a naïve portrait of the area's most infamous sons in the bar. In Wapping, the Captain Kidd pub is named after the notorious pirate, and the Prospect of Whitby, though no longer called the Devil's Tavern, still likes to remind us of the fate of some of its more disreputable patrons by way of a token hangman's noose hanging over the river. Sometimes the East End finds it difficult to bury its violent and crime-ridden past.

Not everything is so obvious. The house where the doomed Milsteins ran their restaurant and gambling club still stands anonymously on Hanbury Street, as does the rear of Henry Wainwright's warehouse on Whitechapel Road where Harriet Lane was so horribly dismembered.

But most places have gone altogether; Israel Lipski's lodgings have been rebuilt and Nova Scotia Gardens, where 'the Italian Boy' and others perished at the hands of the London burkers, exists only in the pages of the history books. Brilliant Chang's home in Limehouse, the centre of his drug-trafficking business, has long disappeared under mid-twentieth-century redevelopment, as has Green Dragon Alley on nearby Narrow Street where the notorious Spring-heeled Jack frightened a young woman into semi-consciousness. Ikey Solomon's jewellers in Bell Lane is so long gone that it would be impossible to know today exactly where it once stood, and there is no 'Tiger Bay' or Dorset Street rookery to steer clear of. Once to be seen almost everywhere, hardly any examples of the 1970s graffiti declaring George Davis's innocence survive.

But the East End does not need so many reminders of the friction and turbulence of its violent history, because these elements continue to this day. Sadly, homelessness has become a noticeable presence on the streets of London, despite still being punishable by law under the 1824 Vagrancy Act, and the East End, with its numerous homeless shelters speaking to the philanthropy of the past, is a notable focus. Hardly a convenience store front, tube entrance or cash machine is without a destitute man or woman begging for a little change. Some of them, when excessively inebriated or intoxicated by more than just alcohol, pace these busy thoroughfares engaged in heated argument or outright quarrels, and quieter streets are often witness to a loitering soul waiting for a drug dealer, followed by a furtive exchange and the screeching wheels of a boy-racer car. At weekends, revellers, many from outside the area, ignore Tower Hamlets' drinking control areas as they boisterously lurch from one pub or nightspot to the other, leaving a trail of discarded cans, bottles or even vomit in their wake. This does not appear to paint a pretty picture of the East End, and, admittedly, the seedy world just described is a concentration of the area's roughness, usually seen in specific areas; but all of those scenarios play out there, and they are occasionally unavoidable.

AFTERWORD

A random sample from several editions of the *East London Advertiser*, spanning the month of November 2016 (during its 150th anniversary), reveals a snapshot of the current range of crime in the East End deemed worthy of press coverage. The violence of West Ham United fans in recent matches leads to the expulsion of many from future games, and the possible banning of up to 200 more, in order to prevent clashes with rival supporters at an upcoming match against Stoke City.[3] A 16-year-old boy is fighting for his life after being stabbed in the neck outside All Saints DLR station in Poplar, the motive unknown.[4] A murder, that of Luther Edwards during a boxing night at Bethnal Green's York Hall, is still under investigation after three months, and CCTV footage showing two men has been released by police to encourage members of the community to volunteer information; however, the fact that witnesses are reluctant to come forward for fear of reprisals suggests gang involvement. A 15-year-old boy is facing charges of 'encouraging, preparing or instigating acts of terrorism'.[5] Poplar, Limehouse and Bethnal Green are being menaced by a robber who has targeted several properties, including two Islamic centres, and made his escape each time on a motorcycle. A police officer has been stabbed near the Bow Bells pub. (This story made wider headlines: the officer survived and a knife was found on Fairfield Road in Bow soon after, and a man was arrested for attempted murder.[6]) O'Leary Square off Sidney Street is the scene of a police drugs raid which has revealed a cannabis 'factory'; neighbours had been well aware that for some time the flat was being used for the dealing of drugs, including heroin. And finally, in a reflection of the East End's 'other' role as a major financial hub, analysis by Blur Group of the government's Annual Fraud Indicator reveals that a shocking £67 million is currently being lost by companies in the East End – including those in the Canary Warf financial complex – through procurement fraud.[7]

This may seem a modest selection of stories, but in one month's worth of local coverage, there was little else pertaining to crime in the

287

pages of the borough's main newspaper. This makes for a surprising contrast with the *East London Advertiser* of the past, where crime reports and serious local issues comprised large chunks of the paper and were reported unflinchingly; in fact, for several decades there was even a dedicated section called 'In the Courts', which briefly outlined a selection of cases heard in the local magistrates' courts on any given week, documenting small-time burglaries, thefts, frauds and assaults. In that one-month period of November 2016, there was little that demonstrated Tower Hamlets' high antisocial behaviour rate, or the continual police war on the drugs menace, or gang crime. What there was in abundance was news about local schools, community group events, charity functions, help groups, local politics, visiting dignitaries and, as this was an anniversary year, many choice stories selected from the *Advertiser*'s substantial archives. The paper's content was accentuating the positives of east London, showing that, despite the problems it still faces with poverty, housing and crime, it is actually a place where community is strong, which has many systems in place to support those in need of help, and where there are many willing to fight to make sure those systems do not fade away.

The East End can alternately be unrelentingly harsh, like a pounding fist, as well as deeply supportive and selfless; it can be shockingly ignorant and bigoted, and incredibly open and tolerant; it can be dirty and dangerous, and bright and optimistic; and it has bounced between all of these things with tremendous vigour since its earliest incarnation, and will, I'm sure, continue to do so. This book has chosen to reflect on one aspect of the East End's turbulent history, perhaps one with which it has all too often been associated, sometimes to the exclusion of all else – but there is still much to feel positive about. The Whitechapel Art Gallery, the Bishopsgate Institute and the local Ideas Stores offer today's visitor abundant leaflets and booklets pertaining to local arts and community events across the cultural spectrum. The East End is often the muse for students of the Sir John Cass School of Art (part of the London Metropolitan University), the fruits of which are sometimes displayed in the institution's window. Weavers Fields in Bethnal Green hosts the annual Boishakhi Mela, celebrating the start of the Bangladeshi new year, a colourful explosion of culture, music and food. Columbia Road Flower Market, close to where the notorious Nova Scotia Gardens once stood, blooms and thrives, one of many markets which still enrich the East End as they have done in various ways for centuries.

Unlike some parts of London, the East End's tendency to shift frequently on its cultural axes means that it is always facing challenges, and it continues to react and respond to them in its own positive or exasperating ways. It is London's own naughty and confused adolescent, fighting against a maturity that threatens settled conformity, yet, no matter how wickedly or infuriatingly it behaves, one knows there is good in it, and with a little smile or a wink, all is forgiven. Until the next time.

Endnotes

Introduction

1. Charles Dickens, *The Pickwick Papers* (London: Chapman and Hall, 1836–37).
2. Gardiner's was a clothing store, sometimes referred to as the 'Harrods of the East End' and a much-loved local landmark thanks to its prominent clock tower. It was closed down in 1971 and was demolished after a major fire caused extensive and irreparable damage to the building the following year.
3. Robert Sinclair, *East London: The East and North East Boroughs* (London: Robert Hale, 1950).
4. General William Booth, *In Darkest England and the Way Out* (London: Salvation Army, 1890).
5. When formed in 1965, Tower Hamlets amalgamated the former metropolitan boroughs of Bethnal Green, Stepney and Poplar.

1 Beyond the City Wall

1. John Stow, *The Survey of London* (Oxford: Clarendon, 1908).
2. England's first Articles of War, published in 1653, were actually written for the Royal Navy and provided a statute regulating the behaviour of all members of the navy. They became an Act of Parliament following the Restoration and were further amended in 1749 in order to tighten naval discipline; however, concerns over the severity of punishments resulted in changes in 1779. The articles remained in force until the 2006 Armed Forces Act.
3. Madge Darby, *Piety and Piracy: The History of Wapping and St Katharine's* (London: The History of Wapping Trust, 2011).
4. The location of Execution Dock has been variously given as the Sun Wharf building in Narrow Street, Limehouse, the Captain Kidd pub, or the Town

of Ramsgate pub, both on Wapping High Street. The Prospect of Whitby pub on Wapping Wall has a noose hanging over the river to mark one potential location. John Roque's 1746 map of London places the no longer extant 'Execution Dock Stairs' approximately where the Thames police station is today.

5. Leigh Yetter (ed.), *Public Executions in England, 1573–1868, Parts I and II* (London: Pickering and Chatto, 2009–10).

6. *The City of London as in Queen Elizabeth's Time*, based on a map of London attributed to Ralph Agas and engraved by John Strype for the 1720 update of *The Survey of London*.

7. Later Petticoat Lane and, since 1831, Middlesex Street.

8. This church, first recorded in 1340 and built as a chapel of ease to relieve growing demand on St Dunstan's in Stepney, was painted with a bright coating of whitewash made of lime and chalk: the white appearance swiftly earned it the name 'White Chapel', from which the area gets its name.

9. William Bohun, *Privilegia Londoni or The Laws, Customs and Privileges of the City of London* (London: Browne, 1702).

10. The act, passed by Parliament in 1539, was introduced to reassert the traditional Catholic doctrine as the basis of the English Church and enforce existing heresy laws. Formally titled 'An Act Abolishing Diversity in Opinions', it was also known as 'the bloody whip with six strings'.

11. James Anthony Froude, *History of England from the Fall of Wolsey to the Death of Elizabeth* (Cambridge: Cambridge University Press, 1858).

12. John Foxe, *Acts and Monuments, Vol. VIII*, ed. Josiah Pratt (Religious Tract Society, 1877).

13. The exact location is unclear. Two possibilities have been mooted by researchers: on the north side of Whitechapel Road, approximately where Whitechapel Underground Station now stands, or slightly further west, on the south side, close to the present site of the Royal London Hospital. Recent research for Crossrail suggests the latter location is more likely.

14. Christopher Philpotts, *Red Lion Theatre, Whitechapel* (Crossrail Documentary Research Report, prepared by MoLAS).

15. The octagonal foundations of the Theatre in New Inn Yard are thought to have been uncovered during archaeological digs in 2008. Similar investigations located the foundations of the Curtain, a square structure, at Holywell Lane in 2012.

16. Martha Fletcher Bellinger, *A Short History of the Theatre* (New York: Henry Holt and Company, 1927).

17. St Paul's Cross, or 'Powles Crosse' was an open-air pulpit in the grounds of Old St Paul's Cathedral where, since the thirteenth century at least, the 'folkmoot' (a general assembly of the people) had been held. It was destroyed by Puritans in 1643 during the first English Civil War. A new Paul's Cross was erected in 1908, although it has never revived its former use as a place of public preaching. Thomas White, *A Sermon Preached at Paul's Cross . . . in the Time of the Plague* (London, 1578).

18. John Northbrook, *A Treatise Against Dicing, Dancing, Plays, and Interludes, with Other Idle Pastimes* (London, 1577; reprinted for the Shakespeare Society, 1843).

19. John Dover Wilson, 'The Puritan Attack Upon the Stage', in A.W. Ward and A.R. Waller (eds), *The Cambridge History of English Literature* (Cambridge: Cambridge University Press, 1908).

20. W.H. Overall and H.C. Overall (eds), *'Plays and Players': Analytical Index to the Series of Records Known as a Rememberancia, 1579–1664* (London: E.J. Francis, 1878).
21. East London History Group, 'The Population of Stepney in the Early Seventeenth Century', *East London Papers* 11:2 (1968).
22. Stow, *The Survey of London*.
23. After 1777 it became known as the Prospect of Whitby, named after a ship that often moored nearby.
24. Melissa Hope Ditmore, *Encyclopaedia of Prostitution and Sex Work* (Westport: Greenwood Publishing Group, 2006).
25. Ruth Mazo Karras, *Common Women: Prostitution and Sexuality in Medieval England* (Oxford: Oxford University Press, 1998).
26. Francis Beaumont, *The Knight of the Burning Pestle* (first performed 1607, published 1613).
27. Ronald Hutton, *The Rise and Fall of Merry England: The Ritual Year, 1400–1700* (Oxford: Oxford University Press, 2001).
28. Letter from John Chamberlain to Sir Dudley Carleton, 1617, in John Richardson, *The Annals of London: A Year by Year Record of a Thousand Years of History* (London: Cassell, 2000).
29. Catherine Arnold, *City of Sin: London and Its Vices* (London: Simon and Schuster, 2010).
30. Samuel Pepys, *The Diary of Samuel Pepys* (London: George Bell & Sons, 1893).
31. Denver Alexander Brunsman, *The Evil Necessity: British Naval Impressment in the Eighteenth-century Atlantic World* (Chapel Hill: University of Virginia Press, 2013).
32. Tim Harris, *London Crowds in the Reign of Charles II: Propaganda and Politics from the Restoration until the Exclusion Crisis* (Cambridge: Cambridge University Press, 1990).
33. Richard L. Grieves, *Glimpses of Glory: John Bunyan and English Dissent* (Redwood City: Stanford University Press, 2002).
34. Melissa Mowry, *The Bawdy Politic in Stuart England, 1660–1714: Political Pornography and Prostitution* (Farnham: Ashgate Publishing, 2004).
35. Elizabeth Creswell was also one of the most successful prostitutes and brothel-keepers during this period, running bawdy houses in such diverse locations as Moorfields, Clerkenwell, Millbank and Lincoln's Inn Fields. Like Damaris Page, her brothels were patronised by the king and widely used by men from the royal court.
36. Pepys, *The Diary*.
37. William Jackson, *The New and Complete Newgate Calendar: Or Villainy Displayed in all Its Branches, Containing Accounts of the Most Notorious Malefactors from the Year 1700 to the Present Time, Vol. 1* (London: A. Hogg, 1795).
38. Ibid.

2 Economic Conflict

1. *Old Bailey Proceedings*, February 1723: William Summerfield (t17230227–11).
2. The name 'Spittle Field' originated from the Priory and Hospital of St Mary without Bishopsgate which was founded there by Walter Brune and his wife Roisia in 1197. It was commonly referred to as St Mary Spital, hence the later corruption.

3. Part of Flower and Dean Street still exists as Lolesworth Close; Thrawl Street survives in name only as a road winding through a housing estate, while Dorset Street was effectively wiped off the map by modern redevelopment in 2016.

4. *Old Bailey Proceedings*, February 1680: Frances Philips, William Harris, John Anderson, Benson (t16800226–7).

5. *Old Bailey Proceedings*, December 1682: John Hutchings, Joseph Redwell, Henry Paffet, Richard Kent and Thomas Williams (t16821206–11).

6. *Old Bailey Proceedings*, May 1682: Peter Anderson (t16830524–1).

7. Quoted in Frank McLynn, *The Road Not Taken: How Britain Narrowly Missed a Revolution, 1381–1926* (London: Random House, 2012).

8. Ibid.

9. *Old Bailey Proceedings*, February 1723: Jonathan Batt (t17230227–67).

10. *Old Bailey Proceedings*, February 1728: James Stagles (t17280228–49).

11. T.F.T. Baker (ed.), *A History of the County of Middlesex: Volume 11, Stepney, Bethnal Green* (London: Victoria County History, 1998).

12. Much of Turpin's legend, both factual and fictional, can be traced to Richard Bayes's *Genuine History of the Life of Richard Turpin*, published in 1739 immediately after Turpin's trial, which hurriedly put together the man's story to satisfy a curious public in the wake of his execution.

13. Jackson, *The New and Complete Newgate Calendar*.

14. *London Gazette*, 22 February 1734.

15. *The Life and Adventures of Dick Turpin* (London: James Cattnach, 1820).

16. Paul Donnelley, *Essex Murders* (Barnsley: Wharncliffe Books, 2007).

17. The pub, later known as the Old Red Lion, was rebuilt numerous times, the last being a nineteenth-century building which stood at the corner of Whitechapel High Street and Leman Street. It did have a plaque inside, commemorating Turpin's brief association with the pub, although much of its content is said to have been erroneous. Having been closed down for many years, the Old Red Lion was demolished to make way for improvements to the Aldgate East Underground station exit in *c.* 2004.

18. Contemporary press reports give the name Robert, which has been repeatedly used in subsequent accounts. Matthew King has often been called Tom.

19. *Derby Mercury*, 12 May 1737; *Newcastle Courant*, 14 May 1737.

20. James Moore, *Murder at the Inn: A History of Crime in Britain's Pubs and Hotels* (Stroud: History Press, 2015).

21. *Gentleman's Magazine*, 7 April 1739.

22. A pub, the Captain Kidd, was built into a former warehouse, near to the former site of Execution Dock, to commemorate the famous pirate in the 1980s.

23. Kevin Carpenter, *Penny Dreadfuls and Comics: English Periodicals for Children from Victorian Times to the Present Day* (London: V&A Publications, 1983).

24. F.H.W. Sheppard (ed.), *The Survey of London, Vol. 27: Spitalfields and Mile End New Town* (London County Council, 1957).

25. Samuel Eliot Morison, *The Oxford History of the American People* (Oxford: Oxford University Press, 1968).

26. 'Industries: Silk-weaving' in William Page (ed.), *A History of the County of Middlesex: Volume 2, General; Ashford, East Bedfont With Hatton, Feltham, Hampton With Hampton Wick, Hanworth, Laleham, Littleton* (London: Victoria County History, 1911).

27. John Strype (ed.), *A Survey of the Cities of London and Westminster, Vol. 2, Book IV* (1720).
28. M. Beloff, *Public Order and Popular Disorder, 1660–1714* (Oxford: Oxford University Press, 1938).
29. Thanks to determined campaigning in the late 1970s, many of these properties survive (now sympathetically restored) despite decades of neglect and misuse. Now listed buildings, some of the finest examples can be seen in Fournier Street, the heart of the Spitalfields preservation district. No. 18 Folgate Street, once owned by American artist Denis Severs, has become a museum piece, with various rooms decorated in the seventeenth-century style and tableaux that suggest that the French silk-weaving Jervis family have just left.
30. Strype, *A Survey of the Cities of London and Westminster.*
31. The building still survives today. In 1809 it became a Wesleyan chapel, bought by the London Society for Promoting Christianity Amongst the Jews, and ten years later it was converted to a Methodist chapel. In 1897, it became the Spitalfields Great Synagogue, reflecting the vast influx of Jews in the area, but by the 1960s it had become largely unused and neglected. In 1976 it became the London Jamme Masjid mosque (now Brick Lane Jamme Masjid), again reflecting the changing cultural makeup of the area. No other building in the East End reflects the ever-changing populace more than this.
32. The building of the new churches was funded by a tax on coal, a duty previously assigned to the rebuilding of St Paul's Cathedral after the Great Fire of 1666. Despite the Commission's title alluding to fifty new churches, only twelve were built outright, with a further seven being bought up and either rebuilt or remodelled.
33. *Manufacturer*, 15 December 1719.
34. Printed for W. Boram, Paternoster Row, London, 1719.
35. *Weekly Journal or Saturdays Post*, 13 June 1719.
36. *Old Bailey Proceedings*, July 1719: John Larmony and Mary Martoon (t17190708–57).
37. *Weekly Journal or Saturdays Post*, 13 June 1719.
38. *London Journal*, 13 August 1720.
39. *Daily Post*, 14 May 1720.
40. *Applebee's Original Weekly Journal*, 16 July 1720.
41. Correspondent of Sir Robert Walpole, quoted in George E.F. Rudé, *Hanoverian London 1714–1808* (London: Martin Secker and Warburg, 1971).
42. Quoted in James Peller Malcolm (ed.), *London Redivivum, or an Antient History and Modern Description of London, Vol. 4* (London: Nichols and Son, 1807).
43. Arthur Redford, *Labour Migration in England, 1800–50* (Manchester University Press, 1976).
44. *Caledonian Mercury*, 3 August 1736.
45. *Old Bailey Proceedings*, October 1736: Robert Page, William Orman Rod, Thomas Putrode (t17361013–5).
46. *Old Bailey Proceedings punishment summary*, 13 October 1736 (s17361013–1).
47. *Ipswich Journal*, 31 July 1736.
48. Christopher Haydon, *Anti-Catholicism in Eighteenth-century England, c. 1714–80: A Political and Social Study* (Manchester University Press, 1993).

49. The Weaver's Arms appears to be the most common title: there were three pubs in Whitechapel bearing the name (in Vallance Road, Spelman Street and Backchurch Lane), two in Bethnal Green (on Bethnal Green Road and Warley Street) and one on Hanbury Street in Spitalfields.
50. Bernard Mandeville, *The Fable of the Bees: Or, Private Vices, Public Benefits* (London: J. Tonson, 1724).
51. *Gentleman's Magazine*, 3 October 1763.
52. *Leeds Intelligencer*, 3 September 1769.
53. John Marriott, *Beyond the Tower: A History of East London* (New Haven and London: Yale University Press, 2011).
54. *Old Bailey Proceedings*, 18 October 1769: John D'Oyle, John Valline (t17691018–22).
55. *Derby Mercury*, 3 October 1769.
56. *Ipswich Journal*, 7 October 1769.
57. *Salisbury and Winchester Journal*, 11 December 1769; *Derby Mercury*, 15 December 1769.

3 Mounting Problems

1. Patrick Colquhoun, *A Treatise on the Commerce and Police of the River Thames: Containing an Historical View of the Trade of the Port of London . . .* (London: A.J. Monclair and Patterson Smith, 1800).
2. The London Infirmary was founded at Moorfields in 1740 and moved to existing premises in Whitechapel, on Prescott Street, in 1741. The site moved again to a completely new building on Whitechapel Road in 1757, by which time it had acquired the name of the London Hospital.
3. Sometime in the late 1700s Ducking Pond Lane was renamed North Street and finally became Brady Street in 1875. Ducking Pond Row had been renamed Buck's Row by the1850s and now survives as Durward Street.
4. Homann Heirs' 'Map of London and Southwark', published in 1736 shows no pond, but it is apparent in John Roque's map of 1746. By the time of Horwood's map of 1799, it had disappeared.
5. John Cordy Jeaffreson (ed.), *Middlesex County Records, Vol. 3, 1625–67* (London: Middlesex County Record Society, 1888).
6. Spruce's Island was a small tract of land located close to what would become the northern entrance to the Thames Tunnel, now part of the London Overground, at Wapping. Modern-day Prussom Street recalls the earlier name of the site, Prusom's.
7. E. Lynn Linton (ed.), *Witch Stories* (London: Chapman and Hall, 1861).
8. Anon., *The Witch of Wapping, or an Exact and Perfect Relation of the Life and Devilish Practices of Joan Peterson* (London: Thomas Spring, 1652; reprinted 1843).
9. Ibid.
10. Sir William Blackstone, *Commentaries on the Law of England, Vol. 4* (Oxford: Clarendon Press, 1769).
11. *Old Bailey Proceedings*, December 1769: William Eastman (t17691206–31).
12. *Ipswich Journal*, 4 May 1771.

13. *Old Bailey Proceedings*, July 1771: Henry Stroud, Robert Cambell, Anstis Horsford (t17710703–59).
14. *Bath Chronicle and Weekly Gazette*, 2 May 1771.
15. *Ipswich Journal*, 4 May 1771
16. *Reading Mercury*, 15 July 1771.
17. *Old Bailey Proceedings*, July 1768: Peter Conway, Thomas Cruise (t17680706–4).
18. *Old Bailey Proceedings*, January 1770: Peter Conway, John Chapman, William Paterson, John Milbank (t17700117–14).
19. *Oxford Journal*, 21 July 1770.
20. *Derby Mercury*, 17 July 1770.
21. *Derby Mercury*, 27 July 1770.
22. *Ipswich Journal*, 21 July 1770.
23. *Derby Mercury*, 27 July 1770.
24. Jonathan Wild (1683–1725) was the self-styled 'thief-taker general' a gang leader and thief who operated on both sides of the law. He exploited the legal system to his advantage, sometimes collecting rewards for crimes he himself had committed. His methods also included bribing prison authorities and blackmail, as well as retaining particular thieves as part of his operation, only to hand them over to the authorities and claim the reward when he felt they had outlived their usefulness. Ultimately, Wild's duplicity would catch up with him and he was charged with a number of crimes, convictions for which earned him the death penalty. He was hanged at Tyburn in front of a tremendous crowd.
25. The wall around the City was systematically demolished throughout the eighteenth century and its gates, although outliving much of the wall, were removed during the 1760s. Aldgate was dismantled in 1761.
26. [G.D. Yeats], *A Biographical Sketch of the Life and Writings of Patrick Colquhoun* (London: G. Smeeton, 1818); Colquhoun, *A Treatise on the Police of the Metropolis*.
27. Ibid.
28. *Saunder's Newsletter*, 17 January 1799.
29. *Oxford Journal*, 19 January 1799.
30. *Old Bailey Proceedings*, January 1799: James Ayres (t17990109–5)
31. Fiona Rule, *London's Docklands* (Hersham: Ian Allen 2009).
32. The London Docks were opened in Wapping in 1805; also in 1805 came the East India Docks at Blackwall, followed by St Katharine's by the Tower of London in 1828.
33. Edward Lloyd, *The String of Pearls, or, the Demon Barber: A Domestic Romance, The People's Periodical and Family Library* (1846–47).
34. Peter Haining, *The Mystery and Horrible Murders of Sweeney Todd, the Demon Barber of Fleet Street* (London: F. Muller, 1979) and *Sweeney Todd: The Real Story of the Demon Barber of Fleet Street* (London: Robson, 2007).
35. 'Revealed: The truth about the REAL Sweeney Todd'; *Daily Mail Online*, 19 January 2008.
36. Ibid.
37. Haining, *The Mystery and Horrible Murders of Sweeney Todd*.
38. Judith Sackville-O'Donnell, *The First Fagin: The True Story of Ikey Solomon* (Melbourne: Acland Press, 2002).

39. Camden Pelham, *The Chronicles of Crime: Or the New Newgate Calendar, Vol. 2* (London: Thomas Tegg, 1841).
40. *Old Bailey Proceedings*, 6 June 1810: Joel Joseph, Isaac Solomon (t18100606–89).
41. Hulks were decommissioned ships that were no longer deemed fit for regular use, stripped of their essentials and moored in ports to be used for storage and other purposes. Use of such vessels as prisons began in 1776 as a temporary measure, but ended up lasting for eighty years. Those in Britain were predominantly based at Chatham and Portsmouth, although some, such as the HMS *Prudent* and HMS *Savage*, were moored at Woolwich.
42. Pelham, *The Chronicles of Crime*.
43. Ibid.
44. Henry Mayhew, *London Labour and the London Poor, Vol. 4* (London: Griffin, Bohn and Co., 1862).
45. R.C. Sharman (ed.), *Australian Dictionary of Biography, Vol. 2* (Melbourne University Press, 1967).
46. Published by Joseph Knight (London: Paternoster Row, 1829).
47. *Old Bailey Proceedings*, 8 July 1830: Isaac Solomon, receiving (t18300708–140), simple larceny (t18300708–177); Sharman, *Australian Dictionary of Biography, Vol. 2*.
48. Geoffrey Nunberg, *The Way We Talk Now: Commentaries on Language and Culture from NPR's Fresh Air* (Boston: Houghton Mifflin, 2001).
49. Bryce Courtenay, *The Potato Factory* (New Hampshire: Heinemann, 1995). Judith Sackville-O'Donnell, quoted in 'Ikey stirs up storm 200 years on', Larry Schwartz, *The Age*, online at www.theage.com.au/articles/2004/07/13/1089694358255.html (accessed 20 August 2016).
50. Howard Mancing, *The Cervantes Encyclopedia* (Santa Barbara: ABC-CLIO / Greenwood, 2003).

4 The Growth of Infamy

1. Thomas De Quincey, 'On Murder Considered as One of the Fine Arts', *Blackwood's Magazine*, collected edition, Vol. IV (1857).
2. J. Ewing Ritchie, *The Night Side of London* (London: William Tweedie, 1858).
3. *Morning Chronicle*, 10 December 1811.
4. *Evening Mail*, 9 December 1811.
5. *Morning Chronicle*, 9 December 1811.
6. *Globe*, 9 December 1811.
7. *Public Ledger and Daily Advertiser*, 9 December 1811.
8. *Morning Post*, 10 December 1811.
9. *Bell's Weekly Messenger*, 22 December 1811.
10. *Globe*, 9 December 1811.
11. *Morning Chronicle*, 11 December 1811.
12. *Evening Mail*, 20 December 1811.
13. *Morning Chronicle*, 21 December 1811.
14. *Morning Post*, 21 December 1811.
15. *Evening Mail*, 23 December 1811.
16. De Quincey, 'On Murder Considered as One of the Fine Arts'.
17. *Morning Post*, 30 December 1811.

18. Lord Thomas Macaulay, 'Review of *The History of the Revolution in England in 1688* by Sir James Mackintosh', *Edinburgh Review* (July 1835; collected in Lord Thomas Macaulay, *Macaulay's Essays and Lays of Ancient Rome* (London, 1843)).

19. *Morning Chronicle*, 27 December 1811.

20. P.D. James and T.A. Critchley, *The Maul and the Pear Tree* (London: Constable, 1971).

21. *Morning Chronicle*, 1 January 1812.

22. *Evening Mail*, 1 January 1812.

23. Peter Linebaugh, *Ned Ludd & Queen Mab: Machine-breaking, Romanticism, and the Several Commons of 1811–12* (Oakland: PM Press, 2012).

24. Situated around Sun Tavern Fields, and commemorated by King David Lane which runs between Cable Street and The Highway (formerly Ratcliffe Highway).

25. 'The Lascars', from the *Sailor's Magazine and Nautical Intelligencer, Vol. V* (1843).

26. *London Courier and Evening Gazette*, 30 September 1813.

27. *Morning Chronicle*, 30 September 1813.

28. G. Benton and E. Gomez, *The Chinese in Britain, 1800–Present: Economy, Transnationalism, Identity* (New York: Springer, 2007).

29. Ibid.

30. W.B. Gurney, *The Trials at Large of Joseph Merceron, Esq.* (London: W. Wright, 1819).

31. Ibid.

32. Sidney Webb and Beatrice Webb, *English Local Government from the Revolution to the Municipal Corporations Act: The Parish and the County* (London: Green, 1906).

33. Melanie Barber, Gabriel Sewell and Stephen Taylor, *From the Reformation to the Permissive Society: A Miscellany in Celebration of the 400th Anniversary of Lambeth Palace Library* (Woodbridge: Boydell and Brewer, 2010).

34. Gurney, *The Trials at Large of Joseph Merceron, Esq.*

35. Webb and Webb, *English Local Government from the Revolution to the Municipal Corporations Act.*

36. Gurney, *The Trials at Large of Joseph Merceron, Esq.*

37. Neil R.A. Bell, *Capturing Jack the Ripper* (Stroud: Amberley, 2014).

38. Ibid.

39. Chris Hitchens, 'The Metropolitan Police Force: Its Creation and Records of Service' (The National Archives Podcast Series, no. 18).

40. This would later be reorganised when H-Division became Whitechapel and K-Division became Bow. J-Division (Bethnal Green) would be added in 1886.

41. In 1827 and 1828, William Burke and William Hare expanded the common method of supplying anatomical schools with cadavers by murdering their subjects as opposed to exhuming them. The law caught up with them and Burke was executed in 1829, although Hare managed to evade capture and his later whereabouts were never satisfactorily ascertained.

42. In 1808 the death penalty was removed for pickpocketing and other lesser offences. The Judgement of Death Act of 1823 gave judges the power to commute the death penalty, save for acts of treason and murder.

43. Nigel Wier, *British Serial Killers* (Bloomington: Authorhouse, 2011).
44. *Evening Mail*, 2 December 1831.
45. *Morning Post*, 3 November 1831.
46. *Morning Advertiser*, 4 November 1831.
47. *Examiner*, 20 December 1831.
48. *London Courier and Evening Gazette*, 3 November 1831.
49. *Old Bailey Proceedings*, January 1832: Edward Cook, Elizabeth Ross (t18320105-22).
50. *Cambridge Chronicle and Journal*, 13 January 1832.
51. *Examiner*, 18 December 1831.
52. *Pierce Egan's Weekly Courier*, 18 January 1829.
53. Baker (ed.), *A History of the County of Middlesex*.
54. J.J. Smith (ed.), *Celebrated Trials of all Countries, and Remarkable Cases of Criminal Jurisprudence* (Philadelphia: E.L. Carey and A. Hart, 1835).
55. *Old Bailey Proceedings*, December 1831: John Bishop, Thomas Williams, James May (t18311201-17).
56. Pelham, *The Chronicles of Crime*.
57. Ibid.
58. *Evening Mail*, 5 December 1831.

5 A Downward Slide

1. Anon., *Spring-heeled Jack: The Terror of London* (published in forty parts by the Newsagents Publishing Company, 1863).
2. Lionel Fanthorpe and Patricia Fanthorpe, *The World's Most Mysterious People* (Toronto: Dundurn Press, 1995).
3. Martin Coverley, *Occult London* (Harpenden: Oldcastle Books, 2012).
4. *Staffordshire Advertiser*, 24 February 1838.
5. *London Courier and Evening Gazette*, 22 February 1838.
6. *London Evening Standard*, 22 February 1838.
7. *Morning Advertiser*, 23 February 1838.
8. *London Evening Standard* and *Bell's Weekly Messenger*, 26 February 1838.
9. *London Courier and Evening Gazette*, 9 March 1838.
10. *Annual Register, Vol. 80* (London: Thomas Curson Hansard, 1839).
11. *Morning Post*, 13 March 1838.
12. *Examiner*, 25 March 1838.
13. *Kentish Mercury*, 17 March 1838.
14. *London Evening Standard*, 28 February 1838.
15. *Bell's New Weekly Messenger*, 4 March 1838.
16. Advert published in the *Morning Advertiser*, 7 April 1838.
17. Census data show that the population in 1801 stood at 103,871 and by 1851 had increased to 330,548.
18. Andrew August, *Poor Women's Lives: Gender, Work and Poverty in Late-Victorian London* (New Jersey: Fairleigh Dickinson University Press, 1999).
19. Rule, *London's Docklands*.
20. Gareth Stedman Jones, *Outcast London: A Study in the Relationship Between Classes in Victorian Society* (Oxford: Oxford University Press, 1971).
21. *Morning Chronicle*, 20 November 1841.

22. John G. Bennett, *E1: A Journey through Whitechapel and Spitalfields* (Nottingham: Five Leaves, 2009).
23. *Morning Chronicle*, 17 October 1850.
24. *London Evening Standard*, 1 January 1848.
25. *Kentish Independent*, 24 February 1855.
26. Nassau Senior and Edwin Chadwick, *Poor Law Commissioner's Report of 1834* (London: H.M. Stationery Office, 1834).
27. William Collingridge, *Report of the Medical Officer of Health for the City of London* (London: Charles Skipper & East, 1905).
28. Metropolitan Police, 'Registers of Common Lodging Houses' (LCC/PH/REG/01/001–10, London Metropolitan Archives).
29. 'Second Report from Select Committee on Metropolis Improvements', *Parliamentary Papers 1837–38, Vol. XVI.*
30. Metropolitan Police, 'Registers of Common Lodging Houses' (LCC/PH/REG/01/001–10, London Metropolitan Archives).
31. 'Second Report from Select Committee on Metropolis Improvements'.
32. James Greenwood, *The Seven Curses of London* (London: Osgood, 1869).
33. *London Daily News*, 14 May 1846.
34. *Old Bailey Proceedings*, October 1846: Anne Sinner (t18461026–2032).
35. *London Daily News*, 2 June 1847.
36. *Morning Advertiser*, 9 September 1848.
37. *Bell's New Weekly Messenger*, 5 December 1847.
38. *Old Bailey Proceedings*, April 1849: George Davis, Margaret M'Carthy, Ann Wood (t18490409–1003).
39. Henry Mayhew, *London Labour and the London Poor, Vol. 1: The London Street-folk* (London: George Woodfall and Son, 1851).
40. *Morning Advertiser*, 15 November 1847.
41. *Era*, 8 December 1850.
42. *Morning Post*, 1 February 1850.
43. Mayhew, *London Labour and the London Poor, Vol. 1.*
44. Ibid.
45. Metropolitan Police, 'Registers of Common Lodging Houses' (LCC/PH/REG/01/001–10, London Metropolitan Archives).
46. Wilmott owned nos 11, 12, 12a, 13, 15 and 18 Thrawl Street at various times; Mayhew, *London Labour and the London Poor, Vol. 1*; Metropolitan Police, 'Registers of Common Lodging Houses' (LCC/PH/REG/01/001–10, London Metropolitan Archives).
47. Howard J. Goldsmid, *Dottings of a Dosser: Being Revelations of the Inner Life of Low London Lodging-Houses* (London: T. Fisher Unwin, 1886).
48. *The Times*, 4 September 1888.
49. Samuel Rid, *Martin Mark-All, Beadle of Bridewell* (London: J. Budge and R. Bonian, 1610).
50. *Clerkenwell News*, 2 January 1861.
51. Benjamin Scott, Appendix III, 'Comparative Statement of Indictable Offences in the Metropolitan Police District and the City of London For the Eight Years 1858–65', in *A Statistical Vindication of the City of London, or Fallacies Exploded and Figures Explained* (London: Longmans, Green, Reader and Dyer, 1867).

52. *East London Observer*, 23 March 1861.
53. *Morning Advertiser*, 27 March 1861.
54. *Luton Times and Advertiser*, 6 April 1861.
55. *Old Bailey Proceedings*, 8 April 1861: Emma Augusta Papworth (t18610408–345).
56. *Lloyd's Weekly Newspaper*, 10 March 1861.
57. *East London Observer*, 10 August 1861.
58. *East London Observer*, 28 September 1861.
59. *East London Observer*, 21 December 1861.
60. Ibid.
61. *London Evening Standard*, 7 September 1863.
62. *Morning Post*, 7 September 1863.
63. *Glasgow Saturday Post, and Paisley and Renfrewshire Reformer*, 27 August 1864.
64. *Marylebone Mercury*, 20 August 1864.
65. *Thanet Advertiser*, 3 September 1864.
66. *Reynolds's Newspaper*, 21 August 1864.
67. *London Evening Standard*, 2 May 1862.
68. *East London Observer*, 3 May 1862.
69. *East London Observer*, 30 September 1871.

6 Cruel Beasts

1. 'Dwellings of the Poor in Bethnal Green', *Illustrated London News*, 24 October 1863.
2. *Bell's Weekly Messenger*, 31 January 1863.
3. *North London News*, 16 May 1863.
4. *Illustrated Weekly News*, 16 May 1863.
5. *East London Observer*, 26 December 1863.
6. *Clerkenwell News*, 23 June 1866.
7. 'Dwellings of the Poor in Bethnal Green', *Illustrated London News*, 24 October 1863.
8. *London Daily News*, 13 August 1866.
9. Ibid.
10. Sarah Wise, *The Blackest Streets: The Life and Death of a Victorian Slum* (London: The Bodley Head, 2009).
11. *Morning Advertiser*, 20 December 1864.
12. *Lloyd's Weekly Newspaper*, 6 December 1868.
13. *Illustrated Weekly News*, 27 June 1863.
14. *London Evening Standard*, 20 June 1863.
15. David Cannadine and David Reeder (eds), *Exploring the Urban Past: Essays in Urban History by H.J. Dyos* (Cambridge: Cambridge University Press, 1982).
16. Thomas Archer, *The Pauper, the Thief and the Convict* (London: Groombridge and Sons, 1865).
17. *Reynolds's Newspaper*, 18 August 1861.
18. Blanchard Jerrold, *London: A Pilgrimage* (London: Grant and Co., 1872).
19. *Morning Post*, 30 September 1865.
20. *Surrey Comet*, 10 April 1869.
21. *Shoreditch Observer*, 25 November 1865.

22. Charles Dickens, *The Mystery of Edwin Drood* (London: Chapman and Hall, 1870).
23. *East London Observer*, 2 November 1872.
24. *Sportsman*, 6 May 1868.
25. *East London Observer*, 11 July 1868.
26. Anon., 'East London Opium Smokers', *London Society*, July 1868.
27. Kay Van Ash and Elizabeth Sax Rohmer, *Master of Villainy: A Biography of Sax Rohmer* (Bowling Green: Bowling Green University Press, 1972).
28. Arthur Conan Doyle, *The Man With the Twisted Lip* (first published in *The Strand Magazine*, December 1891).
29. Oscar Wilde, *The Picture of Dorian Gray*, ch. XVI (first published complete in *Lippincott's Monthly Magazine*, July 1890).
30. Harold Begbie, *The Life of General William Booth, the Founder of the Salvation Army* (London: Macmillan, 1920).
31. The site of Booth's early meetings is commemorated by a statue on the Mile End Road, erected in 1979, which was joined by a similar statue of his wife, Catherine, in 2015. The former site of the tent is now Vallance Gardens, still an open piece of land, on Vallance Road.
32. Begbie, *The Life of General William Booth, the Founder of the Salvation Army*.
33. Ian Spencer Hornsey, *A History of Beer and Brewing* (London: Royal Society of Chemistry, 2003).
34. Cyril Arthur Edward Ranger Gull, *The Great Acceptance: The Life Story of F.N. Charrington* (London: Hodder and Stoughton, 1913).
35. Ibid.
36. Charrington, quoted in Ron Lee Davis, *Courage to Begin Again* (Eugene: Harvest House Publishing, 1988).
37. Paul Begg, *Jack the Ripper: The Definitive History* (Edinburgh: Pearson Education, 2003).
38. Gull, *The Great Acceptance*.
39. *East London Observer*, 16 November 1861.
40. *East London Observer*, 9 December 1865.
41. *East London Observer*, 3 August 1867.
42. *Bell's Weekly Messenger*, 18 June 1864.
43. *Old Bailey Proceedings*, 2 May 1870: Henry Parker (t18700502–399).
44. *Illustrated Weekly News*, 3 November 1866.
45. *Morning Advertiser*, 7 January 1869.
46. *East London Observer*, 17 August 1861.
47. *Tower Hamlets Independent and East End Local Advertiser*, 9 January 1869.
48. *East London Observer*, 26 November 1870.
49. *London Daily News*, 4 January 1877.
50. *East London Observer*, 13 April 1878.
51. *East London Observer*, 12 September 1874.
52. *East London Observer*, 17 February 1877.
53. Thomas Barnardo (1845–1905) began training at the London Hospital Medical College in 1866, becoming drawn into charity work in the area, particularly for impoverished and homeless children. He visited beer houses, small theatres and homes, distributing cheap bibles, and in doing so attracted a certain

amount of antagonism – like William Booth he was attacked on numerous occasions. Barnardo's gravitation towards the plight of children in particular stemmed from his involvement in the Ernest Street Ragged School, as well as his first experience of the 'lays' in Petticoat Lane where destitute children slept.

7 'Vulgarity, Rudeness and Immorality'

1. *Illustrated Police News*, 26 July 1890.
2. The Pavilion on Whitechapel Road was one of the East End's most popular theatres and was at one time known as the 'Drury Lane of the East' due to its massive stage and generous seating capacity of 3,500. Much of the Pavilion's success stemmed from its long-standing entrepreneurial manager, Isaac Cohen, who owned the theatre from 1870 to 1904. After his retirement its fortunes began to falter, beginning after the First World War when it briefly became a Cine-Variety Theatre. But its role soon changed again and for the last twenty years of its working life, the Pavilion became a Yiddish theatre before closing its doors for the last time in 1934. It was not demolished until 1961 and the site has remained empty to this day.
3. *The Times*, 14 September 1875.
4. *London Daily News*, 13 September 1875.
5. *London Evening Standard*, 15 September 1875.
6. Geoffrey Howse, *Foul Deeds and Suspicious Deaths in London's East End* (Barnsley: Wharncliffe Books, 2003).
7. Thomas Wainwright was given a seven-year prison sentence for being an accessory after the fact of Harriett Lane's murder. Alice Day, who had no knowledge of the crime at the time she was arrested, had been dismissed early in the case.
8. *Illustrated Police News*, 1 January 1876.
9. The *Illustrated Police News* was founded in 1864 and benefited from the often sensationalist nature of its highly illustrated front covers, a trend set from 1842 by the popular *Illustrated London News*. Appealing to a predominantly working-class readership, it would later go on to report crime and social issues with lurid gusto, and its handling of the 'alien immigration question' in the early twentieth century promoted xenophobic paranoia. It ceased publication in 1938.
10. *Illustrated Police News*, 1 December 1877.
11. *Old Bailey Proceedings*, December 1877: Joseph Millward (t18771210–95).
12. *Illustrated Police News*, 6 October 1877.
13. Ibid.
14. *Illustrated Police News*, 20 July 1878.
15. *East London Observer*, 23 August 1879.
16. Eric Partridge, *The New Partridge Dictionary of Slang and Unconventional English: J–Z* (Gurgaon, India: Taylor and Francis, 2006).
17. *Ludlow Advertiser*, 15 December 1894.
18. Daryl Harris, Russell Turner, Ian Garrett and Sally Atkinson, *Understanding the Psychology of Gang Violence: Implications for Designing Effective Violence Interventions* (Ministry of Justice Research Series 2/11, March 2011).
19. *London Evening Standard*, 3 March 1882.

20. Donald McCormick, *The Identity of Jack the Ripper* (London: Jarrold, 1959).
21. Wise, *The Blackest Streets*.
22. Ibid.
23. Goldsmid, *Dottings of a Dosser*.
24. Ibid.
25. *Derby Daily Telegraph*, 12 December 1885.
26. *Pall Mall Gazette*, 6 July 1885.
27. *Pall Mall Gazette*, 8 July 1885.
28. *Pall Mall Gazette*, 6 July 1885.
29. *Old Bailey Proceedings*, October 1885: Rebecca Jarrett, William Thomas Stead, Sampson Jacques, William Bramwell Booth, Elizabeth Combe (t18851019–1031).
30. O. Baylen, 'Stead, William Thomas (1849–1912)', *Oxford Dictionary of National Biography* (Oxford: Oxford University Press, 2004).

8 'The Social Cancer Spreading in Our Midst'

1. *Pall Mall Gazette*, 7 August 1885.
2. *Jewish Chronicle*, 18 March 1881.
3. John Klier and Shlomo Lambroza (eds), *Pogroms: Anti-Jewish Violence in Modern Russian History* (Cambridge: Cambridge University Press, 1992).
4. *Jewish Chronicle*, 6 May 1881.
5. William J. Fishman, *East End Jewish Radicals, 1875–1914* (London: Duckworth, 1975).
6. Charles Booth, *Life and Labour of the People of London, Vol. 1* (London: Macmillan, 1892).
7. *Pall Mall Gazette*, 7 August 1885.
8. *Poilishe Yidl*, 3 October 1884.
9. *Morning Post*, 30 May 1882.
10. *Reynolds's Newspaper*, 23 December 1888.
11. Hermann Adler, 'Report to the Home Office on the Problem of Prostitution in the Jewish Community', in James Knowles (ed.), *The Nineteenth Century, Vol. 23* (London: Kegan, Paul, Tench, 1888).
12. *St James's Gazette*, 26 August 1885.
13. *Yorkshire Post and Leeds Intelligencer*, 30 June 1887.
14. *Pall Mall Gazette*, 13 August 1887.
15. *Old Bailey Proceedings*, August 1887: Israel Lipski (t18870725–817).
16. *Pall Mall Gazette*, 19 August 1887.
17. *Illustrated Police News*, 27 August 1887.
18. *Evening News*, 24 August 1887.
19. *Morning Post*, 26 August 1887.
20. MEPO 3/144/221/A49301C, ff. 204–6 (National Archives).
21. *Old Bailey Proceedings*, January 1888: Henry Blaming (t18880130–250).
22. *Old Bailey Proceedings*, April 1888: Robert Matthews (t18880423–438).
23. *Old Bailey Proceedings*, April 1888: Elizabeth Williams (t18880423–458).
24. Ibid.
25. William J. Fishman, *East End 1888* (London: Duckworth, 1988).
26. *East London Observer*, 4 February 1888.

27. *Eastern Post & City Chronicle*, 18 August 1888.
28. *Eastern Post & City Chronicle*, 7 April 1888.
29. *East London Advertiser*, 7 April 1888.
30. *East London Observer*, 31 March 1888.
31. Walter Dew, *I Caught Crippen* (London: Blackie and Son, 1938).
32. Hayes (also described as Hames) had also been assaulted the previous Christmas and had spent a fortnight in the infirmary as a result; *Lloyd's Weekly Newspaper*, 8 April 1888.
33. This was at 18 George Street.
34. 'Inquest report', *The Times*, 9 April 1888.
35. Ibid.
36. *East London Advertiser,* 14 April 1888.
37. *Weekly Herald*, 17 August 1888.
38. 'Inquest report', *The Times*, 10 August 1888.
39. Report by Inspector Edmund Reid, 24 August 1888, HO 144/220/A49301B, f. 177 (National Archives).
40. Report by Inspector Edmund Reid, 24 September 1888, HO 144/220/A49301B, f. 178 (National Archives).
41. 'Inquest report', *Daily Telegraph*, 23 August 1888.
42. *Eastern Post*, 18 August 1888.
43. *Echo*, 17 August 1888.
44. *Echo*, 13 August 1888.
45. *East London Advertiser*, 25 August 1888.

9 The Nemesis of Neglect

1. George R. Sims ['Dagonet'], *Sunday Referee*, 16 September 1888.
2. Situated behind Whitechapel Underground station, it is now known as Durward Street; the name was changed in 1892 to avoid associations with the murder there.
3. Both Emma Smith and Martha Tabram had two children from their marriages.
4. *Weekly Herald*, 7 September 1888.
5. *Daily Telegraph*, *Irish Times*, *The Echo*, 4 September 1888; *East London Advertiser*, *Croydon Advertiser*, 8 September 1888.
6. *Star*, 1 September 1888.
7. *Sheffield and Rotherham Independent*, 1 September 1888.
8. *Star*, 5 September 1888.
9. At the time of the murder, 29 Hanbury Street was home to seventeen residents across three floors and an attic. The backyard where Annie Chapman's body was found was easily accessible from the front of the house, as the number of people living there meant that the front door was rarely locked, a fact known to local prostitutes who were often found in the house with their clients. No. 29 was demolished in 1970.
10. *Lloyd's Weekly Newspaper*, 9 September 1888.
11. *Morning Advertiser*, 9 September 1888.
12. Cullen received three months' hard labour for the assault on Betsy Goldstien; Paul Begg, Martin Fido and Keith Skinner, *The Complete Jack the Ripper A–Z* (London: John Blake, 2010).

305

13. *Star*, 8 September 1888.
14. *Eastern Argus & Borough of Hackney Times*, 8 September 1888.
15. *Eastern Argus & Borough of Hackney Times*, 15 September 1888.
16. *Austin Statesman*, 5 September 1888.
17. *Star*, 6 September 1888.
18. *Leytonstone Express and Independent*, 8 September 1888.
19. Report by Acting Superintendent W. Davis, 7 September 1888, MEPO 3/140, ff. 235–8 (National Archives).
20. *Irish Times*, 20 September 1888.
21. *East London Observer*, 15 September 1888.
22. *Punch, or the London Chivari*, 29 September 1888.
23. MEPO 3/144/221/A49301C, ff. 204–6 (National Archives).
24. Report by Sir Charles Warren, 6 November 1888, HO 144/221/A49301C, ff. 173–81 (National Archives).
25. The 'Dear Boss letter', as it is frequently known, was published in the press on 1 October and released on posters soon after, along with the text of a postcard, also written by 'Jack the Ripper', which was received on 1 October. This most infamous letter is currently retained in the National Archives in London (MEPO 3/3183, ff. 2–4).
26. CLRO Police Box 3.23 No. 395 (London Metropolitan Archives).
27. *Star*, 20 October 1888.
28. *Macclesfield Courier and Herald*, 27 October 1888.
29. Canon Barnett (1844–1913) became vicar of St Jude's in 1873, choosing the parish specifically to initiate social reform in the area along with his wife Henrietta. The Barnetts were instrumental in setting up Toynbee Hall, Britain's first university settlement, as well as the Whitechapel Art Gallery.
30. *The Times*, 16 November 1888.
31. In public grave no. 210752. Since 1996 there has been a small commemorative plaque marking the approximate place of burial. The graves of the Ripper's victims have been marked with small plaques or headstones.
32. *East London Advertiser*, 8 September 1888.
33. Public grave no. 49336, square 318.
34. *Eastern Post & City Chronicle*, 13 October 1888.
35. *Barking and East Ham Advertiser*, 24 November 1888.
36. *Evening News*, 13 October 1888.
37. *Portsmouth Evening News*, 1 November 1889.
38. *Atchison Daily Globe*, 21 November 1888.
39. *Evening News*, 21 November 1888.
40. *Daily News*, 10 November 1888.
41. Ibid.
42. The Pinchin Street torso case, as well as being tentatively associated with the Whitechapel murders, has been linked to a bizarre series of crimes known today as the Thames Torso Murders. Between 1887 and 1889, numerous pieces of women were found in or near the River Thames, enough remains usually being found to piece the bodies back together again, albeit without a head, which was always missing. One horrible find was made in the foundations of New Scotland Yard, which was under construction at that time.
43. *East London Observer*, 14 September 1889.

10 Black on the Map

1. *St James's Gazette*, 4 April 1887.
2. *Pall Mall Gazette*, 7 August 1884.
3. David Dixon, *From Prohibition to Regulation: Bookmaking, Anti-gambling, and the Law* (Oxford: Clarendon Press, 1991).
4. *Pall Mall Gazette*, 21 May 1889.
5. *Pall Mall Gazette*, 21 January 1889.
6. *Morning Post*, 6 September 1887.
7. *Illustrated Police News*, 30 November 1889.
8. *Morning Post,* 10 August 1889.
9. *St James's Gazette*, 4 April 1887.
10. Quoted in Todd M. Endelman, *The Jews of Britain, 1656 to 2000* (Berkeley, CA: University of California Press, 2002).
11. *St James's Gazette*, 7 April 1887.
12. *Illustrated Police News*, 13 February 1886.
13. Two days before the 13 November riots, the Metropolitan Radical Association had announced plans to stage a demonstration. Word quickly spread, and soon representations of the Home Rule Union, assorted socialist and anarchist groups, the Socialist Democratic Federation, and the unemployed had joined. Metropolitan Police Commissioner Charles Warren decided to put 5,000 constables on duty, with a battalion of Grenadier Guards and a regiment of Life Guards on standby, in case of trouble. It was estimated that up to 50,000 marchers converged upon Trafalgar Square and the authorities' heavy response inflamed the demonstrators. The violence was considerable and by the time order had been restored, 100 people had been taken to hospital with injuries, seventy-seven police officers were hurt, forty rioters were arrested and there were seventy-five complaints of police brutality. Two men died.
14. The match girls' strike of 1888 involved the mass walkout of over 1,400 young female employees at Bryant and May's match factory in Bow, in protest over fourteen-hour working days, poor pay, excessive fines and the severe health complications of working with white phosphorus. Such grievances came to a head in July 1888 with the dismissal of one of the workers, and the refusal to work began. The strike ended when the women's demands for fair conditions were met. The dock strike of 1889, widely considered a milestone in the development of the British trade union movement, saw a walkout by over 100,000 dock-workers from the Port of London over rates of pay, demanding the 'docker's tanner', or a guaranteed wage of sixpence per hour. The strike was accompanied by large marches through the East End.
15. John Henry Mackay, *The Anarchists: A Picture of Civilization at the Close of the Nineteenth Century* (Boston: Benj. R Tucker, 1891).
16. *The Times*, 21 March 1889.
17. *East London Advertiser*, 27 April 1889.
18. *The Times*, 26 April 1889.
19. *Star*, 24 September 1888.
20. *Pall Mall Budget*, 9 October 1890.
21. Ibid.
22. Sheppard (ed.), *The Survey of London, Vol. 27.*

23. Jerry White, *Rothschild Buildings: Life in an East-End Tenement Block 1887–1920* (Sydney: Law Book Co. of Australasia, 1980).
24. *Illustrated Police News*, 15 October 1892.
25. *Tamworth Herald*, 15 October 1892.
26. Charles Booth, *Labour and Life of the People, Vol. 1: East London* (London: Macmillan, 1889).
27. Ibid.
28. Charles Booth Online Archives, B351, pp. 23–4.
29. Charles Booth Online Archives, B351, pp. 123–4.
30. Charles Booth Online Archives, B351, p. 131.
31. Charles Booth Online Archives, B351, pp. 102–3.
32. Charles Booth Online Archives, B350, pp. 50–1.
33. *Scotsman*, 9 August 1897.
34. *Old Bailey Proceedings*, September 1897: Louis Lewinsky (t18970914–583).
35. *The Times*, 12 January 1899.
36. *Sheffield Evening Telegraph*, 24 January 1899.
37. *Dover Express*, 17 February 1899.
38. *Daily Mail*, 16 July 1901.
39. 'The Worst Street in London – Jack McCarthy's Reply'; pamphlet published in 1901, full transcription online at *Casebook: Jack the Ripper*: www.casebook.org/victorian_london/the-worst-street-in-london.html (accessed 13 April 2017).
40. *The Times*, 3 June 1901.
41. *The Times*, 20 June 1901.
42. *Old Bailey Proceedings*, April 1894: John Collins (t18940402–364).
43. *Daily Express*, 6 February 1903.
44. *Grantham Journal*, 5 January 1889.
45. *Cardiff Times*, 3 June 1899.
46. *Dundee Evening Telegraph*, 29 July 1899.
47. The north side of Dorset Street was demolished in 1928 to make way for the Spitalfields Fruit and Wool Exchange; the south side was cleared in 1963 in further market development. The whole area, including the rear of the Fruit and Wool Exchange, was again redeveloped in 2015, effectively wiping the former 'worst street in London' from the map.
48. *Shields Daily Gazette*, 2 December 1904.
49. Begg, Fido and Skinner, *The Complete Jack the Ripper A–Z*.
50. Crippen, an American homoeopath and medicine dispenser who was wanted for the murder of his wife Cora, had fled to Canada by ship with his mistress, Ethel Le Neve. Whilst in transit, the captain of the vessel, the *Montrose*, became suspicious of the pair and telegraphed the British authorities. Dew, after boarding a faster ship and intercepting the *Montrose*, was able to make the arrest. Crippen was the first criminal caught using the telegraph system.
51. Begg, Fido and Skinner, *The Complete Jack the Ripper A–Z*.
52. By Michael Caine in 1988's TV series *Jack the Ripper* and by Johnny Depp in the 2001 movie *From Hell*, respectively.
53. Dew, *I Caught Crippen*.
54. Ibid.

55. *Pall Mall Gazette*, 29 October 1891.
56. Tom Wescott, *The Bank Holiday Murders: The True Story of the First Whitechapel Murders* (Crime Confidential Press, 2014).
57. *Daily News*, 29 March 1882.
58. Ibid.
59. Jack London, *The People of the Abyss* (London: Macmillan, 1903).
60. *Reynolds's Newspaper*, 2 December 1900.
61. Begg, Fido and Skinner, *The Complete Jack the Ripper A–Z*.
62. *Lloyd's Weekly Newspaper*, 2 December 1900.
63. *Cornishman*, 6 December 1900.
64. *Old Bailey Proceedings*, February 1901: Barnett Abrahams (t19010204–156).
65. *Illustrated Police News*, 15 December 1900.
66. *Western Gazette*, 7 December 1900.
67. *Northern Echo*, 3 December 1900.
68. *Reynolds's Newspaper*, 2 December 1900.
69. *Western Gazette*, 7 December 1900.
70. *London Daily News*, 23 October 1901.
71. Ibid.
72. Frederick Wensley, *Detective Days* (London: Cassel, 1931).
73. Raphael Samuel, *East End Underworld: Chapters in the Life of Arthur Harding* (London: Routledge & Kegan Paul, 1981).
74. Ibid.

11 Gangs and Guns

1. Wensley, *Detective Days*.
2. George W. Cornish, *Cornish of the Yard* (London: The Bodley Head, 1935).
3. *Old Bailey Proceedings*, November 1902: Max Moses, Samuel Oreman, Barnett Brozishewski (t19021117–41).
4. *London Daily News*, 25 November 1902.
5. *Portsmouth Evening News*, 30 June 1904.
6. *Shepton Mallet Journal*, 1 July 1904.
7. *London Daily News*, 29 August 1907.
8. *London Daily News*, 22 January 1907.
9. *St James's Gazette*, 11 November 1904.
10. F.D. Sharpe, *Sharpe of the Flying Squad* (London: John Long, 1938).
11. Brian McDonald, *Gangs of London: 100 Years of Mob Warfare* (Lancashire: Milo Books, 2010).
12. *Old Bailey Proceedings*, June 1908: George Askew (t19080623–37).
13. *London Daily News*, 21 September 1907.
14. *Hull Daily Mail*, 6 January 1911.
15. The International Working Men's Educational Club was taken over by the 'Knights of Labour' in 1891. After being evicted from the premises the following year, the club went through several temporary locations before settling on Jubilee Street in 1906.
16. Bernard Porter, 'Piatkoff, Peter (fl. 1901)', *Oxford Dictionary of National Biography* (Oxford: Oxford Unversity Press, 2011).
17. *Western Times*, 26 January 1909.

18. *Shoreditch Observer*, 30 January 1909.
19. L. Muravyova and L. Sivolap-Kaftanova, *Lenin in London: Memorial Places*, trans. Jane Sayer (Moscow: Progress, 1983).
20. *London Daily News*, 2 June 1906.
21. *Nottingham Evening Post*, 25 January 1909.
22. Winston Churchill, *Thoughts and Adventures* (London: Macmillan, 1942).
23. Ed Glinert, *The London Compendium* (London: Penguin, 2012).
24. *London Daily News*, 5 January 1911.

12 Mob Town

1. *Illustrated Police News*, 22 June 1912.
2. Clearance of the Nichol district, declared a slum in 1890, began in 1891, and included the demolition of over 730 houses believed to have been occupied by 5,719 people. In its place was constructed the Boundary Estate, the London County Council's first large-scale housing scheme. Along with widened roadways and more commodious dwellings (deemed revolutionary in their day), a raised central area from which the streets radiated was constructed, using rubble from the demolished properties, which would later become the site of a small bandstand. Seen as an important early housing project, many of the buildings of the estate are now Grade II listed.
3. McDonald, *Gangs of London*.
4. Samuel, *East End Underworld*.
5. *London Daily News*, 18 December 1911.
6. James Morton, *East End Gangland* (London: Warner Books, 2000).
7. McDonald, *Gangs of London*.
8. Samuel, *East End Underworld*.
9. *London Daily News*, 27 September 1911.
10. *Tamworth Herald*, 30 September 1911.
11. *Old Bailey Proceedings*, December 1911: Robert Wheeler, William Spencer, Stephen Cooper, Thomas Taylor, Charles Callaghan, William Newman, William Andrews, Arthur Tressadern (t19111205–53).
12. *London Daily News*, 18 December 1911.
13. McDonald, *Gangs of London*.
14. *London Daily News*, 28 December 1911.
15. M.W. Oldridge, *Murder and Crime: Whitechapel and District* (Stroud: History Press, 2011).
16. *Old Bailey Proceedings*, January 1912: Myer Abramovich (t19120130–46).
17. *Dundee Evening Telegraph*, 4 January 1912.
18. *London Daily News*, 26 January 1912.
19. *London Daily News*, 5 April 1912.
20. *Shoreditch Observer*, 1 June 1912.
21. Two, St Boniface on Adler Street and the German Lutheran Church on Alie Street, still survive. The German Evangelical Reformed Church (St Paul's) on Goulston Street was bombed during enemy action in 1941 and the site is now occupied by the London Metropolitan University.
22. *Portsmouth Evening News*, 12 May 1915.
23. *Newcastle Journal*, 13 May 1915.

24. *Derry Journal*, 14 May 1915.
25. Ibid.
26. *Manchester Evening News*, 12 May 1915.
27. *Daily Mirror*, 14 May 1915.
28. *Western Gazette*, 14 May 1915.
29. *Daily Mirror*, 13 May 1915.
30. *Daily Mirror*, 14 May 1915.

13 Anti-Heroes

1. *Dundee Evening Telegraph*, 24 December 1915.
2. Samuel, *East End Underworld*.
3. *Dundee Evening Telegraph*, 24 December 1915.
4. This requirement for a gap in serving hours, a notable quirk in British life for many generations, would remain in law until the passing of the Licensing Act of 1988, when all-day opening became permitted.
5. *Dundee Evening Telegraph*, 24 December 1915.
6. *Daily Mirror*, 25 February 1916.
7. *Daily Mirror*, 6 September 1917.
8. *Daily Mirror*, 10 October 1918.
9. *Western Times*, 29 October 1918.
10. *Aberdeen Evening Express*, 19 July 1917.
11. *Shepton Mallet Journal*, 21 May 1915.
12. *Daily Mirror*, 25 September 1917.
13. James Denman and Paul McDonald, 'Unemployment Statistics from 1881 to the Present Day', *Labour Market Trends*, January 1996.
14. Sean Martin, 'WWI 100th Anniversary: How the Great War Led to a Culture of Organised Crime in the UK', *International Business Times*, 4 August 2014.
15. *Daily Mirror*, 11 April 1924.
16. *Dundee Evening Telegraph*, 10 April 1924.
17. *Daily Mirror*, 11 April 1924.
18. *The Times*, 25 April 1922.
19. Rebecca West, quoted in Marek Kohn, *Dope Girls: The Birth of the British Drug Underground* (London: Granta Books, 2013).
20. Ibid.
21. *Sunday Post*, 13 April 1924.
22. *Western Daily Press*, 11 April 1924.
23. Morton, *East End Gangland*.
24. McDonald, *Gangs of London*.
25. Reggie Kray and Ronnie Kray with Fred Dinenage, *Our Story* (London: Sidgwick and Jackson, 1988).
26. Lenny McLean (1949–98), known as 'The Guv'nor', as well as being a fighter, minder, criminal and businessman, also had a minor acting career in film and television. His best-known role was 'Barry the Baptist' in Guy Ritchie's popular 1998 gangster film *Lock, Stock and Two Smoking Barrels*.
27. Lenny McLean with Peter Gerrard, *The Guv'nor* (London: John Blake, 2003).
28. Bryan Magee, *Clouds of Glory: A Hoxton Childhood* (London: Pimlico, 2004).

311

29. This story was told to the author by long-term Bethnal Green resident Dennis Ellam in 2015.
30. The author's great-uncle, Bert Clark, knew Newman in his heyday and the darts story is one of several that were passed down through the family. The incident in the butcher's shop was apparently witnessed by the author's grandfather.
31. Kray and Kray with Dinenage, *Our Story*.
32. Jacob Comer's parents, originally Comacho, had first renamed themselves Colmore, and later Comer, in order to integrate into English society, a not unusual decision made by many Jewish immigrant families in Britain.
33. Morton, *East End Gangland*.
34. *Evening Standard*, 6 January 1986.
35. G.D.H. Cole and M.I. Cole, *The Condition of Britain* (London: Victor Gollancz, 1937).
36. *Jewish Chronicle*, 16 April 1937.
37. Marriott, *Beyond the Tower*.
38. *Western Daily Press*, 1 September 1936.
39. *Yorkshire Post and Leeds Intelligencer*, 30 September 1936.
40. *Yorkshire Evening Post*, 3 October 1936.
41. *Northern Whig*, 5 October 1936.
42. *Sheffield Independent*, 5 October 1936.
43. The act also banned the wearing of uniforms at political rallies or marches.
44. *Gloucestershire Echo*, 13 October 1936.
45. *Nottingham Evening Post*, 23 November 1936.
46. *Gloucestershire Echo*, 4 February 1941.
47. *Express and Echo*, 25 November 1940.
48. *Hackney Gazette*, 22 March 1946.
49. *Daily Mirror*, 28 September 1940.
50. *Daily Mirror*, 8 May 1940.
51. *Derby Daily Telegraph*, 15 January 1943.
52. *Daily Mirror*, 23 December 1940.
53. *Evening Despatch*, 22 May 1943.
54. *The Times*, 26 November 1941.
55. *People*, 15 December 1940.
56. Frankie Fraser (1923–2014) was a south London gangster most famous for being part of the gang run by Eddie and Charlie Richardson in the 1950s and 1960s. Certified insane on two separate occasions (hence the nickname), Fraser spent a total of forty-two years in prison.
57. Interview with Frankie Fraser, *The Krays and Fred Dinenage*, Talent TV South (broadcast 15 March 2010).

14 Gangland Legend

1. Kray and Kray with Dinenage, *Our Story*.
2. John Bennett, *Krayology* (London: Mango Books, 2016).
3. James Morton and Jerry Parker, *Gangland Bosses: The Lives of Jack Spot and Billy Hill* (London: Sphere, 2005).
4. Billy Hill (1911–84) was born in Fitzrovia, west London, into an established criminal family. He started out as a house burglar in the 1920s before

gravitating towards more aggressive 'smash and grab' raids on jewellers and furriers. He made a living during the war by working in the black market and supplying forged documents to deserters, and later fled to South Africa following a charge for burglary. Extradited back to England he found himself imprisoned for another robbery and afterwards met his wife, Gypsy. In the 1960s he was involved in highly organised gambling scams which made him enough money to retire to Tangier, where he and Gypsy opened a bar, Churchill's, in 1966.

5. Phyllis Young, 'Report of Investigation into Conditions of the Coloured Colonial Men in the Stepney Area' (London: Public Record Office, March 1944).

6. Ibid.

7. *East London Advertiser*, 31 October 1947.

8. James Morton, *East End Gangland* (London: Little, Brown, 2000).

9. *East London Advertiser*, 20 June 1958.

10. Ibid.

11. *East London Advertiser*, 21 February 1958.

12. *East London Advertiser*, 20 June 1958.

13. *East London Advertiser*, 27 June 1958.

14. Funded by Bernhard Baron, a cigarette manufacturer, the settlement opened in 1929 to cater for Jewish needs at all stages of life. Amongst the services it offered were a clinic for expectant mothers, a kindergarten, several youth clubs, religion classes, free legal advice and a burial scheme; it is now private flats. Berner Street was renamed Henriques Street in 1962 on the death of Sir Basil Henriques, the Jewish magistrate and philanthropist who lived at the settlement with his wife.

15. *East London Advertiser*, 18 July 1958.

16. *East London Advertiser*, 7 November 1958.

17. Sukhdev Sandhu, 'Come Hungry, Leave Edgy', *London Review of Books* (February 2003).

18. Interview with the author, published in Bennett, *E1*.

19. Charles and Violet moved, along with their three young sons, from Hoxton to 178 Vallance Road, Bethnal Green, in 1939. Close by lived Violet's parents and by the end of the war, her siblings, Joe, May and Rose, were occupying the neighbouring houses, giving this now redeveloped section of Vallance Road the local nickname of 'Lee Street', or 'Lee Corner.' It would be the family home until 1967.

20. Reggie was arrested at the age of twelve for firing an air-rifle from the window of a moving train; both twins received two-year suspended sentences at Old Street Magistrates' Court for assaulting a police officer in November 1950.

21. Their time in the army included a month in Wormwood Scrubs for assaulting a police officer and eight months in Shepton Mallet military prison. Additionally they spent long periods in detention barracks and are often cited as two of the last prisoners to be held at the Tower of London.

22. John Pearson, *The Profession of Violence* (London: Weidenfeld & Nicolson, 1972).

23. The incident was portrayed in the 1990 film *The Krays* (dir. Peter Medak), with Ronnie (Gary Kemp) wielding the sword. In reality, Ronnie did not drive the

sword through a man's hand as depicted in the movie, but merely chased the gang from the club with it, attacking their car as they attempted to drive away.

24. *News Chronicle*, 28 May 1958.
25. *Daily Telegraph*, 28 May 1958.
26. Blasker died in 1974; Blasker Walk on the Isle of Dogs was named after him following a campaign by local residents. He was highly popular with his patients and an affectionate overview of his career can be found online at island history.wordpress.com/2014/02/16/lead-kindly-light (accessed 17 April 2017).
27. Readers may recall that this was once the notorious Dorset Street; the Pen Club was housed in a former common lodging house.
28. Morton, *East End Gangland*.
29. *East London Advertiser*, 11 March 1960.
30. MEPO 2/9974, f. 1C (National Archives).
31. Report by Detective Superintendent Tommy Butler, 6 May 1960, MEPO 2/9974, f. 3A (National Archives).
32. Reggie Kray, *Born Fighter* (London: Arrow Books, 1991).
33. The Betting and Gaming Act came into force on 1 January 1961, allowing gambling for small sums, and from May 1961 betting shops were allowed to open. The result was the expansion of licensed betting in the UK, the installation of casinos in many clubs, the arrival of bingo halls and a downturn in the popularity of greyhound racing.
34. The royal couple had been due to attend the premiere of the film *Sparrows Can't Sing* at the Odeon Mile End Road in 1963, which was followed by an after-show party at the Kentucky, organised by the Krays. Princess Margaret apparently had the flu and so did not attend, but Snowdon was at the screening.
35. For a much more detailed account of the Boothby affair, see John Pearson, *Notorious: The Immortal Legend of the Kray Twins* (London: Century, 2010).
36. McCowan, the son of Sir David James Cargill McCowan, 2nd baronet, was unable to prove his succession to the title on his father's death and was known as 'presumed 3rd baronet'.
37. Statement by Hew McCowan taken at City Road police station, 6 January 1965, MEPO 2/10763, ff. 1–11 (National Archives).
38. He had acquired convictions for sodomy in July 1953 and gross indecency in November 1955, as well as two other convictions for breaking the terms of his probation and driving without a licence with intent to deceive; McCowan's criminal record, MEPO 2/10763 (National Archives).
39. David Bailey, *David Bailey's Box of Pinups* (London: Weidenfeld and Nicolson, 1965).
40. A highly detailed breakdown of that night's events, drawn from the Scotland Yard files held at the National Archives, Kew, can be found in Bennett, *Krayology*.
41. Statement of Detective Inspector Edward Tebbell, taken at Bethnal Green police station, 2 July 1968, MEPO 2/10923, ff. 141–3 (National Archives).
42. MEPO 2/10922, f. 11Q (National Archives).
43. This incident, which took place on 8 March 1966, resulted in gunshot injuries to Eddie Richardson and 'Mad' Frankie Fraser; most involved were charged and sentenced to imprisonment for affray. Cornell, a member of the Richardson gang,

was not present, so the death of Dickie Hart, apparently a friend of the Krays, made it unfortunate that when Cornell chose to drink in the East End the following night, he was, as 'last man standing', in the wrong place at the wrong time.

44. *Sunday Express*, 11 March 1966.
45. *Daily Mirror*, 10 March 1966.
46. *Daily Mirror*, 25 May 1966.
47. *Sunday Express*, 20 June 1966.
48. Kray and Kray with Dinenage, *Our Story*.
49. Albert Donoghue with Martin Short, *The Enforcer* (London: John Blake, 2002).
50. John Dickson, *Murder Without Conviction* (London: Sidgwick and Jackson, 1986).
51. Foreman would later admit that Mitchell's body was disposed of in the English Channel, along with those of several other individuals, including Tommy 'Ginger' Marks and Jack 'The Hat' McVitie.
52. Donoghue with Short, *The Enforcer*.
53. *Daily Mirror*, 5 March 1966.
54. *Guardian*, 5 March 1969.
55. Bennett, *Krayology*.

15 A Low Ebb

1. *Daily Mirror*, 5 July 1972.
2. *Guardian*, 18 January 1965.
3. Freddie Foreman, *Freddie Foreman: The Godfather of British Crime* (London: John Blake, 2007).
4. Freddie Foreman and Tony Lambrianou, *Getting It Straight: Villains Talking* (London: Sidgwick and Jackson, 2001).
5. Kray and Kray with Dinenage, *Our Story*.
6. A famous epilogue to this tale, sometimes described as 'the magic bullet' story, has it that Ronnie gave Dixon the bullet as a souvenir of how lucky he had been. Further claims suggest that Dixon wore it around his neck from then on as a reminder.
7. Albert Wickstead, *Gangbuster* (London: Futura, 1985).
8. *Daily Mirror*, 5 July 1972.
9. Morton, *East End Gangland*.
10. *Daily Mirror*, 5 July 1972.
11. Rose Davis's obituary, *Daily Telegraph*, 3 February 2009.
12. 'BBC On This Day: 19 August 1975 – Davis campaigners stop Test match', online at news.bbc.co.uk/onthisday/hi/dates/stories/august/19/newsid_2534000/2534763.stm (accessed 18 April 2017).
13. Andrew Malone, 'Why Bank Robber George Davis Wasn't So Innocent After All, Reveals his Ex-Wife', *Mail Online*, 6 February 2009, online at dailymail.co.uk/femail/article–1138290/Why-bank-robber-George-Davis-wasnt-innocent-reveals-ex-wife.html (accessed 15 August 2016).
14. 'Fitting Up George Davis', *UPAL Magazine*, issue 9, August 1975.
15. *East London Advertiser*, 14 May 1976.
16. 'George Davis is Innocent' appeared on their debut album *Tell Us the Truth*, released in 1978.

17. Quoted in Malone, 'Why Bank Robber George Davis Wasn't So Innocent After All, Reveals his Ex-Wife'.
18. Morton, *East End Gangland*.
19. Surviving examples can be seen in Poplar, in Salmon Lane and on a railway bridge in Bow Common Lane.
20. Malone, 'Why Bank Robber George Davis Wasn't So Innocent After All, Reveals his Ex-Wife'.
21. White, *Rothschild Buildings*.
22. *The Times*, 20 April 1972.
23. *East London Advertiser*, 29 November 1973.
24. *East London Advertiser*, 8 June 1973.
25. John Pearson, *The Cult of Violence* (London: Orion Books, 2001).
26. Brunswick Buildings and Davis Mansions were demolished in the late 1970s and early 1980s, but Wentworth Dwellings, after standing empty and almost derelict for many years after their closure in 1982, were renovated. Part of it is now called Merchant House.
27. *East London Advertiser*, 7 April 1978.
28. *East London Advertiser*, 21 April and 6 October 1978.

16 Culture and Conflict

1. Reverend Kenneth Leech, quoted in John Eade (ed.), *Tales of Three Generations of Bengalis in Britain: Oral History and Socio-cultural History Project* (London: Nirmal Committee – Swadhinata Trust, 2006).
2. Terry Fitzptrick, quoted in ibid.
3. Nooruddin Ahmed, quoted in ibid.
4. Bethnal Green and Stepney Trades Council, *Blood on the Streets: A Report by Bethnal Green and Stepney Trades Council on Racial Attacks in East London* (London: Bethnal Green and Stepney Trades Council, 1978).
5. Terry Fitzpatrick, quoted in Eade (ed.), *Tales of Three Generations of Bengalis in Britain*.
6. *East London Advertiser*, 18 June 1976.
7. *Tower Hamlets Voice*, Issue 1, February 1975.
8. *East London Advertiser*, 21 May 1976.
9. *East London Advertiser*, 4 June 1976.
10. *East London Advertiser*, 20 August 1976.
11. *East London Advertiser*, 11 June 1976.
12. Ibid.
13. Letter from Reverend Kenneth Leech, *The Times*, 14 June 1978.
14. Bethnal Green and Stepney Trades Council, *Blood on the Streets*.
15. Reverend Kenneth Leech, quoted in Eade (ed.), *Tales of Three Generations of Bengalis in Britain*.
16. Report from May 1977, Papers, publications, press cuttings, correspondence regarding London squatting groups, 1970–1980, ASS/7 (Bishopsgate Institute Library).
17. Bethnal Green and Stepney Trades Council, *Blood on the Streets*.
18. John Newbigin, quoted in Eade (ed.), *Tales of Three Generations of Bengalis in Britain*.

316

19. Nazli Kibria, *Muslims in Motion: Islam and National Identity in the Bangladeshi Diaspora* (Newark: Rutgers University Press, 2011).
20. *East End Citizen*, 11 May 2016, online at eastendcitizen.co.uk/2016/05/11/altab-ali-commemoration-day-whitechapel-protests-racially-motivated-murder/ (accessed October 2016).
21. Taj Stores first opened its doors on Hunton Street (off Buxton Street) in 1936 before moving to larger premises on Brick Lane in 1956, and again in 1979. The Clifton was established in 1974 but no longer operates.
22. *East London Advertiser*, 16 June 1978.
23. *East Ender*, 17 June 1978.
24. *Hackney Gazette*, 17 November 1978.
25. *East Ender*, 31 March 1979.

17 Fighting the Good Fight

1. Nick Ryan, 'Children of the Abyss', *Telegraph Magazine*, 2005, available online at www.nickryan.net/ASIAN%20GANGS.pdf (accessed 3 October 2016).
2. Quoted in Janet Foster, *Docklands: Cultures in Conflict, Worlds in Collision* (London: Routledge, 1999).
3. Quoted in Tom Walker, 'The Battle of Wapping', *Socialist Worker*, No. 2235 (January 2011).
4. 'BBC On This Day, 15 February 1986 – Printers and Police Clash in Wapping', online at news.bbc.co.uk/onthisday/hi/dates/stories/february/15/newsid_3455000/3455083.stm (accessed 3 September 2016).
5. Andrew Neil, quoted in 'Wapping: Legacy of Rupert's Revolution', *Observer*, 15 January 2006.
6. *Commercial Motor*, 2 May 1987.
7. Roy Greenslade, 'Is It Time to Reconsider the Death of Michael Delaney?', *Guardian*, 2 March 2012.
8. Deborah Cameron, 'The Ghost in the Ripper Machine', *Guardian*, 15 March 1988. Jane Caputi, *The Age of Sex Crime* (Bowling Green State University: Popular Press, 1987).
9. Cameron, 'The Ghost in the Ripper Machine'.
10. *East London Advertiser*, 23 May 1980.
11. A former East End wrestler, Taheny later appeared in several films as a bit-part actor, most notably as 'Salt Peter' in Guy Ritchie's gangster movie *Snatch* (2000).
12. Richard Madeley, 'Jack the Ripper is Back!', *East London Advertiser*, 2 May 1975.
13. *East London Advertiser*, 23 October 1987.
14. Ibid.
15. *Hackney Gazette*, 30 September 1988.
16. *East London Advertiser*, 30 September 1988.
17. Interview from 'Shadow of the Ripper', BBC2, UK broadcast date 7 September 1988.
18. *East London Advertiser*, 7 October 1988.
19. 'Action Against the Ripper Centenary: A Statement', received by Tower Hamlets Library and Archives, 12 September 1988.
20. *East London Advertiser*, 30 September 1988.
21. *Big Issue*, 26 July 1993.

22. *Independent on Sunday*, 27 June 1993.
23. The East End tours were frequently run by the historian and academic, Professor Bill Fishman (1921–2014). 'The Cloak and Dagger Club', a society formed in 1994 to examine the Whitechapel murders and their social impact on the East End, had their first meetings there.
24. *East London Advertiser*, 18 March 1993.
25. *East London Advertiser*, 16 May 1993.
26. *East London Advertiser*, 30 May 1996.
27. The mosque's beginnings were modest: in 1910 a meeting was held to raise funds for the building of an Islamic centre in London, for at this time Friday prayers were taking place in hired halls. As more and more Muslim sailors began to settle in the East End, religious provision became a pressing need and in 1938, three houses were purchased in Commercial Road, and were eventually opened in 1941 as the East London Mosque. This state of affairs was maintained until 1975 when the Commercial Road buildings were bought by the Greater London Council under compulsory purchase – the GLC were obviously aware of the need to replace the mosque, which by then had become essential to the still-growing Muslim community, and duly provided a patch of disused land on the corner of Fieldgate Street and Whitechapel Road (the result of a Second World War bomb), installing large portakabins so that the mosque could continue. The current building replaced the temporary structures ten years later.
28. *East London Advertiser*, 25 April 1986.
29. *Evening Standard*, 14 July 1989.
30. Tony Thompson, *Gangland Britain* (London: Hatchett, 1996).
31. Ibid.
32. *East London Advertiser*, 28 July 1989.
33. Thompson, *Gangland Britain*.
34. Combat 18 was formed in 1992 by Charlie Sargent and Harold Covington, and quickly attracted national attention for its threats of violence against ethnic minorities and leftists. The '18' signified Hitler's initials, represented numerically.
35. Nick Lowles, *White Riot: The Violent Story of Combat 18* (Bury: Milo Books, 2001).
36. 'Thugs Attack Freedom', *Freedom*, Vol. 54, No. 7, 3 April 1993.
37. 'Arson Attack on Freedom Building', *Freedom*, Vol. 54, No. 12, 12 June 1993.
38. Andrew Flood, 'Can the European Fascists Take Power in the 1990s?', *Workers Solidarity*, No. 38, 1993.
39. *Guardian*, 30 June 2000.
40. *Independent*, 24 April 1999.
41. Ibid.
42. *Independent*, 30 June 2000.
43. Azizur Rahman, 'Drug Use: Musings of an East London British-Bengali in Tower Hamlets', *Talking Drugs*, 16 July 2012, online at talkingdrugs.org/drug-use-musings-of-an-east-london-british-bengali-in-tower-hamlets (accessed 2 October 2016).
44. 'It's a War on Turf Wars in London's Crime-Ridden East End', *East London Advertiser*, 23 February 2012.

318

45. Ryan, 'Children of the Abyss'.
46. *Independent*, 29 August 1998.
47. Ibid.
48. The list, published 1 January 2013, can be found online at londonstreetgangs. blogspot.co.uk (accessed 18 October 2016).
49. *East London Advertiser*, 22 May 2014.
50. *Daily Mirror*, 1 June 2015.
51. *East London Advertiser*, 27 July 2016.

18 A Battle of Wills

1. 'Class War Wins Round one in Poor Door Battle', *Class War*, online at http:// www.classwarparty.org.uk/class-war-wins-round-one-poor-doors-battle/ (accessed 5 December 2016).
2. *East London Advertiser*, 1 April 1993.
3. Ryan, 'Children of the Abyss'.
4. Tower Hamlets Partnership and NHS, 'Tower Hamlets Substance Misuse Strategy 2011–14', online at www.towerhamlets.gov.uk/pdf/Draft%20 Substance%20Misuse%20Strategy%20Summary.pdf (accessed 18 April 2017).
5. Tower Hamlets Partnership and NHS, 'Tower Hamlets Substance Misuse Strategy 2016–19', online at www.towerhamlets.gov.uk/Documents/ Consultation/Substance_Misuse_Summary_2016_19.pdf (accessed 3 October 2016).
6. Metropolitan Police, 'Tower Hamlets Borough Profile: 2009', online at s3.amazonaws.com/zanran_storage/www.met.police.uk/ContentPages/ 682431375.pdf (accessed 29 September 2016).
7. *East London Advertiser*, 23 April 2013.
8. Tower Hamlets Drug Action Team, 'Exploratory Research Study into the Substance Misuse and Health Related Needs of Migrant and Trafficked Women engaged in prostitution in Tower Hamlets and the City, Service Specification and Terms of Reference' (2005).
9. J. Bindel and H. Atkins, *Streets Apart: Outdoor Prostitution in London* (London: The POPPY Project, Eaves Housing for Women, 2007).
10. K. Neumann, 'Insight into the Current State of Prostitution and the Potential Impact of the Olympics in the Host Five Boroughs' (London: Toynbee Hall, 2009).
11. London Borough of Tower Hamlets, 'Violence against Women and Girls, Consultation Report' (2016), online at democracy.towerhamlets.gov.uk/ mgConvert2PDF.aspx?ID=95178 (accessed 8 August 2016).
12. *Docklands and East London Advertiser*, 6 May 2012.
13. Alan White, 'The Streetwalkers of Whitechapel Have Been Badly Let Down', *New Statesman*, 5 July 2012.
14. *Guardian*, 24 July 2014.
15. 'Texan Billionaire Friend of Royalty Targets Class War', *Class War*, 22 May 2015, online at www.classwarparty.org.uk/texan-billionaire-friend-of-royalty-targets-class-war (accessed 18 April 2017).
16. *Guardian*, 4 October 2015.
17. Ibid.

Afterword

1. Tom Cullen, *Autumn of Terror: Jack the Ripper, His Crimes and Times* (London: The Bodley Head, 1965).
2. Bennett, *E1*.
3. *Docklands and East London Advertiser*, 3 November 2016.
4. *Docklands and East London Advertiser*, 17 November 2016.
5. *Docklands and East London Advertiser*, 10 November 2016.
6. Ibid.
7. *Docklands and East London Advertiser*, 3 November 2016.

Bibliography

Books and articles

Adler, Hermann. 'Report to the Home Office on the Problem of Prostitution in the Jewish Community', in James Knowles (ed.) *The Nineteenth Century, Vol. 23* (London: Kegan, Paul, Tench, 1888).

Annual Register, Vol. 80 (London: Thomas Curson Hansard, 1839).

Anon. *The Witch of Wapping, or an Exact and Perfect Relation of the Life and Devilish Practices of Joan Peterson* (London: Thomas Spring, 1652; reprinted 1843).

Anon. *Adventures, Memoirs, Former Trial, Transportation, & Escapes of that Notorious Fence, and Receiver of Stolen Goods, Isaac Solomons* (London: Joseph Knight, 1829).

Archer, Thomas. *The Pauper, the Thief and the Convict* (London: Groombridge and Sons, 1865).

Arnold, Catherine. *City of Sin: London and Its Vices* (London: Simon and Schuster, 2010).

August, Andrew. *Poor Women's Lives: Gender, Work and Poverty in Late-Victorian London* (New Jersey: Fairleigh Dickinson University Press, 1999).

Bailey, David. *David Bailey's Box of Pinups* (London: Weidenfeld and Nicolson, 1965).

Baker, T.F.T. (ed.). *A History of the County of Middlesex: Vol. 11, Stepney, Bethnal Green* (London: Victoria County History, 1998).

Barber, Melanie, Gabriel Sewell and Stephen Taylor. *From the Reformation to the Permissive Society: A Miscellany in Celebration of the 400th Anniversary of Lambeth Palace Library* (Woodbridge: Boydell and Brewer, 2010).

Baylen, O. 'Stead, William Thomas (1849–1912)', *Oxford Dictionary of National Biography* (Oxford: Oxford University Press, 2004).

BIBLIOGRAPHY

Beaumont, Francis. *The Knight of the Burning Pestle* (1613).

Begbie, Harold. *The Life of General William Booth, the Founder of the Salvation Army* (London: Macmillan, 1920).

Begg, Paul. *Jack the Ripper: The Definitive History* (Edinburgh: Pearson Education, 2003).

Begg, Paul, Martin Fido and Keith Skinner. *The Complete Jack the Ripper A–Z* (London: John Blake, 2010).

Bell, Neil R.A. *Capturing Jack the Ripper* (Stroud: Amberley, 2014).

Bellinger, Martha Fletcher. *A Short History of the Theatre* (New York: Henry Holt, 1927).

Beloff, M. *Public Order and Popular Disorder, 1660–1714* (Oxford: Oxford University Press, 1938).

Bennett, John G. *E1: A Journey through Whitechapel and Spitalfields* (Nottingham: Five Leaves, 2009).

—*Krayology* (London: Mango Books, 2016).

Benton, G. and E. Gomez. *The Chinese in Britain, 1800–Present: Economy, Transnationalism, Identity* (New York: Springer, 2007).

Bindel, J. and H. Atkins. *Streets Apart: Outdoor Prostitution in London* (The POPPY Project, Eaves Housing for Women, 2007).

Blackstone, Sir William. *Commentaries on the Law of England, Vol. 4* (Oxford: Clarendon Press, 1769).

Bohun, William. *Privilegia Londoni or The Laws, Customs and Privileges of the City of London* (London: Browne, 1702).

Booth, Charles. *Labour and Life of the People, Vol. 1: East London* (London: Macmillan, 1889).

Booth, General William. *In Darkest England and the Way Out* (London: Salvation Army, 1890).

Brunsman, Denver Alexander. *The Evil Necessity: British Naval Impressment in the Eighteenth-century Atlantic World* (Chapel Hill: Virginia University Press, 2013).

Burke, Edmund (ed.). *The Annual Register* (London: Longmans, Green, 1800).

Cannadine, David and David Reeder (eds). *Exploring the Urban Past: Essays in Urban History by H.J. Dyos* (Cambridge: Cambridge University Press, 1982).

Caputi, Jane. *The Age of Sex Crime* (Bowling Green State University Popular Press, 1987).

Carpenter, Kevin. *Penny Dreadfuls and Comics: English Periodicals for Children from Victorian Times to the Present Day* (London: V&A Publications, 1983).

Churchill, Winston. *Thoughts and Adventures* (London: Macmillan, 1942).

Cole, G.D.H and M.I. Cole. *The Condition of Britain* (London: Victor Gollancz, 1937).

Collingridge, William. *Report of the Medical Officer of Health for the City of London* (London: Charles Skipper & East, 1905).

Colquhoun, Patrick. *A Treatise on the Police of the Metropolis* (London: H. Fry for C. Dilly, 1796).

Conan Doyle, Arthur. *The Man with the Twisted Lip* (first published in *The Strand Magazine*, December 1891).

Cornish, George W. *Cornish of the Yard* (London: The Bodley Head, 1935).

Courtenay, Bryce. *The Potato Factory* (New Hampshire: Heinemann, 1995).

Coverley, Martin. *Occult London* (Harpenden: Oldcastle Books, 2012).

BIBLIOGRAPHY

Cullen, Tom. *Autumn of Terror: Jack the Ripper, His Crimes and Times* (London: The Bodley Head, 1965).

Darby, Madge. *Piety and Piracy: The History of Wapping and St Katharine's* (London: The History of Wapping Trust, 2011).

De Quincey, Thomas. 'On Murder Considered as One of the Fine Arts', *Blackwood's Magazine*, collected edition, vol. IV (1857).

Dew, Walter. *I Caught Crippen* (London: Blackie and Son, 1938).

Dickens, Charles. *The Mystery of Edwin Drood* (London: Chapman and Hall, 1870).

Dickson, John. *Murder Without Conviction* (London: Sidgwick and Jackson, 1986).

Ditmore, Melissa Hope. *Encyclopaedia of Prostitution and Sex Work* (Westport: Greenwood Publishing Group, 2006).

Dixon, David. *From Prohibition to Regulation: Bookmaking, Anti-gambling, and the Law* (Oxford: Clarendon Press, 1991).

Donnelley, Paul. *Essex Murders* (Barnsley: Wharncliffe Books, 2007).

Donoghue, Albert with Martin Short. *The Enforcer* (London: John Blake, 2002).

Eade, John (ed.). *Tales of Three Generations of Bengalis in Britain: Oral History and Socio-cultural History Project* (London: Nirmal Committee – Swadhinata Trust, 2006).

East London History Group. 'The Population of Stepney in the Early Seventeenth Century', *East London Papers*, 11:2 (1968).

Endelman, Todd M. *The Jews of Britain, 1656 to 2000* (Berkeley: University of California Press, 2002).

Fanthorpe, Lionel and Patricia Fanthorpe. *The World's Most Mysterious People* (Toronto: Dundurn Press, 1995).

Fishman, William J. *East End Jewish Radicals, 1875–1914* (London: Duckworth, 1975).

— *East End 1888* (London: Duckworth, 1988).

Foreman, Freddie. *Freddie Foreman: The Godfather of British Crime* (London: John Blake, 2007).

Foreman, Freddie and Tony Lambrianou. *Getting It Straight: Villains Talking* (London: Sidgwick and Jackson, 2001).

Foster, Janet. *Docklands: Cultures in Conflict, Worlds in Collision* (London: Routledge, 1999).

Foxe, John. *The Acts and Monuments of John Foxe*, ed. Josiah Pratt (London: The Religious Tract Society, 1877).

Froude, James Anthony. *History of England from the Fall of Wolsey to the Death of Elizabeth* (Cambridge: Cambridge University Press, 1858).

Glinert, Ed. *The London Compendium* (London: Penguin, 2012).

Goldsmid, Howard J. *Dottings of a Dosser: Being Revelations of the Inner Life of Low London Lodging-houses* (London: T. Fisher Unwin, 1886).

Greenwood, James. *The Seven Curses of London* (London: Osgood, 1869).

Grieves, Richard L. *Glimpses of Glory: John Bunyan and English Dissent* (Redwood City: Stanford University Press, 2002).

Gull, Cyril Arthur Edward Ranger. *The Great Acceptance: The Life Story of F.N. Charrington* (London: Hodder and Stoughton, 1913).

Gurney, W.B. *The Trials at Large of Joseph Merceron, Esq.* (London: W. Wright, 1819).

BIBLIOGRAPHY

Haining, Peter. *The Mystery and Horrible Murders of Sweeney Todd, the Demon Barber of Fleet Street* (London: F. Muller, 1979).

— *Sweeney Todd: The Real Story of the Demon Barber of Fleet Street* (London: Robson, 2007).

Harris, Daryl, Russell Turner, Ian Garrett and Sally Atkinson. *Understanding the Psychology of Gang Violence: Implications for Designing Effective Violence Interventions* (Ministry of Justice Research Series 2/11, March 2011).

Harris, Tim. *London Crowds in the Reign of Charles II: Propaganda and Politics from the Restoration until the Exclusion Crisis* (Cambridge: Cambridge University Press, 1990).

Haydon, Christopher. *Anti-Catholicism in Eighteenth-century England, c. 1714–80: A Political and Social Study* (Manchester University Press, 1993).

Hitchens, Chris. 'The Metropolitan Police Force: Its Creation and Records of Service' (The National Archives Podcast Series, no. 18, 2011).

Hornsey, Ian Spencer. *A History of Beer and Brewing* (London: Royal Society of Chemistry, 2003).

Howse, Geoffrey. *Foul Deeds and Suspicious Deaths in London's East End* (Barnsley: Wharncliffe Books, 2003).

Hutton, Ronald. *The Rise and Fall of Merry England: The Ritual Year, 1400–1700* (Oxford: Oxford University Press, 2001).

Jackson, William. *The New and Complete Newgate Calendar: Or Villainy Displayed in all Its Branches, Containing Accounts of the Most Notorious Malefactors from the Year 1700 to the Present Time, Vol. 1* (London: A. Hogg, 1795).

James, P.D. and T.A. Critchley. *The Maul and the Pear Tree* (London: Constable, 1971).

Jeaffreson, John Cordy (ed.). *Middlesex County Records, Vol. 3, 1625–67* (London: Middlesex County Record Society, 1888).

Jerrold, Blanchard. *London: A Pilgrimage* (London: Grant, 1872).

Kibria, Nazli, *Muslims in Motion: Islam and National Identity in the Bangladeshi Diaspora* (Newark: Rutgers University Press, 2011).

Klier, John and Shlomo Lambroza (eds). *Pogroms: Anti-Jewish Violence in Modern Russian History* (Cambridge: Cambridge University Press, 1992).

Kohn, Marek. *Dope Girls: The Birth of the British Drug Underground* (London: Granta Books, 2013).

Kray, Reggie. *Born Fighter* (London: Arrow Books, 1991).

Kray, Reggie and Ronnie Kray with Fred Dinenage. *Our Story* (London: Sidgwick and Jackson, 1988).

Linebaugh, Peter. *Ned Ludd & Queen Mab: Machine-breaking, Romanticism, and the Several Commons of 1811–12* (Oakland: PM Press, 2012).

Lloyd, Edward. *The String of Pearls, or, the Demon Barber: A Domestic Romance, The People's Periodical and Family Library* (London: 1846–47).

London, Jack. *The People of the Abyss* (London: Macmillan, 1903).

Lowles, Nick. *White Riot: The Violent Story of Combat 18* (Bury: Milo Books, 2001).

Lynn Linton, E. (ed.). *Witch Stories* (London: Chapman and Hall, 1861).

Macaulay, Lord Thomas. 'Review of *The History of the Revolution in England in 1688* by Sir James Mackintosh', *Edinburgh Review* (July 1835; collected in Lord Thomas Macaulay, *Macaulay's Essays and Lays of Ancient Rome* (London, 1843)).

324

BIBLIOGRAPHY

McCormick, Donald. *The Identity of Jack the Ripper* (London: Jarrold, 1959).

Mackay, John Henry. *The Anarchists: A Picture of Civilization at the Close of the Nineteenth Century* (Boston: Benj. R Tucker, 1891).

McDonald, Brian. *Gangs of London: 100 Years of Mob Warfare* (Lancashire: Milo Books, 2010).

McLean, Lenny with Peter Gerrard. *The Guv'nor* (London: John Blake, 2003).

McLynn, Frank. *The Road Not Taken: How Britain Narrowly Missed a Revolution, 1381–1926* (London: Random House, 2012).

Magee, Bryan. *Clouds of Glory: A Hoxton Childhood* (London: Pimlico, 2004).

Malcolm, James Peller (ed.). *London Redivivum, or an Ancient History and Modern Description of London, Vol. 4* (London: Nichols and Son, 1807).

Mancing, Howard. *The Cervantes Encyclopedia* (Santa Barbara: ABC-CLIO / Greenwood, 2003).

Mandeville, Bernard. *The Fable of the Bees: Or, Private Vices, Public Benefits* (London: J. Tonson, 1724).

Marriott, John. *Beyond the Tower: A History of East London* (New Haven and London: Yale University Press, 2011).

Mayhew, Henry. *London Labour and the London Poor, Vol. 1: The London Street-folk* (London: George Woodfall and Son, 1851).

— *London Labour and the London Poor, Vol. 4* (London: Griffin, Bohn, 1862).

Mazo Karras, Ruth. *Common Women: Prostitution and Sexuality in Medieval England* (Oxford: Oxford University Press, 1998).

Moore, James. *Murder at the Inn: A History of Crime in Britain's Pubs and Hotels* (Stroud: History Press, 2015).

Morison, Samuel Eliot. *The Oxford History of the American People* (Oxford: Oxford University Press, 1968).

Morton, James. *East End Gangland* (London: Warner Books, 2000).

Mowry, Melissa. *The Bawdy Politic in Stuart England, 1660–1714: Political Pornography and Prostitution* (Farnham: Ashgate Publishing, 2004).

Muravyova, L. and L. Sivolap-Kaftanova. *Lenin in London: Memorial Places*, trans. Jane Sayer (Moscow: Progress, 1983).

Northbrook, John. *A Treatise Against Dicing, Dancing, Plays, and Interludes, with Other Idle Pastimes* (London, 1577; reprinted for the Shakespeare Society, 1843).

Nunberg, Geoffrey. *The Way We Talk Now: Commentaries on Language and Culture from NPR's Fresh Air* (Boston: Houghton Mifflin, 2001).

Oldridge, M.W. *Murder and Crime: Whitechapel and District* (Stroud: History Press, 2011).

Overall, W.H. and H.C. Overall (eds). *'Plays and Players': Analytical Index to the Series of Records Known as a Rememberancia, 1579–1664* (London: E.J. Francis, 1878).

Partridge, Eric. *The New Partridge Dictionary of Slang and Unconventional English: J–Z* (Gurgaon, India: Taylor and Francis, 2006).

Pearson, John. *The Cult of Violence* (London: Orion Books, 2001).

— *Notorious: The Immortal Legend of the Kray Twins* (London: Century, 2010).

Pelham, Camden. *The Chronicles of Crime: Or the New Newgate Calendar, Vol. 2* (London: Thomas Tegg, 1841).

Pepys, Samuel, *The Diary of Samuel Pepys* (London: George Bell & Sons, 1893).

Philpotts, Dr Christopher. *Red Lion Theatre, Whitechapel* (Crossrail Documentary Research Report, prepared by MoLAS, 2004).

Redford, Arthur. *Labour Migration in England, 1800–50* (Manchester University Press, 1976).

Richardson, John. *The Annals of London: A Year by Year Record of a Thousand Years of History* (London: Cassell, 2000).

Rid, Samuel. *Martin Mark-All, Beadle of Bridewell* (London: J. Budge and R. Bonian, 1610).

Ritchie, J. Ewing. *The Night Side of London* (London: William Tweedie, 1858).

Rose, Millicent. *The East End of London* (London: Cresser Press, 1951).

Rudé, George E.F. *Hanoverian London 1714–1808* (London: Martin Secker and Warburg, 1971).

Rule, Fiona. *London's Docklands* (Hersham: Ian Allen, 2009).

Ryan, Nick. 'Children of the Abyss', *Telegraph Magazine* (2005).

Sackville-O'Donnell, Judith. *The First Fagin: The True Story of Ikey Solomon* (Melbourne: Acland Press, 2002).

Samuel, Raphael. *East End Underworld: Chapters in the Life of Arthur Harding* (London: Routledge & Kegan Paul, 1981).

Scott, Benjamin. *A Statistical Vindication of the City of London, or Fallacies Exploded and Figures Explained* (London: Longmans, Green, Reader and Dyer, 1867).

Senior, Nassau and Edwin Chadwick. *Poor Law Commissioner's Report of 1834* (London: H.M. Stationery Office, 1834).

Sharman, R.C. (ed.). *Australian Dictionary of Biography, Vol. 2* (Melbourne University Press, 1967).

Sharpe, F.D. *Sharpe of the Flying Squad* (London: John Long, 1938).

Sheppard, F.H.W. (ed.). *The Survey of London, Vol. 27: Spitalfields and Mile End New Town* (London County Council, 1957).

Sinclair, Robert. *East London: The East and North East Boroughs* (London: Robert Hale, 1950).

Smith, J.J. (ed.). *Celebrated Trials of All Countries, and Remarkable Cases of Criminal Jurisprudence* (Philadelphia: E.L. Carey and A. Hart, 1835).

Stedman Jones, G. *Outcast London: A Study in the Relationship Between Classes in Victorian Society* (Oxford: Oxford University Press, 1971).

Stow, John. *The Survey of London* (Oxford: Clarendon, 1908).

Strype, John (ed.). *A Survey of the Cities of London and Westminster, Vol. 2, Book IV* (1720).

Thompson, Tony. *Gangland Britain* (London: Hatchett, 1996).

Van Ash, Kay and Elizabeth Sax Rohmer. *Master of Villainy: A Biography of Sax Rohmer* (Bowling Green: Bowling Green University Press, 1972).

Webb, Sidney and Beatrice Webb. *English Local Government from the Revolution to the Municipal Corporations Act: The Parish and the County* (London: Green, 1906).

Wensley, Frederick. *Detective Days* (London: Cassel, 1931).

Wescott, Tom. *The Bank Holiday Murders: The True Story of the First Whitechapel Murders* (Crime Confidential Press, 2014).

White, Jerry. *Rothschild Buildings: Life in an East-End Tenement Block 1887–1920* (Sydney: Law Book Co. of Australasia, 1980).

Wickstead, Albert. *Gangbuster* (London: Futura, 1985).

Wier, Nigel. *British Serial Killers* (Bloomington: Authorhouse, 2011).

Wilde, Oscar. *The Picture of Dorian Gray* (first published complete in *Lippincott's Monthly Magazine*, July 1890).

Wilson, John Dover. 'The Puritan Attack Upon the Stage' in A.W. Ward and A.R. Waller (eds), *The Cambridge History of English Literature* (Cambridge: Cambridge University Press, 1908).

Wise, Sarah. *The Blackest Streets: The Life and Death of a Victorian Slum* (London: The Bodley Head, 2009).

[Yeats, G.D.] *A Biographical Sketch of the Life and Writings of Patrick Colquhoun* (London: G. Smeeton, 1818).

Yetter, Leigh (ed.). *Public Executions in England, 1573–1868, Parts I and II* (London: Pickering and Chatto, 2009–10).

Websites

www.british-history.ac.uk – British History Online contains a wealth of material on metropolitan history and contains complete online versions of *The Survey of London.*

www.britishnewspaperarchive.co.uk – the British Newspaper Archive is a subscription-only searchable collection of national newspapers, containing 708 titles (a total of over 17 million pages) from 1710 to the present day.

www.casebook.org – Casebook: Jack the Ripper is an online resource containing a wealth of material on the Whitechapel murders and east London history, including many transcribed newspapers and rare contemporary documents.

www.eastlondonhistorysociety.org.uk – the website of the society, founded in 1952, containing historical images, maps, articles and other material.

www.nickryan.net – contains a selection of writer/producer Ryan's journalism on gang and drug culture, focusing particularly on the East End.

www.oldbaileyonline.org – free-to-access database of 197,745 criminal trials held at London's central criminal court between 1674 and 1913, including trial transcripts, original report images and other material related to the trials and punishments served.

www.swadhinata.org – the Swadhinata Trust, a London-based secular Bangladeshi heritage group, works to promote Bangladeshi history and heritage amongst young people. Its website contains complete interviews from its oral history project focusing on Bangladeshi life around Brick Lane.

www.thekrays.net – created by family and associates of the Krays, the website contains numerous articles on the twins, Britain's gangland and a wealth of original documents and memorabilia.

Illustration Credits

Index

INDEX

332

INDEX

INDEX

INDEX